THINGS HIDDEN

OTHER FRANCISCAN MEDIA TITLES FROM
RICHARD ROHR

Breathing Under Water: Spirituality and the Twelve Steps

The Great Themes of Scripture: New Testament

The Great Themes of Scripture: Old Testament

Hope Against Darkness: The Transforming Vision of Saint Francis in an Age of Anxiety

Jesus' Plan for a New World: The Sermon on the Mount

Preparing for Christmas: Daily Meditations for Advent

Silent Compassion: Finding God in Contemplation

Why Be Catholic?

Wild Man to Wise Man: Reflections on Male Spirituality

Wondrous Encounters: Scripture for Lent

Yes, And…: Daily Meditations

Eager to Love: The Alternative Way of Francis of Assisi

THINGS
HIDDEN

SCRIPTURE
AS
SPIRITUALITY

RICHARD ROHR

Franciscan
MEDIA
Cincinnati, Ohio

Scripture passages are the author's own translation, unless otherwise indicated.
All rights reserved.

Cover design by Candle Light Studios
Cover photo by Liselotte Carlson
Book design by Jennifer Tibbits

LIBRARY OF CONGRESS CATALOGING-IN-PUBLICATION DATA
Rohr, Richard.
Things hidden : scripture as spirituality / Richard Rohr.
p. cm.
Includes bibliographical references and index.
ISBN 978-0-86716-659-0 (pbk. : alk. paper) 1. Bible—Theology. 2.
Spirituality. I. Title.

BS543.R64 2007
220.6—dc22

2007035512

ISBN 978-0-86716-659-0

Published by Franciscan Media
28 W. Liberty St.
Cincinnati, OH 45202
www.FranciscanMedia.org

Printed in the United States of America.
Printed on recycled paper.

14 15   11 10 9

to STEPHEN & MARY JO PICHA

Their love for the message,
for the Center for Action and Contemplation,
and for me,
Allows my words, hopefully God's too,
to reach so many people,
And who share with me the "grandchildren"
I would never have,
Grace Ann and Luke Jonah.

"I will speak to you in parables and reveal to you
things hidden since the foundation of the world."

—Psalm 78:2, quoted in Matthew 13:35

"It is not because you do not know the truth that
I write to you, but rather because you know it
already."

—1 John 2:21

contents

introduction
connecting the dots   1

chapter one
information is not necessarily transformation   7

chapter two
getting the "who" right   27

chapter three
people who have faces   53

chapter four
the boxing ring   71

chapter five
good power and bad power   85

chapter six
the razor's edge: knowing and not knowing   109

chapter seven
evil's lie   133

chapter eight
the resented banquet   155

chapter nine
the mystery of the cross   185

chapter ten
mutual indwelling   207

notes   223

annotated bibliography   225

appendix a   228

appendix b   232

index   233

What is this awesome mystery
that is taking place within me?
I can find no words to express it;
my poor hand is unable to capture it
in describing the praise and glory that belong
to the One who is above all praise,
and who transcends every word…
My intellect sees what has happened,
but it cannot explain it.
It can see, and wishes to explain,
but can find no word that will suffice;
for what it sees is invisible and entirely formless,
simple, completely uncompounded,
unbounded in its awesome greatness.
What I have seen is the totality recapitulated as one,
received not in essense but by participation.
Just as if you lit a flame from a flame,
it is the whole flame you receive.

—St. Symeon the New Theologian (949–1022)[1]

introduction
connecting the dots

> "We teach not the way that philosophy is taught, but in the way that the Spirit teaches. We desire to teach spiritual things spiritually."
>
> —1 Corinthians 2:13

> "In your goodness, you let the blind speak of your light."
>
> —Nicholas of Cusa

I am writing this book based on a set of talks I gave in 1998, the twenty-fifth anniversary of my first taped talks, *The Great Themes of Scripture,* given in 1973 at Mount St. Joseph College, in Cincinnati, Ohio. The editors at St. Anthony Messenger Press asked me to reflect again on what I thought were the "great themes" twenty-five years later. This book is my attempt.

I dare to write not because I strongly trust in my own ability to write, but with a much stronger faith in the objective presence of the "Stable Witness" within who "will teach you everything" (John 14:26) and whose "law is already written on your hearts" (Jeremiah 31:33). All that a spiritual teacher really does is "second the motions" of the Holy Spirit.

The first motion is already planted within us by God at our creation (Jeremiah 1:5; Isaiah 49:1), and that is probably what gives spiritual wisdom both such inner conviction and such outer authority. I have always said that the best compliment I ever get is when people tell me something to this effect: "Richard, you did not teach me anything totally new. Somehow I already knew it, but it did not become conscious or real for me until you said it."

That is the divine *symbiosis* between mutual members of the body of Christ, or the "midwifery" of Socrates, who believed that he was merely delivering the baby that was already inside the person. On some level, spiritual cognition is invariably experienced as "re-cognition." Even Peter said that his work was largely "recalling" and "reminding" (see 2 Peter 1:12–15) his people. For some reason, we have forgotten that. It makes us preachers and teachers take ourselves far too seriously, and it makes believers far too reliant upon external authority.

I am also convinced by what Malcolm Gladwell, in his 2006 bestseller, *Blink*, calls the phenomenon of "thin slicing" in our human search for patterns and wisdom. He believes that what we call insight or even genius comes from the ability of some people to "sift through the situation in front of them, throwing out all that is irrelevant, while zeroing in on what really matters. The truth is that our unconscious is really good at this, to the point where thin-slicing often delivers a better answer than more deliberate and exhaustive ways of thinking."[1]

I would hope that I am doing some sort of thin-slicing here, and that it will open you to real spiritual transformation and "what really matters." Frankly, my disappointment in so much scriptural preaching and teaching is that it never seems to get to this level of patterning, but often just remains on the level of anecdote, historical and critical analysis. It's often inspiration and even good theology, but it seldom seems to connect the dots and see the developing tangents. Connecting those dots is absolutely necessary, or we will have no markers by which to recognize the regressive passages that back away from those same tangents. We must see where the dots are leading us.

Our unwillingness, or our inability, to thin-slice the texts and then discern the tangents has created widespread fundamentalist Christianity, Judaism and Islam, which, ironically, usually miss the "fundamentals"! *If you do not know the direction and the momentum, you will not recognize the backpedaling.* You will end up making very accidental themes into "fundamentals" while missing the biggies! One dot is not wisdom: You can prove anything you want from a single Scripture quote.

My assumption throughout this book is that the biblical text also mirrors the nature of human consciousness itself. It includes within itself passages that develop the prime ideas and passages that fight and resist those very advances. You might even call it faith and unfaith— both are locked into the text.

The journey into the mystery of God is necessarily a journey into the "unfamiliar." While much of the Bible is merely a repetition of familiar terrain, where nothing new is asked of history or nothing new given to the soul, there are also those frequent breakthroughs, which we would rightly call "revelations" from the Spirit (because you would never come to them by your own "small mind").

But once you observe the trajectory, you are always ready to be surprised and graced by the Unfamiliar, which is why it is called "faith," to begin with. That is what we will attempt to do here. It might first feel scary, new or even exciting, but if you stay with the unfolding texts, you will have the courage to know them also as your own deepest hopes or intuitions. Such is the dance between outer authority and inner authority, the Great Tradition and inner experience. This is the balance we will seek here.

Unlike many who might go book by book through the Bible, I'm going to try to show how the prime ideas of Scripture are already indicated in (1) capsulated form at the beginning in the Hebrew Scriptures. From that early statement of the theme, we will proceed with something akin to a (2) character or theme development through the whole middle part of the Bible. By the end, especially in the Risen Christ and in Paul's theology of the Risen Christ, we have sort of the (3) crescendo, the full revelation of One we can trust to be a nonviolent and thoroughly gracious God, who is inviting us into loving union.

It takes all of the Bible to get beyond the punitiveness and pettiness that we project onto God and that we harbor within ourselves. But for now we have to keep connecting the dots. Remember, *how you get there determines where you will finally arrive.* The process itself is important and gives authority to the outcome. The medium does become the message, as Marshall McLuhan famously said in the 1960s. The two-steps-backward texts give us even deeper urgency to go forward and much deeper understanding when we get there.

My desire here is to make some clear connections with what I perceive to be the prime ideas in the Judeo-Christian Scriptures with a practical and pastoral spirituality for believers today. Although my tangent definitely coalesces in Jesus, whom we Christians call the Christ, I would like to believe that a lover of the Hebrew Scriptures will also find much to relish here.

I love the clear continuities between the two Testaments and clearly see Jesus as first of all a Jew, who brilliantly thin-sliced his own tradition and gave us a wonderful lens by which to love the Jewish tradition and keep moving forward with it in an inclusive way (which became its child, Christianity).

Although I am clearly a Catholic, I would hope that my Protestant and Anglican brothers and sisters would also find much to guide and inspire them here. There is clearly an "emerging church" that is gathering the scriptural, the contemplative, the scholarly and the justice-oriented wisdom from every part of the Body of Christ.

The ecumenical character and future of Christianity is becoming rather obvious. It is really the religious side of globalization. We cannot avoid one another any longer, and we do only at our own loss (1 Corinthians 12:12–30), and to the loss of the gospel.

Finally, you will note that I use many Scripture citations with only a small comment, hoping that such a small comment will tease and invite you into deeper involvement with the text and context for yourself. I would love to make you love Scripture, and go there for yourself, to find both your own inner experience named, and some outer validation of the same.

Only when the two come together, inner and outer authority, do we have true spiritual wisdom. We have for too long insisted on outer authority alone, without any teaching of prayer, inner journey and maturing consciousness. The results for the world and for religion have been disastrous.

I am increasingly convinced that the word *prayer*, which has become a functional and pious thing for believers to do, is, in fact, a *descriptor for inner experience.* That is why all spiritual teachers mandate prayer so much. They are saying, "Go inside and know for yourself!" We will understand prayer and inner experience this way throughout this book. As Jesus graphically puts it, prayer is "going to your private room and shutting the door and [acting] in secret" (Matthew 6:16). Once you hear it this way, it becomes pretty obvious.

My citations are paraphrased from any number of excellent Bible translations, and to be honest, some of them are my own, but not without study, and, I hope, inspiration.

I offer these reflections to again unite what should never have been separated: Sacred Scripture and Christian spirituality.

Father Richard Rohr, O.F.M.
Center for Action and Contemplation
Albuquerque, New Mexico
Springtime 2007

chapter one
information is not necessarily transformation

"Overexplanation separates us from astonishment."

—Eugene Ionesco

We need transformed people today, and not just people with answers. I begin with the above epigraph from Ionesco, the French-Romanian playwright, to cover my bases from the start! I do not want my too many words here to separate you from astonishment or to provide you with a substitute for your own inner experience. Theology and Bible answers have done that for too many.

This marvelous anthology of books and letters called the Bible is all for the sake of astonishment! It's for divine transformation *(theosis)*, not intellectual or "small-self" coziness.

The British-American author D.H. Lawrence said that "the world fears a new experience more than anything. Because a new experience displaces so many old experiences." Ideas are not a problem. "The world can pigeonhole any idea," he said. They are easily discounted and "dodged."[1] But a true *inner experience* is something else, again. It changes us, and human beings do not like to change. Rosemary Haughton rightly speaks of the same as "the knife edge of experience."[2]

The biblical revelation invites us into a genuinely new experience. Wonderfully enough, human consciousness in the twenty-first century is more than ever ready for such an experience—and also very needy of it! The trouble is that we have made the Bible into a bunch of ideas—about which we can be right or wrong—rather than an invitation to a *new set of eyes*. Even worse, many of those ideas are the same, old tired ones, mirroring the reward and punishment system of the dominant culture, so that most people don't even expect anything *good* or anything *new* from the momentous revelation that we call the Bible.

The very word that the four Evangelists and Saint Paul chose to name this new revelation was a strange one, *gospel*, which we now translate as "good news." It was actually a word taken from a world dominated by wars and battles. A "gospel" was a returning message of victory announcing a new era to the winning party. Obviously, Jesus' message was seen as something genuinely good and genuinely new. This is still true today—*if we are asking the right questions* and, as Jesus says, if we have a "poverty of spirit" (Matthew 5:3). (That is, if we are not over-entitled, smug or complacent. These types are largely unteachable.)

We all need, forever, what Jesus described as "the beginner's mind" of a curious child. A beginner's mind of what some call "constantly renewed immediacy" is the best path for spiritual wisdom, as this book will try to make clear. If our only concerns are for the spiritual status of our group, or our private "social security" premiums, the Gospels will not be new nor will they be good or even attractive. We will proceed on cruise control, even after reading them. They will be "religion" as we have come to expect it in our particular culture, but not any genuine "astonishment" that rearranges everything.

Some scholars, interestingly enough, have said that Jesus came to end religion. That's not as bad as it sounds. He came to end religion *as it was*. Historic religion, archaic religion, in all the world, was usually an attempt to assure that nothing new would happen. This was certainly true of the Egyptians and their pyramids, the Mayans and their calendar, and it is a constant theme across the ancient cultures of the Middle East. People want their lives and history to be predictable and controllable, and the best way to do that is to try to control and even manipulate the gods. Most religions told humans what spiritual buttons to push to keep history and God predictable.

We must know that for most of human history God was not a likeable, much less a lovable character. That's why every "theophany" in the Bible (an event where God breaks through into history) begins with the same words, "Do not be afraid!" It is the most common one-liner in the Bible. Whenever an angel or God breaks into human life, the first words are invariably, "Do not be afraid." Why? Because people have always been afraid of God—and afraid of themselves, as a result. God was not usually "nice," and we were not too sure about ourselves either.

When God appeared on the scene, it was not felt to be good news by most people; it was bad news. The sense was, "Who has to die now? Who's going to be punished now? What is the price I will have to pay for this?" Most people do not realize that humanity did not, by and large, expect love from God before the biblical revelation. Yet even today most humans feel that God's love and attention must be earned, and then we deeply resent that process, just as we do with our parents. (I know no other way to explain the overwhelmingly passive and even passive-aggressive nature of many churchgoers.)

This pattern of expectation and fear is so in the hardwiring that in the two thousand years since the incarnation of God in Christ, not much has really changed—except in a rather small critical mass of humanity. Most people in my experience are still into fearing God and controlling God instead of loving God. They never really knew it was possible, given the power equation. When one party has all the power—which is most peoples' very definition of God—all you can do is fear and try to control.

The only way that can be changed is for God, from God's side, to change the power equation and invite us into a world of mutuality and vulnerability. Our living image of that power change is called Jesus! In him, God took the initiative to overcome our fear, our need to manipulate God and made honest Divine relationship possible. This unthinkable relationship is already planted in human consciousness with the Jewish idea of "covenant love."

In most ancient religions, God was felt to be "controllable" through human sacrifice, found on all continents. Around the time of Abraham, the sacrificial instinct matures a bit and gets transferred to the poor goats, sheep and bullocks; animals had to be sacrificed to please this fearsome God. I still saw it in Africa, India and Nepal, when I visited those places. But "civilized cultures" have pretty much transmuted it into various forms of self-sacrifice and moral heroics—because we all know that *something* has to be sacrificed to bend this God toward us!

We don't really believe that God could naturally know and love what God has created, or that we could actually love (or even like!) God back. This is a fracture at the core of everything and creates the overwhelmingly shame- and guilt-based church and culture we have today in the West. (It was also at the heart of most of the European Reformations—on both sides.)

The amazing wonder of the biblical revelation, that I hope to make clear in this book, is that God is much different than we thought, and also much better than we feared. To paraphrase what a quantum physicist said of the universe, "God is not only stranger than we think but stranger than we *can* think." God is not bad news but, in fact, overwhelmingly comforting and good news.

This is what Walter Brueggemann, in *Theology of the Old Testament*, calls a "credo of five adjectives" that continually recurs in the Hebrew Scriptures: This God that Israel—and Jesus—discovered is consistently seen to be: "merciful, gracious, faithful, forgiving, and steadfast in love."[3]

It has taken us a long time to even *believe* that could be true, but the only people who really *know it to be true for themselves are those who sincerely seek, pray and, often, suffer.* That is "the knife edge of experience," Haughton wrote about. Outside of inner experience of the same, those are just five more pious words. Outside of your own inner experience of this kind of God, most religion will remain merely ritualistic, moralistic, doctrinaire and largely unhappy.

In the pages that follow I'm going to describe the Bible as what historian, social scientist and literary critic Rene Girard rightly calls "a text in travail."[4] The text itself edges forward and sometimes backward, just as humans do. In other words, it doesn't just give you the conclusions, but *it does create a clear set of patterns and a tangent—and our job is to connect the dots forward and backward.* In my opinion, it is only inner experience that can do that job—not just proof texts or external belief systems. Spiritually speaking, it does not help to give people quick conclusions before they have made any inner journeys. They will always misunderstand them or misuse them, and it will "separate them from astonishment."

I am afraid you are burdened with being the receiver station yourself, and no pope or Bible quote can take away that invitation and responsibility. Fortunately, if it is true gospel, it is a "participatory knowing," and you are only one receiver station, holding your small part of the mystery. That should keep us all humble.

I know there were times when all of us have wished the Bible were some kind of "seven habits for highly effective people." *Just give us the right conclusions,* we've thought, instead of all these books of Kings, Leviticus, Chronicles and those Pauline letters that we don't even like. "What's all of this monotonous history and out-of-date science got to do with anything that matters?" That's why an awful lot of people give up on the Bible, and why most Catholics don't even bother with it. (I too often at Mass see their eyes glaze over as the readings from the lectionary begin. You *know* that is true!).

But the genius of the biblical revelation is that it doesn't just give us the conclusions; it gives us (1) the process of getting there, and (2) the inner and outer authority to trust that process. To repeat for the sake of emphasis: Life itself—and Scripture too—is always three steps forward and two steps backward. It gets the point and then loses it or doubts it. In that, the biblical text mirrors our own human consciousness and journey. Our job is to see where the three steps forward texts are heading (invariably toward mercy, forgiveness, inclusion, nonviolence and trust), which gives us the ability to clearly recognize and understand the two steps backward texts (which are usually about vengeance, divine pettiness, law over grace, form over substance and technique over relationship).

This is what you cannot discern if you have no inner experience of how God works in your own life! You will just substitute the text for the real inner spirit. Or as Paul courageously says, "The written letters alone will bring death, but the Spirit gives life" (2 Corinthians 3:6).

We're going to look at the Bible as an anthology of many books. If we believe in inspiration, a trust that the Spirit was guiding this listening and this writing, but like all things human "through a glass darkly," we will allow ourselves to be led. We will trust that there is a development of crucial divine wisdom inside this anthology of books. Woven amidst these developing ideas are what I first called "the great themes of Scripture."

When we get to the Risen Jesus, there is nothing to be afraid of in God. His very breath is identified with forgiveness and the Divine *Shalom* (see John 20:20–23). If the Risen Jesus is the final revelation of the nature of the heart of God, then suddenly we live in a safe and lovely universe. But it is not that God has changed, or that the Hebrew God is a different God than the God of Jesus, it is that *we* are growing up as we move through the texts and deepen our experience. God does not change, but our readiness for such a God takes a long time to change. Stay with the text and with your inner life with God, and your capacity for God will increase and deepen. If you read searching for certain conclusions, to quickly reassure your "false self," as if each line in the Bible was a full dogmatic statement, all spiritual growth will not just stop, but you will become a rather toxic person for yourself and others.

Just as the Bible takes us through many stages of consciousness and salvation history, it takes us individually a long time to move beyond our need to be dualistic, judgmental, accusatory, fearful, blaming, egocentric and earning. The text in travail mirrors and charts our own human travail and will illustrate all these stages from within the Bible! It will offer both the mature and immature responses to almost everything, and you have to learn the difference.

Isn't it a consolation to know that life is not a straight line? Many of us wish and have been told that it should be, but I haven't met a life yet that's a straight line to God. And I have even met Mother Teresa! It's always getting the point and missing the point. It's God entering our lives and then fighting it, avoiding it, running from it. There is the moment of divine communion or intimacy, and then the pullback that says, "That's too good to be true. I must be making it up." Fortunately, God works with all of it, and that's called mercy or steadfast love.

But how do we get to these great themes of Scripture? What are the prime ideas that are liberating human history? Henri de Lubac, a French Jesuit who was one of the great theologians of the Second Vatican Council in the 1960s, said there are two alternating mediocrities in the interpretation of Scripture. He describes the first one as the hackneyed moralisms and pieties of those who have never studied the historical and anthropological setting in which it was first set (the conservative temptation). It's all heart and little head. It's sweet and nice, but it's never going to transform history. It's never going to affect anybody who's got a little education, to put it honestly, and it becomes a cover for an awful lot of pride and prejudice.

The other alternating mediocrity, he says, is the narrow historical, critical interpretation of those who have not had any real God experience (the progressive temptation). It's the usually "enlightened" formulas of those who have no inner experience to awaken the reality of the spiritual world. They do not really love God as much as talk about God. The only possible path is to substitute letter for Spirit, formula for inner authority, education for actual knowing. It is all head and little heart. We find out what the Greek really meant and whether Jesus really said it, all of which often puts the mind back in control, but the heart does not know anything gracious or new.

In this book we're going to try to name a healthy middle, a place between those alternating mediocrities. We're going to bring some healthy cultural studies, psychology and historical awareness to the task, but always point you toward an inner awareness of the Spirit that is guiding you right now. Such humility and trust will keep you humble before the text, and not so needy of quick conclusions.

Then you will know for yourself, and not just because "the Bible says so" or Richard says so. Spiritual maturity, as E.F. Schumacher said in *A Guide for the Perplexed,* is always characterized by a trustful dance between outer authority and inner authority. Conservatives, in my experience, are those who over-rely on outer authority, while liberals tend to over-rely upon their own inner authority. Maturity, as always, is that "third something" in between, a spacious place that is offered by God and grace, leaving neither of us totally comfortable.

I must forewarn the reader that if you commit to really struggling with the text, it's always much more exciting, but could also challenge your way of seeing the Bible and yourself. To learn the context in which Jesus said this or Jeremiah did that, to dig in deeper and understand the why behind the actions of biblical figures, we will often realize how revolutionary and counterintuitive the biblical text often is. Get ready to be changed. The studied text does not let you off the hook the way fundamentalists fear, it just hangs you on the right hook.

Both Albert Einstein and Carl Jung said, in their own way, that the essential human question is, *"Are we related to something infinite or not?"* On the male initiation rites we give, I say, "Are we part of a 'cosmic egg' of meaning? Are we part of an enchanted universe? Or are we just trapped each in our own little desperate search for private meaning?" Biblical revelation says that we are *essentially* related to something Infinite. It says that, in fact, we cannot know the full meaning of our life until we see we are a little strand in a much larger tapestry. Today astrophysicists and social biologists are saying the same thing. Truth is converging like never before.

Inside of the "Circle of Life" we can find our private meaning, but now it is almost given to us as a gift! So the Bible says yes, we are a part of something infinite, and wonderfully so, but we will come to this in a most ingenious way. Eventually we will call it the experience of grace—or undeserved gift. God always and forever comes as one who is *totally hidden and yet perfectly revealed* in the same moment or event. It is never forced on you, and you do not have to see it if you don't want to. What I will call "non-dual thinking" has the greatest chance of seeing the epiphany.

Most of religion, historically, expected we would come to God by finding spiritual locations, precise rituals or right words. Our correct behavior or morality would bring us to God or God to us. Actually almost everybody starts there—looking for the right maps, hoping to pass some kind of cosmic SAT test. The assumption being that if you get the right answers, God will like you. God's love was always highly contingent, and the clever were assumed to be the winners. But the Bible will not make transformation dependent on cleverness at all, but in one of God's favorite and most effective hiding places—*humility.* (Read the opening eight Beatitudes in that light, Matthew 5:1–12.) Such "poverty of spirit," Jesus says, is something we seem to lose as we grow into supposed adulthood (Matthew 18:2; Mark 9:3–6).

The genius of the biblical revelation is that we will come to God through what I'm going to call "the actual," the here and now, or quite simply *what is.* The Bible moves us from sacred *place* (why the temple had to go) or sacred *action* (why the Law had to be relativized) or mental belief systems (why Jesus has no prerequisites in this regard) to time itself as sacred *time*. "I am with you always, yes, to the very end of time" is the last verse of Matthew's Gospel.

It is time itself, and patience with it, which reveals the patterns of grace, which is why it takes most of us a long time to be converted. Our focus eventually moves from preoccupation with perfect actions of any type, to naked *presence itself* (the code word for that is "prayer"). Jesus will often call it "vigilance," "seeing" or "being awake." When you are aware and awakened, you will know for yourself. In fact, "stay awake" is almost the last thing Jesus says to the apostles—twice—before he is taken away to be killed, but then he accepts their inability, and speaks so compassionately to them and to us: "Go ahead and sleep on now, but the hour has come" (Mark 14:35–41).

As Eckhart Tolle points out in *The Power of Now*, you don't have to be in a certain place or even a perfect person to experience the fullness of God. God is always given, incarnate in every moment and present to those who know how to be present themselves. Strangely enough, it is often imperfect people and people in quite secular settings who encounter "The Presence" (*Parousia*, "fullness"). That pattern is rather clear in the whole Bible.

Let's state it clearly: One great idea of the biblical revelation is that God is manifest in the ordinary, in the actual, in the daily, in the now, in the concrete incarnations of life. That's opposed to God holding out for the pure, the spiritual, the right idea or the ideal anything. This is why Jesus stands religion on its head! We Catholics used to even speak of "actual grace" in this light. That is why I say it is our experiences that transform us if we are willing to experience our experiences all the way through.

But it is also why we have to go through these seemingly laborious and boring books of Kings, Chronicles, Leviticus, Numbers and Revelation. We hear in these books about sin and war, adulteries and affairs, kings and killings, intrigues and deceits—the ordinary, wonderful and sad events of human life. Those books, documenting the life of real communities, of concrete ordinary people, are telling us that "God comes to us disguised as our life" (a wonderful line I learned from my dear friend and colleague, Paula D'Arcy). But for most "religious" people this is actually a disappointment! They seemingly would rather have church services.

God's revelations are always concrete and specific. They are not a Platonic world of ideas and theories about which you can be right or wrong. Revelation is not something you measure, but something or Someone you meet! All of this is called the "mystery of incarnation," and it reaches its fullness in the incarnation of God in one ordinary-looking man named Jesus. Walter Brueggemann calls it "the scandal of the particular."[5]

It is not about becoming spiritual beings nearly as much as about becoming human beings. The biblical revelation is saying that we are already spiritual beings; we just don't know it yet. The Bible tries to let you in on the secret, by revealing God in the ordinary. That's why so much of the text seems so mundane, practical, specific and, frankly, unspiritual! Most of us would rather read an inspiring life of a pious saint.

We have created a terrible kind of dualism between the spiritual and the so-called non-spiritual. This dualism precisely is what Jesus came to reveal as a lie. The principle of Incarnation proclaims that matter and spirit have never been separate. Jesus came to tell us that these two seemingly different worlds are and always have been one. We just couldn't see it until God put them together in his one body (see Ephesians 2:11–20).

In the Bible we see God using the very wounded lives of very ordinary people, who would never have passed the tests of later Roman canonization processes. Moses, Deborah, Elijah, Paul and Esther were at least complicit in murdering; David was both an adulterer and a liar; there were rather neurotic prophets like Ezekiel, Obadiah and Jeremiah; an entire history of ridiculously evil kings and warriors—yet all these are the ones God works with.

The Jewish people are always right in the bloody middle of history, undefended with any sophisticated theology or doctrines—only with their belief that Yahweh is with them and was guiding them. I am afraid true biblical faith leaves you very vulnerable to reality, because now there is no place to hide. No wonder we prefer abstractions over the actual! We can hide behind abstractions, but Incarnation leaves you both utterly exposed and constantly invited.

incorporation of negative and self-critical thinking

Once you agree to experience your experiences, once you accept that God is found in the actual, there is something else: *You have to experience the negative side of the actual along with the positive!* No wonder we split, avoid and deny, no wonder we prefer abstract ideas, where we can dismiss the unacceptable material. But the Hebrew Scriptures, most amazingly, incorporate the negative. Jesus does the same when he is "tempted by the devil for forty days" (remember, temptation implies at least some level of attraction and conflict).

The Jewish people, in a sense against all odds and expectations, kept their complaining and avoiding, kept their arrogant and evil kings and their very critical prophets inside of their Bible. They read about them publicly and still do, and we read them also. These are passages that didn't tell the Jewish people how wonderful they were, but told them how terrible they were!

What you have built into the Hebrew Bible and strongly expressed by Jesus and the prophets is the *capacity for self-critical thinking. It is the first step beyond the dualistic mind and teaches us patience with ambiguity and mystery.* Critical thinking is a characteristic of the Western mind that produced the scientific and industrial revolutions, as well as the Protestant reformations. The Jewish and Christian religions always have the power to correct themselves from inside, because of these kinds of sacred texts.

This is quite rare in the history of religion. This is the self-criticism necessary to keep religion from its natural tendency toward arrogant self-assurance. It undercuts the possibility of any long-lasting group idolatry, even though it also deteriorates into cynicism, skepticism and post-modernism.

The Jewish people possessed an uncommon power to stand their ground, with God alone, before negative realities. That's quite the opposite of what we often have today, which can feel like "making a religion out of your better moments." *They made a religion out of their worst moments, which is probably why they have lasted so strongly to this day, even after the Holocaust.*

You've got to realize how daring Jewish religion was and is. Imagine, before they crossed the Red Sea, Moses telling them, "You have nothing to do but keep still, Yahweh will do the fighting for you" (Exodus 14:14). Or "No one has ever trusted in Yahweh and been put to shame" (Psalm 25:3).

These kinds of assertions leave you naked before your enemies and before the moment. No wonder one-third of the Psalms are psalms of lamentation. Much of Christian history has found itself unable to do the same, while considering itself superior to Judaism. (We will discuss that in chapter nine.)

Our temptation now and always is not to trust in God *but to trust in our faith tradition of trusting in God.* They are not the same thing! Often our faith is in our tradition in which we can talk about all of our past saints and theologians who have trusted in God. That's a very clever way to avoid the experience itself, to avoid scary encounters with the living God, to avoid the ongoing Incarnation. We tend to trust the past for its own sake, as if God came to earth to protect human traditions, or that past time is somehow holier than present time. Jesus specifically says that is not true (see Matthew 15:3).

I must say that I love Tradition, but it's a tradition of surrender to the wonderful and always too-much mystery of God. In that sense it will always be a Tradition of not-knowing. That's what we call the *apophatic* tradition, or the "cloud of unknowing," and it becomes the very concept of faith, the freedom not to know because *I am known* more fully than I know or even need to know (1 Corinthians 13:12). We do need *enough knowing* to be able to hold and sustain the mystery of not knowing, but let's hold off on that until chapter six.

It is amazing how religion has turned this biblical idea of faith around to mean its exact opposite: into a tradition of certain knowing, presumed predictability and complete assurance about whom God likes and whom God does not like. I guess *we* think we have God in our pocket. We know what God is going to say next, because we think our particular denomination has it all figured out. In this schema, God is no longer free and must follow our rules and our decisions. If God is not free, we are in trouble, because every time God forgives or shows mercy, God is breaking God's own rules and showing terrible inconsistency!

The amazing thing about the Hebrews is that they did not repress their reality. They refused to let themselves be consoled by superstitious myths. In a certain way, Israel did not distance itself from its own con- tradictions or the contradictions of life, from the horrors and abysses of human history—which finally became "the cross" in Jesus. But these hard realities had already been presented in the stories of Job, their own experience of exodus and exile, and their constant invasion or occupa- tion by foreign powers. They often must have felt like saying to God what Teresa of Avila is supposed to have said: "If this is the way you treat your friends, I would hate to see your enemies."

the cosmic egg

For our overall purposes in this book, I would like you to picture an image that I've used in some of my other works that I call "The Cosmic Egg." Picture three domes of meaning. The smallest dome of meaning is my private story, "This is me," "My story." Probably no people have had the language or the freedom for that level of personal meaning as have people during the last thirty or so years in the United States of America. It's the talk-show language. It's subjective, interpersonal, self-help, psychological language. It is very good, as far as it goes.

Most people in history didn't even have access to this language and largely survived by hanging onto the larger domes. We've only recently discovered it, although it has its Christian beginning in Augustine's *Confessions* and John of the Cross's brilliant charting of inner states. This language does answer a lot of questions, so we are reveling in it right now.

The trouble is that it is so rich it is becoming a substitute for true transcendence. My story, you see, is not yet totally *The* Story. It creates individuals, and even good individuals, but not holiness or true wholeness, or even people who understand their place in society or history.

So there is a second and larger dome of meaning that encloses the first, "This is us," "Our story." This is where most people have lived their lives in all of human history: their ethnicity, their gender, their group, their religion, their occupation. We farmers, we Polish people, we Catholic people, whatever your group identity might be is the way most people in history have seen themselves. That is why they need to defend their group so irrationally. It is all they have. It is groupthink.

I still see this in many parts of the world where people have no time, or even no vocabulary, for their private or personal story. Their only identity is the identity of the group. This, of course, becomes scary because such groups are highly malleable and very subject to fear and violence from supposed threats to their group, as we see in much of the world today. They often have little self-knowledge, and the only way out is if they are bound to the first or the third domes of meaning.

The biblical tradition honors both of these domes of meaning; though it doesn't name them as "domes," it takes each of them seriously. "This is me" and "This is us" are both part of the narrative; the life of the individual and the life of the nation are both arenas for God's action, but then it adds something more. They are "connected to something Infinite," too.

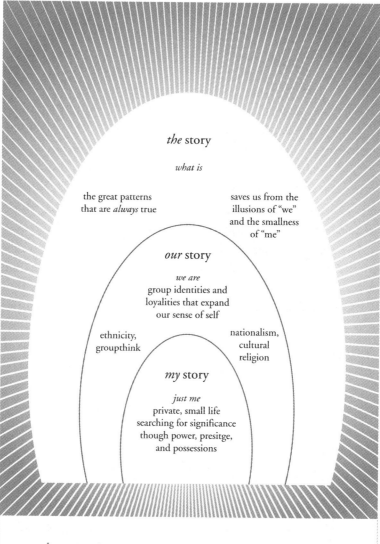

the story

what is

the great patterns
that are *always* true

saves us from the
illusions of "we"
and the smallness
of "me"

our story

we are
group identities and
loyalities that expand
our sense of self

ethnicity,
groupthink

nationalism,
cultural
religion

my story

just me
private, small life
searching for significance
though power, presitge,
and possessions

the cosmic egg

healthy and biblical religion
includes the whole cosmic egg

The New Age temptation, and the sophisticated liberal temptation, is to live only in the first dome of meaning, in the realm of my private experience. That's far too small. Basically, to just keep telling your story becomes boring and narcissistic after a while. The question always, for everyone, is "How does this fit into a larger context?" "What do I do with my experience for the sake of others and for the sake of the future?"

More conservative, traditional people tend to get lost in the second dome of meaning: group loyalty, group identity. "My country right or wrong" or "My religion without any inner experience of the same" would be examples of this level of thought. Everything can become bowing before the leader or identity of the group. Many conservative Catholics are unable to admit the absurd things that past popes have said and done. Many conservative Americans are incapable of criticizing their own political party, the military or the president of the United States.

I think people at either of these extremes become ideologues, which means that one replaces real experience with predetermined conclusions. They have their answers before listening to and learning from the information. Both need a larger dome of meaning to save them from themselves.

The third dome of meaning that encloses and regulates the two smaller ones is called "The Story." By this, I mean *the patterns that are always true*. I hesitate to tell this to "true believers," but this is much larger and more shared than any one religion or denomination. All healthy religion would on some levels be telling The Story, as our Second Vatican Council authoritatively taught us (see *Nostra Aetate*, 1–2). For example, forgiveness always heals; it does not matter whether you are Hindu, Buddhist, Catholic or Jewish. Forgiveness is one of the patterns that is always true, it is part of The Story. There is no specifically Catholic way to feed the hungry or to steward the earth. Love is love, even if the motivation might be different.

The biblical tradition takes all three levels seriously: My Story, Our Story and *The* Story. Biblical revelation is saying that the only way you dare move up to The Story and understand it with any depth is that you must walk through and take responsibility for *your personal* story and also for *your group* story. You've got to listen to your own experience, to your own failures, to your own sin, to your own salvation, and you've got to recognize that you're a part of history, a part of a culture, a religious group, for good and for bad. You cannot heal or *look honestly at* what you do not acknowledge.

Fundamentalist religion tries to jump up to the third level of *The* Story, without doing the painful, personal work of my story and the social, historical and critical work of our story. This is why it is so superficial and so un-self-critical.

The genius of the biblical revelation is that, instead of simply giving us "seven habits for highly effective people," it gives us permission and even direction to take conscious ownership of *our own* story at every level, every part of our life and experience. God will use all of this material, even the negative parts, to bring us to life and love.

Now *that's* really good news! Suddenly we can take our own lives seriously, the good and the bad parts, because God has done it first! We are neither trapped inside of our little culture and group identity, or our private pain and hurts. We are people of the Big Picture and live inside of a lovely cosmic egg of full meaning, where nothing is eliminated and all is used to bring us to life. Jesus taught us to call that the kingdom of God.

Sacred wounding. All of our smaller levels take on a transcendent meaning when we can connect them to The Story. Even our wounds become sacred wounds by reason of seeing them inside of this Big Picture. For Christians, we learn to identify our own wounds with the wounding of Jesus and the sufferings of the universal Body of Christ (see Philippians 3:11–12; Colossians 1:24–25).

One of the enlightened themes that develops in the Judeo-Christian tradition and reaches its fullness in the crucified Jesus is the recognition of the cosmic and personal significance of human pain and suffering. We will especially see it in the four "Servant Songs" of Isaiah (found in chapters 42—53), in the story of Jonah and in the book of Job.

Jesus quotes Isaiah more than any other prophet; he builds on what his Jewish tradition already recognized. For example, one could say that the story of Job is both the summit and the summary of Old Testament faith response to suffering. One could also say that the story of Jesus is the same story as Jeremiah, the prophet who speaks but is not appreciated. Jesus is Job—crucified!

Pain teaches a most counterintuitive thing—that we must go down before we even know what up is. In terms of the ego, most religions teach in some way that all must "die before they die." Suffering of some sort seems to be the only thing strong enough to destabilize our arrogance and our ignorance. I would define suffering very simply as "whenever you are not in control."

If religion cannot find a meaning for human suffering, humanity is in major trouble. All healthy religion shows you what to do with your pain. Great religion shows you what to do with the absurd, the tragic, the nonsensical, the unjust. *If we do not transform our pain, we will most assuredly transmit it.*

If we cannot find a way to make our wounds into sacred wounds, we invariably become negative or bitter. Indeed, there are bitter people everywhere, inside and outside of the church. As they go through life, the hurts, disappointments, betrayals, abandonments, the burden of their own sinfulness and brokenness all pile up, and they do not know where to put it.

If there isn't some way to find some deeper meaning to our suffering, to find that *God is somehow in it*, and can even use it for good, we will normally close up and close down. The natural movement of the ego is to protect itself so as not to be hurt again.

Biblical revelation is about transforming history and individuals so that we don't just keep handing the pain onto the next generation. That tit-for-tat, quid-pro-quo mentality has controlled most of human history. Exporting our unresolved hurt is almost the underlying story line of human history, so you see why people still need healthy spirituality and healthy religion.

The biblical narrative is saying that there is coherence inside of the seeming incoherence of history. The Jewish people believed that our smaller stories have a Bigger Story holding them together. We're going to look for the interpretive clues for that Bigger Story. For me, those are the prime ideas of Scripture, and we are going to continue to try to connect those dots.

I think as Catholics we're in a very special position to be able both to *teach and experience* these great themes of the Bible. We've been given the tools for a very honest critical-historical analysis of the Scriptures ever since the 1940s. Alongside of it, we have our mystical tradition, our social justice tradition, our contemplative (non-dualistic) tradition. This frees us to read the Bible with a healthy head and a happy heart at the same time, both critically and spiritually.

I hope that throughout this book I can somehow speak, if possible, both to your head and to your heart, and to leave you in that in-between space, where you are not too much in control—and God can be.

chapter two
getting the "who" right

"Let us create humanity in our own image, in the likeness of ourselves."

—Genesis 1:26

"Ever since God created the world, God's everlasting
power and deity—however invisible—have been
there for the mind to see in the things God has
made."

—Romans 1:20

We will begin our attempt to connect the dots with the book that is not
the oldest or the first written; in fact, it might have been compiled in its
present form as late as 500 BC, but Genesis is still the famous book that
holds our creation story. Its brilliance gets us off to a very good start.

The Genesis creation story of the Judeo-Christian tradition is really
quite extraordinary compared to other native creation stories. Some
people have creation happening by spontaneous combustion, or emerging out of a hole in the ground, or by a mythological figure, or even by
an act of violence. But our creation story says that we were created in

the very "image and likeness" of God, and out of generative love, as you see above and repeated elsewhere (Genesis 1:27; 9:6). This starts us out on an absolutely positive and hopeful foundation, which cannot be overstated.

We have heard this phrase so often that we don't get the existential shock of what "created in the image and likeness of God" is saying about us! I always tell people if we would just try to believe it, we could save ourselves ten thousand dollars in therapy! If this is true, it says that our family of origin is divine. Our core is original blessing, not original sin. This says that our starting point is totally positive, or as the first chapter of the Bible says, it is "very good" (1:31). We do have someplace good to go home to. If the beginning is right, the rest is made considerably easier, plus we know the clear direction of the tangent.

The Bible will build on this foundational goodness, a true identity "hidden in the love and mercy of God,"[1] as Thomas Merton once said. That is the place we are always trying to get back to, because there are many detours along the way, and many "devils" planting the same doubt they suggested to Jesus, "*If* you are a son (or daughter) of God" (Matthew 4:3, 6). All of the Bible is trying to illustrate through various stories humanity's *objective unity with God.*

In fact, it is sad to me that several of the European reformers, who purported to believe in the Scriptures, still had such a very negative view of humanity. They had tragic starting places like "total depravity" of the person, and so on. No wonder so many Western people seem to hate Christianity; we became exactly what they most feared might be true. Any good news became unhearable on the practical and human level.

With a lack of mysticism and any contemplative mind in some denominations, I find that many Christians still have no knowledge of the soul's objective union with God (e.g., 1 John 3:2; 2 Peter 1:4). They often actually fight me on it, quoting to me that "all things human are evil and depraved," or "humans are like piles of manure, covered over by Christ." Such a negative starting point will have a very hard time creating loving or responsive people, just as when Rome tells homosexual persons that they are "intrinsically disordered." How do you ever undo such foundational damnation?

To preach and know the gospel we must get the "who" right! What is the self we are working with? Who are you? Where do you objectively abide? Where did you come from? Is your DNA divine or is it satanic?

The great illusion that we must all overcome is the illusion of separateness. It is almost the only task of religion—to communicate not worthiness but union, to reconnect people to their original identity "hidden with Christ in God" (Colossians 3:3). The Bible calls that state of separateness "sin," and its total undoing is stated frequently as God's clear job description: "My dear people, we are already the children of God; it is only what is in the future that has not yet been revealed, and then all we know is that we shall be like him" (1 John 3:2).

The word *sin* has so many unhelpful connotations in most of our minds that it's very problematic today. For most of us it does not connote a state of alienation or separateness. Instead, it connotes little naughty behaviors and personal moral unworthiness.

But these are merely the symptoms and not the state itself! Disconnected people *will* do stupid things. But it is the state of believed or chosen autonomy that must be addressed; it is any life lived outside "the garden" that is the core and foundational meaning of sin. We cannot ever get worthy, but we can get reconnected to our Source (see the "True Self/False Self" talks from the Center for Action and Contemplation for more on this).

Sin is primarily describing a state of living outside of union, when the part poses as the Whole. It's the loss of any inner experience of who you are in God. That "who" is nothing you can earn or obtain. It's nothing you can accomplish or work up to. Why? *Because you've already got it.*

The biblical revelation is about awakening, not accomplishing. It is about realization and not performance principles. *You cannot get there, you can only be there,* but that foundational Being-in-God, for some reason, is too hard to believe, and too good to be true. Only the humble can receive it, because it affirms more about God than it does about us, which we will talk more about in chapter eight.

The ego, however, makes it all into achievement and attainment, and at that point religion becomes a worthiness contest, in which everybody loses, which they realize, if they are honest. Many people give up on the whole spiritual journey when they see that they can't live up to the performance principle. They don't want to be hypocrites. I see this especially in males.

Yet union with God is really about awareness and realignment, a Copernican revolution of the mind and heart that is sometimes called conversion. (Sixteenth-century Copernicus, of course, was the first to claim that the world revolves around the sun, not vice-versa, a truly shocking revelation!) From conversion, that deep and wondrous inner knowing, a whole new set of behaviors and lifestyle will surely follow. It is not that *if* I am moral, *then* I will be loved by God, but rather I must first come to experience God's love, and then I will—almost naturally— be moral.

Why do we always put the cart before the horse? God is the horse, and we are always the cart, but remember the ego (read "false self" or "lesser self") always wants to be in control.

To achieve that realization, I'd like to invite you to see both the Hebrew Scriptures and the Christian Scriptures as one complete book, an anthology of inspired stories, with a beginning, middle and end. Read it as one guided text.

Read it as inspiration primarily meaning that God is slowly evolving the reader's consciousness, so that it can receive an ever-clearer understanding of itself as the beloved of God. Biblical texts, when read with "poverty of spirit" (Matthew 5:3), explain us and history to ourselves. When read with a sense of entitlement, as if we are owed something, it unfortunately gives us a false ability to explain God to others.

God does not change in the text, but we do. The written words are inspired precisely insofar as they inspire and change *us!* And here I am using the literal meaning of the word *inspire,* "they breathe into us" a Larger Life. If the written words do not accomplish that—then they are not at all "inspired"—at least for us.

I have met too many people who believe in all kinds of inspired texts, but are lifeless and "without the breath" that was blown into the nostrils of Adam (Genesis 2:7). "They approach me, but only in words," or what both Isaiah and Jesus called "lip service" (Isaiah 29:13; Matthew 15:8).

God's "invasion" of the soul gradually makes us more and more aware, and capable of ever deeper love. The Bible offers immense liberation, a freedom that is almost too much for us. Note the scary offer at the very beginning: "You may eat of *all* of the trees in the garden" (Genesis 2:16) except one! That's more freedom than you or I would ever risk.

God is not afraid of mistakes, it seems. God knows that God can turn everything around—into good. There are no dead ends in the economy of grace that this text will create. So God allows us to play the field and eat of almost all the trees in the garden. This is scary, but Paul, as usual, offers the crescendo statement of the same: "For freedom Christ has set us free" (Galatians 5:1). Jesus lives it in his climactic forgiving breath (John 20:22), wherein he eternally frees humanity from its shame and guilt.

Consider it this way: *God's main problem is how to give away God!* But God has great difficulty doing this. You'd think everybody would want God. But the common response is something like this: "Lord, I am not worthy. I would rather have religion and morality, which give me the impression that I can win a cosmic contest by my own efforts."

Probably the Annunciation story (Luke 1:26–38) is the crescendo point of the theme of total grace and gift. Did you ever notice that Mary does not say she's "not worthy?" She just asks for clarification. She only asks "How" because that might ask something more of her. *She never asks if, whether or why!*

That is quite extraordinary and reveals her egolessness. She becomes the archetype of perfect receptivity. It takes all of the Bible to work up to one perfect vessel that knows how to say an unquestioning yes to an utterly free gift. Every other "election" scene is stymied by the stylized line that sounds so right, "Lord, I am not worthy." "Of course you are not," the Gospel seems to say, "but that was never the question, anyway!"

original shame

The first act of divine revelation is creation itself. I call it the very first Bible of nature itself, which was written approximately fourteen billion years before the Bible of words. God initially speaks through *what is*, as we see Paul affirming in the epigraph at the beginning of this chapter.

Yet it is interesting that in the biblical account creation is done developmentally over seven days, almost as if there was an ancient intuition of what we would eventually call evolution, a rather convincing explanation of God's unfolding creation to which most Christians do not object, regardless of its few vocal critics.

Clearly this creation happened over time, and the only spiritual assertion of Genesis is that God started it all. The exact how, when and where is not its concern, only the *that*. Genesis makes no claim to being a scientific account; it is clearly a spiritual account of the meaning, glory and source of creation. But dualistic minds cannot easily integrate ideas, they prefer to think either/or. Early-stage thinking is almost entirely dualistic because it knows by differentiation. The minds of saints and mystics, on the other hand, tend to be quite non-dual. They see wholes instead of parts.

Have you noticed, however, that on the third, fourth, fifth, sixth and seventh days it says that what God created was "good" (1:9–31)? But most people have never noticed that on the first and second days it does not say it was good! The first day is the separation of darkness from light, and the second day is the separation of the heavens above from the earth below (1:3–8). The Bible does not say that is good—because it isn't! The precise reason that Jesus is the icon of salvation for so many of us is because he does hold them together so beautifully, telling us we can do the same.

The rest of the work of the Bible will be about putting those seeming opposites of darkness and light, heavens and earth, flesh and spirit, back together in one place. They have really never been separate, but remember, "sin" thinks so. It is my own Franciscan tradition, especially that of Saints Francis and Bonaventure, who taught this unity so well. They saw all created things as mirroring and reflecting the Creator. That is called "incarnational spirituality" or "creation spirituality."

The "human ones" will be the place where the "angels will ascend and descend" (John 1:51). This is where creation will come to full and free consciousness, but everything reflects the Creator in some way. It creates what some would call the seven links in "The Great Chain of Being": earth, water, plants, animals, humans, angels and saints and the Divine itself.

The humiliation that you and I carry and that most people refuse to accept is that we humans are a mass of contradictions. We are first of all a blessing, but everyone knows we are also a mixed blessing. We called this basic state of humanity a state of "original sin," a term and doctrine that many do not like. Maybe original "shame" would have described it better. All I know is that we do have a sense of being inadequate—that is obvious.

It often feels like there is a tragic flaw somewhere near our core. Greek and Shakespearean drama say the same, as does Paul in heart-wrenching fashion (see Romans 7:14–25 for a meditation on this).

Unfortunately the word *sin* in our vocabulary implies culpability or personal fault, and that is not at all what the doctrine wants to say. In fact, the precise meaning of original sin is that you are *not* culpable for it, but you must recognize that a wound is there, and that *all* people share in it.

In that sense, it should make you much more patient and empathetic with reality. It names your inner conflict, so you will not be surprised or scandalized when it shows itself. The doctrine of original sin puts humanity on an honest and compassionate stage, right at the beginning.

Adam and Eve, the archetypal humans, are just acting out the mass of contradictions that we all are. That they are seen by some as corporate personalities for the whole is evident by such passages as this: "If the soul needs its own embodiment, so does the Spirit: the first Adam became a living soul, but the last Adam [Christ] has become a life-giving Spirit" (1 Corinthians 15:45).

Clearly Paul sees both Adam and Christ as summaries and representatives of all humanity. What happens in them is what must happen and will happen to the soul. It is not just then, it is always *now*.

The doctrine of original sin is actually a consolation, because if you know you are a mixed blessing, that you are filled with contradictions, a mystery to yourself, then you won't pretend that you can totally eliminate all that you consider unworthy of yourself. As Jesus said in the Parable of the Weeds and the Wheat, "let them both grow together until the harvest" (Matthew 13:30).

Such unnecessary "cleansing" was the hubris and the illusion in recent history of Nazism on the right, and communism on the left and of puritanical believers in almost all religions. Without such humility, they become zealots and ideologues, more than incarnational believers. They are not much open to mystery, compassion or patience.

In the same parable, Jesus advises something I wish someone had told me when I was young, "Don't pull out the weeds, or you might pull out the wheat along with it" (13:29). That's brilliant psychology as well as brilliant spirituality!

In Genesis 1:26 God says, "Let *us* make humanity in our own image, in the likeness of ourselves." It's quite interesting that the plural form is used. It seems almost an intuition of what we will later call the Trinity. One could see this as an early capsulization of what finally becomes the revelation of God as community, God as relationship itself, a God who for Christians is seen as a mystery of perfect giving and perfect receiving, within and without.

I consciously take this pattern of God as a dynamic communion of persons as the central template and pattern of all reality. It will return throughout this book as normative, both source and direction, and should become ever clearer as the text proceeds. It is very interesting that physicists, molecular biologists and astronomers are often more attuned to this universal pattern than many Christian believers.

Consider, however, what God is looking for at this point. God isn't looking for servants. God isn't looking for slaves, workers, contestants to play the game or jump the hoops correctly. God is simply looking for images! God wants images of God to walk around the earth! ("Male and female God created them" it also says in 1:27, which must mean there are two major manifestations of the divine image.)

This is amazing. It's as if God is saying, "All I want are some living icons out there who will communicate who I am, what I'm about and what is happening in God." "You are the ones that I have chosen, that people may know and believe me and understand that it is I" (Isaiah 43:10). Henceforth, all true morality is simply "the imitation of God." Watch what God does, and do the same thing! It is not a "those who do it right get to go to heaven" thing, as much as it is a "those who live like me are in heaven now" thing!

God wants *useable instruments* who will carry the mystery, the weight of glory and the burden of sin simultaneously, who can bear the darkness and the light, who can hold the paradox of incarnation—flesh and spirit, human and divine, joy and suffering, at the same time, just as

Jesus did. Watch what Jesus does, and do the same thing! That, indeed, is hard.

Then and only then will creation be "good" again. It's a limited goodness, to be sure, always a mixture of heaven and earth. This is the only goodness that is available to humans, but it is more than enough. As Jesus himself will later say, "God alone is good" (Mark 10:18). Such a text gives us both glorious but non-inflating goals. There is no appeal to the ego here, only to our need and desire for union—with our own selves and with God.

noah's ark of forgiveness

In Genesis 7 we find the famous story of Noah and the flood. Easily pictured, the story is one that children love. But we miss some excellent pointers if we leave it to children. The story is one of genius. God tells Noah to bring into the ark all the opposites: the wild and the domestic, the crawling and the flying, the clean and the unclean, the male and the female of each animal (Genesis 7:2–15).

In itself, that is understandable. But then God does a most amazing thing. God locks them together inside the ark (Genesis 7:16).

Most people never note that God actually closed them in! God puts all the natural animosities, all the opposites together, and holds them together in one place. I used to think it was about *balancing* all the opposites within me, but slowly I have learned that it is actually "holding" things *unreconciled* that teaches us—leaving them partly unresolved and without perfect closure or explanation. How to live in hope has not been taught well to Christians. The ego always wants to settle the dust quickly and have answers now. But Paul rightly says, "In hope we are saved, yet hope is not hope if its object is seen" (Romans 8:24).

The ark therefore is an image of how God liberates and refines us. The ark is an image of the People of God on the waves of time, carrying the contradictions, the opposites, the tensions and the paradoxes of humanity.

You'd think we would claw one another to death inside, which we have done from time to time. But that gathering of contraries is, in fact, the school of salvation, and the school of love. That's where it happens, in honest community and committed relationships. Love is learned in the encounter with "otherness" as both Martin Buber and Emmanuel Levinas taught. Not coincidentally, they both were Jewish philosophers whose worldview was formed by the Bible.

Eventually we give this mutual deference a word: *forgiveness.* "You should bear one another's burdens, and so fulfill the law of Christ" (Galatians 6:2). Forgiveness becomes central to Jesus' teaching, because to receive reality is always to "bear it," to bear reality for not meeting all, if any, of our needs. To accept reality is to forgive reality for being what it is.

I think forgiveness is the only event in which you simultaneously experience three great graces: God's unmerited goodness, the deeper goodness of the one you have forgiven and then you experience your own gratuitous goodness too. That's the payoff. This makes the mystery of forgiveness an incomparable tool of salvation. There is really nothing else quite like it for inner transformation, which is why all spiritual teachers insist upon it, both in the giving and the receiving.

the garden of knowledge

We hear our story of humanity's original sin in Genesis 2. But this sin, as we've called it, really doesn't look like a sin at all; in fact, wanting knowledge feels like virtue! Hasn't that ever bothered you? "You may eat indeed of all of the trees in the garden, but of the tree of the knowledge of good and evil you are not to eat" (Genesis 2:17). Now why would that be a sin? It sounds like a good thing!

In the seminary we called it moral theology. We ate bushels of the tree of knowledge of good and evil, trying to decide who was good and who was bad. On other levels, it unfortunately refined and even created the very judgmental mind that Jesus strictly warned us against (see Matthew 7:1–2).

But when we lead off with our judgments, love will seldom happen. If the mind that needs to make moral judgments about everything is the master instead of the servant, religion is almost always corrupted.

Some would think that is the whole meaning of Christianity, to be able to decide who's going to heaven and who isn't. This is much more a search for control than it is a search for truth, love or God. It has to do with ego, which needs to pigeonhole everything to give itself that sense of "I know" and "I am in control of the data." Jeremy Young's *The Cost of Certainty* goes into this in helpful detail.

I guess God knew that such would be the direction that religion would take. So God said, "Don't do it. Don't eat of the tree of knowledge of good and evil." What he's trying to keep us from is a lust for certitude, an undue need for explanation, resolution and answers. Frankly, it makes biblical faith impossible.

The major heresy of the Western churches is that they have largely turned around the very meaning of faith, not knowing and not needing to know, into its exact opposite—*demanding to know and insisting that I do know!* The original sin, brilliantly described, warned us against this temptation at the very beginning.

It seems that God is asking humanity to live inside of a cosmic humility. In that holding pattern, we bear the ambiguity, the inconsistencies and the brokenness of all things, instead of insisting on dividing reality into the good guys and the bad guys. It is our ultimate act of solidarity with humanity.

When we are allowed to name the certain bad guys, we all know that persecution and violence will come next; and when we too easily presume that we are one of the good guys, we largely live in illusion and prejudice. I say this as a man of religion, but religion has been the justification of much of the violence in human history. So God had to undercut that very violence at the starting gate.

I came out of the seminary in 1970 thinking that my job was to have an answer for every question. That's probably why I started making tapes and eventually writing books. What I've learned is that not-knowing and often not even needing to know is a deeper way of know-ing and a deeper form of compassion. Maybe that is why Jesus praised faith even more than love; maybe that is why Saint John of the Cross called faith "luminous darkness."

That's why all great traditions teach some form of contemplation, because it is actually a different form of knowledge that emerges inside of the "cloud of unknowing." It is a refusal to eat of the tree of the knowledge of good and evil, and finding freedom, grace and comfort in the not needing to know, which ironically opens us up to a much deeper consciousness that we would call the mind of God. That's because our small mind and lesser self is finally out of the way.

So you see perhaps why false moral certitude is presented at the very beginning of the Bible as the original sin. It clears the way for faith, hope and love, all three (see 1 Corinthians 13:13).

how do we "fall"?

Now let's move to Genesis 3 and look at "the Fall" itself. The Fall is not simply something that happened in one historical moment to Adam and Eve. It's something that happens in all moments and all lives. It must happen and will happen to all of us. In fact, as the English mystic Julian of Norwich said, "First the fall, and then the recovery from the fall, and both are the mercy of God."[2] It is in falling down that we learn almost everything that matters spiritually. As many of the parables seem to say, you have to lose it (or know you don't have it) before you can find it and celebrate fittingly (see all of Luke 15).

The Bible presents us stories in "little theater" to prepare us for the Big Theater, teaching us, in effect, it's not just here, it's everywhere; it's not just this man or woman, it's every man and every woman. For too long, for example, it has been common for Christians to read the Bible complacently, often observing, "That was the problem with Jewish reli-gion back then."

Thus, they cleverly avoid acknowledging that the exact same problem applies today and in their own denomination. If the text is truly inspired, it will always be revealing "the patterns that are always true," even and most especially here and now—in me, and not just back there in them.

In Genesis the Evil One, imaged as a snake, makes Eve suspicious. That starts the unraveling between Eve, Adam and God, just as suspicion does in all relationships. Someone tells you one little bad thing about another person, and that gets our minds going, fitting all sorts of pieces into a pattern all nicely constructed in our head.

It begins with suspicion, the planting of doubt, and it all begins in the mind (see James 4:1–2). Suspicion will almost always find evidence for what it suspects. It inevitably moves toward states of resentment and an inability to trust outside myself. That's the psychology of what's happening here—and it's all in a simple story line.

Then the text says, "the eyes of both of them were opened" (3:7). What they were opened to was a split universe. Teachers of prayer call it the "subject-object split." This happens whenever we stand over and against things, apart and analytical, and can no longer know things by affinity, likeness, or natural connection, but we merely know them as objects out there.

It begins in all human beings somewhere around seven years of age, which is when we "leave the garden." Before that time, like Adam and Eve in the garden, we exist in unitive consciousness. It's where we all begin, when "the father and I are one" (John 10:30), or my mother and I are one, as we enjoy in the first years of life.

We start with unitive consciousness, and eventually the split happens. It has to happen. We *will* eat of the tree of the knowledge of good and evil, and suffer the "wound of knowledge." We will get suspicious of ourselves and of everything else. We will doubt. That's called the state of alienation, and many live their whole lives there.

Alienated people will stop trusting that reality is good, that we are good too and that we belong. Adam and Eve's eyes were opened (Genesis 3:8) to a split universe of suspicion and doubt—of one another, and even doubt of God.

The perfect metaphor for this new split universe, this intense awareness of themselves as separate and cut off, is that "they realized that they were naked" (3:8). Today we would probably call it primal shame. Every human being seems to have it in some form, that deep sense of being inadequate, insecure, separate, judged and apart.

It is almost the human condition, yet it takes a thousand disguises. It creates the yearning for divine recommunion. Yet Adam and Eve "sewed fig leaves together to make themselves loincloths" (Genesis 3:7).

There really is no medicine for this existential shame, apart from Someone who possibly knows all of me and loves me anyway, One who knows me in my nakedness and loves me despite and maybe even *because,* as Thérèse of Lisieux believed. That's what we mean by saying, God alone can "save" you. It is God who says to them, undoing their doubt, "But who told you that you were naked?" (3:11). God creates a doubt, too, but in the opposite direction and in their favor.

When the Significant Other says that you are good, then you are good, indeed. That's what it means, psychologically speaking, to be liberated and loved by God. Anyone else can say it, but you will always doubt it, even though it temporarily feels good, and is the necessary "bottle opener."

Salvation is only secondarily assuring you of an eternal life; it is first of all giving you that life now, and saying, "If now, then also later," and that becomes your deep inner certitude! If God would accept me now when I am clearly unworthy, then why would God change his policy later? You can then begin to rest, enjoy and love life.

This new safe and protective God is now illustrated in a most tender way: God is presented as a divine seamstress. The first image was probably a masculine image of God as creator and now we have God in an almost feminine image. It says, "God sewed together clothes for them out of the skins of animals and they put them on" (3:21).

Surely this is a promise from a protective and nurturing God who takes away their shame and self-loathing. That will become the momentum-building story of the whole Bible, which gradually undoes the common history of a fearsome and threatening deity.

God takes away the shame we have *by giving us back to ourselves*— by giving us God! You don't get any better than that. Human love does the same thing. When someone else loves you, they give you not just themselves, but for some reason they give you back your own self, but now a truer and better self. This dance between the Lover and the beloved is the psychology of the whole Bible, which we will see poetically described in the wonderful single book, the Song of Songs.

Unfortunately, though, in the next chapter of Genesis, we will quickly have the collapse into the scapegoating and murder of Abel by Cain. Once humans are outside of union, symbolized by the garden, the whole pattern of fear, hatred, violence and envy begins.

Much of the rest of the Bible will reveal the conflicts of living outside the garden, in other words, in the dualistic mind of disunion—and yet with the constant invitation back into union. Such evil is inscribed in the text itself, and here it begins with poor Cain, but even him Yahweh gives a mark of protection (4:15) as he moves "east of Eden." I see it as the beginning of the theme of the sacred wounding.

chosenness

The rest of the Bible is largely character development and the transformation of persons. It usually begins with an experience of election or chosenness. You cannot get started, it seems, until you somehow know you are special and empowered. Then the character will indeed develop.

Think of the many, many stories about God choosing people. There's Moses, Abraham and Sarah; there is David, Jeremiah, Gideon, Samuel, Jonah and Isaiah. There is Israel itself. Much later there's Peter and Paul, and, most especially, Mary. God is always choosing people. First impressions aside, God is not primarily choosing them for a role or a task, although it might appear that way. God is really choosing them to be himself in this world.

God needs images. God needs people who are useable as instruments. For starters, though, the instruments have to know that they are not alone, that they are not just doing their own thing, but, rather, that they are doing God's thing. Thus after the standard opening line of "Don't be afraid," the final line is almost always some form of, "I will be with you" (see, for example, Moses in Exodus 3:11).

Being chosen doesn't mean that God likes one more than the other, or that some are better than others. Usually, in fact, they are quite flawed or at least ordinary people, so it is clear that their power is not their own. As Paul will put it, "If anyone wants to boast, they can only boast about the Lord" (1 Corinthians 1:31).

It's not that God likes anyone better or that they are more worthy than the rest. *God's chosenness is for the sake of communicating chosenness to everybody else!* That is the paradox, and it often takes people a long time to learn that (read the Jonah story). You lead others to the depth to which you have been led.

In Romans 11 Paul takes a whole chapter to point out that the Jewish people have been chosen once and for all. That choice will never be withdrawn, he says, but it is only for the sake of the gentiles and the whole world: "all the branches are holy if the root is holy...it is the root that supports you" (11:16, 18). In other words, what first feels like exclusivity is finally and fully for the sake of inclusivity!

Again, it's a slowly learned paradox of which even Paul has to convince Peter (see Galatians 2:11–14). God even has to second the motion before Peter will give in (see Acts 10:9–43). Sometimes even "popes" are slow learners, the text seems to say. At an immature level we prefer "exclusive election," that is, ourselves to the elimination of everybody else.

Here is the principle: You can only transform people to the degree that you have been transformed. You can only lead others as far as you yourself have gone. You have no ability to affirm or to communicate to another person that they are good or special until you know it strongly yourself. Once you get your own "narcissistic fix" as I call it, then you can stop worrying about being center stage, and you have plenty of time and energy to promote other people's empowerment and specialness. Only beloved people can pass on belovedness.

If we do not understand election as "inclusive election" (chosenness is for the sake of communicating the same to others), religion almost always becomes an exclusionary system against the "non-elect," "unworthy" or "impure." Does this need much proof?

It becomes "my belonging system" instead of any good news for the world, which is exactly what Jesus did *not* do. In any kind of "exclusive election," the "chosen" do not see their experience as a gift for others, but merely a gift for themselves. We end up with a very smug and self-satisfied religion.

I would encourage you to take your time and read through both Deuteronomy 7:7–10 and Romans 11. There you'll see how both Moses and Paul beautifully teach what chosenness and election is about. It's not to make you think you are better or to create a society of the superior ones.

If anything, in fact, it is the gathering of the weak and the wounded, to show how God transforms and heals. God gets all the glory. True believers know that they are the "immoral minority" and are being used as starter yeast, savory salt and translucent light (see Matthew 5:13–16; Luke 13:33). How were we able to overlook such clear statements from Jesus at the very beginning of his inaugural address and in his parables? Yeast is not the dough, salt is not the meal, and light illumines something else.

Jesus knew who his best audiovisual aids were for his transformative message: "I did not come for the healthy, but for the sick" (Luke

5:32). The lives of saints never point to themselves, but always and forever beyond themselves to the One who chose them, uses them and loves them.

it's all about union

I want to give three indicators or bookmarks of this deepening plot, this invitation to divine union. They're like little flags all the way through the Bible, and will allow you to read the text much more excitedly, as you yourself discover them.

I will just give some major examples here, but there are many more, especially in the Psalms.

First, there's the symbol of God's constant and gracious invitation to union, God flowing out toward us, God choosing us before we ever choose back. The code word for that is *water*. Watch for it.

We have the Red Sea itself, the water from the rock in the desert (Numbers 20:1–13, where so much is made of Moses doubting it and the people grumbling) the fountain that the temple itself becomes (Ezekiel 47:1–12; Revelation 22:1–2). There is the momentous crossing through the Jordan River (Joshua 3) that John the Baptist builds into his baptismal initiation rite (Mark 1:5), then the water flowing from the side of Christ (John 19:34), the living water that Jesus says he is (John 7:38), the living water that he offers the Samaritan woman at the well (John 4:1–42).

Water is almost always an invitation to that first, subtle religious experience, when the desire just laps up against you and your mind and heart are opened for the first time. It's the first gnawing, inviting sense that there's something more. It's the momentary recognition that the inside of things is even bigger than the outside.

A lot of the medieval mystics, especially women, use this language of God flowing out toward them and through them (Mechtild of Magdeburg, Julian of Norwich, Hildegard of Bingen, Teresa of Avila).

For Christians it becomes the objective trinitarian flow of God's life in us, through us, with us, for us—and usually in spite of us.

It is experienced as an allowing and an enjoying, never a producing or an attainment. So watch for the word and image of water and consider it an invitation.

That brings us to our second bookmark: The code word is *blood*. This invariably symbolizes the transformative experience, the dying before you die that so many religions speak of. The necessary price of newness is always death to oldness. Religion is never afraid to talk about blood-letting, dying, loss of unneeded baggage, letting go—and it is always painful.

Most male initiation rites were needed to "prove" the necessity of that letting-go to the young man (note the Twelve Apostles!), who always resists dying. (There's more on this in my book *Adam's Return: The Five Promises of Male Initiation*.)

"Flowing blood" is an experience that all of us hate and want to run from, but it has to happen. It images the death of the false self, the death of illusion, of the illusions we are addicted to.

In my initiation studies it was noted that women did not historically have initiation rites, but in fact, fertility rites, which taught them the sacred meaning of their monthly flow. Men were circumcised in maybe two-thirds of the cultures of the world, almost to force them to accept the necessity of suffering on the spiritual path. I call this the "path of descent."

The Hebrew Scriptures are filled with images of blood sacrifice. There are the frequent burnt offerings, the paschal lamb that has to be killed, and of course, the many temple sacrifices. By the time of Jesus 90 percent of the economy of the city of Jerusalem was tied up in the hauling, penning, feeding and killing of holocaust victims, and then hauling the dead carcasses back out of the temple. On the great feast days, tens of thousands of goats and bullocks and heifers were killed in the temple (see, for example, 1 Kings 8:63).

We never showed this in any detail in our anesthetized Bible-history books because it was too unbelievable. But to be a priest or Levite was also to be a butcher. A demanding or distant God always needs to be placated with blood, it seems, which unfortunately led to our very limited understanding of what we later called the "atonement theory," which I will discuss at length in chapter nine.

Suffice to say here that we probably could not even imagine or picture *God loving us* without the spilling of blood on God's part (that's how deep the archetypal symbolism flows). As the dualistic mind tends to do, we made the Crucifixion into a tit-for-tat thing instead of a revelation of the eternal nature of the heart of God flowing toward us as water and blood (see John 19:34).

When Jesus comes into the temple and throws out all those tables he, in effect, is undercutting the whole system of sacrificial religion (see Hebrews 10 for a good statement of this). Jesus is "once and for all" saying blood sacrifice is over, as Rene Girard pointed out so well in *Violence and the Sacred.* After all, human, animal and heroic self-"sacrifice" are only vicarious substitutions for the real thing that has to be sacrificed, that we don't want to sacrifice—our false self, our ego, our illusions. That sacrifice is always an experience of death for us, especially if we have courted it for thirty years.

As we go back in the history of religion we find that most every continent, until about the time of Abraham, had human sacrifice. We're still discovering the remains of little girls who were sacrificed in Latin America. On every continent people felt God could not possibly love us unless we gave God our best and our brightest, our eldest son or our virgin daughters.

Somebody had to be given to God because God basically was not seen as being on our side. Unless we know this, we will not see how Jesus turned around the entire history of religion. The symbol, of course, is God spilling his blood to get to us, after millennia of humanity spilling its blood to get to God! Jesus reversed the whole scary process, for those who were willing to read the symbols. *Sym-ballein*, after all, where *symbol* comes from, is Greek for "throwing together" two different notions so we can see their similarity and access a larger whole.

What we have further symbolized in the beautiful Abraham and Isaac story (Genesis 22) is the movement from human to animal sacrifice. The only reason they could write such a story is because humans *did* sacrifice humans! (Note the king of Moab in 2 Kings 3:27.) It was a believable story line. You could say that the reason Isaac went along with it was because he knew the cultural practice, and it was required of him.

In truth, God has been perceived as scary and threatening in most of history. God has never been loveable for most of humanity. Even today you would never fall in love with a God who is basically a terrorist—needy and insecure. You would never spend time with this God. Why would you spend time alone in prayer, unless it was to manipulate or control such a God?

As long as we think God wants physical blood, or maudlin self-sacrifice, instead of the "circumcised heart" (Deuteronomy 10:16) that blood really symbolizes, most of us will probably continue to resist and resent this bookmark.

The third and final bookmark, or code word, to look for is *bread*. This is the positive, nurturing level of religion. It starts with the manna, the miraculous food provided during the journey in the desert (Exodus 16). There are many, many other images of the feeding of prophets, widows and even David and his troops. In every case, we have the text moving toward life-giving strength and intimacy, and not just feeding our needs for security or status.

Food, bread in particular, seems to be used to symbolize fullness and satisfaction in God. It's God feeding us, rather than us being food for God. It's God caring even about our very mundane and immediate needs for "daily bread." God is offering us abundance rather than mere fear-based, subsistence religion, which I often call "fire insurance" religion.

In the New Testament we have the several accounts of the feeding of the thousands by Jesus (Matthew 14:13–21 ff., 15:32 ff.), the breaking of bread on the way to Emmaus (Luke 24:13 ff.), the breakfast by the seashore (John 21:9 ff.), and of course what we call "the Last Supper." This "do this in remembrance" meal becomes the Eucharist, the central defining sacrament of mainline Christians.

Wherever Eucharist is found, you will also find a much stronger incidence of mystical, instead of merely moralistic, Christianity.

So we have water, the first invitation to an inner life of union. Then we have blood, which symbolizes the difficult price of union. Finally, we have bread, the ongoing feeding of that union. Watch for those bookmarks throughout the biblical text, and you will see they are inviting you deeper into union with the God who is always inviting, challenging and consoling. They also create the positive tangents we are trying to discover here.

What the biblical revelation is achieving is basically a very different consciousness, a recreated self, an "identity transplant"—just as today we talk about kidney and heart transplants. The text is inviting us slowly, little by little, into a very, very different sense of who we are.

We are not our own! Or as I tell the men at the initiation rites, "Your life is not about you." We move from the lesser self to the Great Self.

Saint Paul knew this well. He says, "I live now not my own life, but the life of Christ who lives in me" (Galatians 2:20). In the spiritual journey you come to the day where you know you're not just living your own life. You realize that Someone Else is living in you and through you, that you are part of a much Bigger Mystery. You realize that you're a mere drop in a Bigger Ocean, and what's happening in the ocean is happening in you.

This gives you an utterly different sense of yourself as a person, and that is what I mean by an identity transplant, and what the Bible means by conversion. Like Paul's conversion, it takes quite a while for the scales to fall from our eyes (see Acts 9:18), plenty of help from strangers like Ananias (Acts 9:10 ff.), and long, quiet retreats in Arabia (see Galatians 1:17).

Afterward, though, nothing could stop Paul. Read 2 Corinthians 11–12, if you want to see a big human ego (Paul's "I am") that has now put all its energy to the Divine (the "I AM"). Perhaps you cannot have one without the other.

There is only one thing you must definitely know: *"Who am I?"* Or, restated, *"Where do I abide?"* If you can get that right, the rest largely takes care of itself. Paul answers it directly: "You are hidden with Christ in God, and he is your life" (Colossians 3:3–4).

Every time you start hating yourself, think, *Who am I?* The answer will come, "I am hidden with Christ in God" in every part of my life. I am bearing the mystery of the suffering of humanity, its sad woundedness, but I am also bearing the very glory of God, and even "sharing in the divine nature" (2 Peter 1:4).

It seems that God keeps looking at what is good, what is God in me, and of course always finds it entirely loveable. God fixes his gaze intently where I refuse and where I fear to look, on my shared, divine nature as his daughter or son (1 John 3:2). And one day my gaze matches God's gaze (frankly, that is what we mean by prayer). At those times I will find God loveable and myself loveable at the same time. Why? Because it is the same gaze, but they have become symbiotic and look out at life together.

Paul frequently uses the expression "in Christ." We are saved by standing consciously inside the force field that is Christ—not by getting it right in our private selves. We're never going to get it right in the private self. We're never going to put it all together. We're too tiny, too insecure, too ready to beat ourselves up. We can't always be correct, but we can be connected.

All we can do is fall into the Eternal Mercy, where we fall into a net out of which we cannot fall. Eventually, we all know that we are all saved in spite of ourselves, and even worse, much more by doing it wrong than by doing it right! That must be the final death to the ego.

That's the wonder of having extensive times of prayer or those sacred times of childbirth, death accompaniment or sexual intimacy, where you experience being a part of someone else, where you experience that your life is not your own.

These are not *moral* moments; they are *transformative* moments where you come to a different sense of your "I." Our holiness is first of all and really only God's, and that is why it is certain and secure—and always holy. It is a participation, a mutual indwelling, not an achievement or performance on my part.

This dawning realization will find bookmark statements throughout the Jewish and Christian Scriptures, but must also be backed up by your own inner prayer experience, or they will only be words. Nevertheless, let's end with some words that I hope you can hear in a whole new way now:

"God chose us, chose us in Christ, to be holy and perfect, so that we could live through love in God's presence, freely adopting us in Christ for our own good, so that we could exist to give glory to God's utterly free gift, and find freedom in forgiveness" (Ephesians 1:4–7).

chapter three
people who have faces

> "Since then, there has never been such a prophet in
> Israel as Moses, the one who knew Yahweh face to
> face."
>
> —Deuteronomy 34:10

> "Now we are seeing a dim reflection in a mirror, but
> then we shall see face to face. The knowledge I have
> now is imperfect, but then I shall know as fully as I
> am known."
>
> —1 Corinthians 13:12

It seems that this Yahweh who is uncovering and showing himself in the
Bible desires not just images or ideas, but even *persons* with whom God
can be in very concrete and intimate relationship. God is creating, quite
literally, some friends for himself! Jesus became the full representation
of one who accepted and lived that friendship. In fact, he never seemed
to doubt it. That must be at the core of our imitation of Jesus, and
exactly how we become "partners in his triumph" (2 Corinthians 2:14).

Yet God does not settle for mandated or fear-based relationships,
but rather desires willing and free relationships with "friends" (John

15:15). It is called a "new covenant" (Jeremiah 31:31; Luke 22:20), but one that is still a quite new and unbelievable possibility for most people.

In calling forth such freedom and consciousness, and even love, in humanity, God is actually making possible a certain kind of equality between Divinity and humanity, as strange and impossible as that might sound. As Deuteronomy states it, God is creating "a people peculiarly his own" (26:18).

C.S. Lewis's last work of fiction was a book called *Till We Have Faces: A Myth Retold.* In this reinterpretation of the Greek myth of Cupid and Psyche, he illustrated how hard it is for God to give us a "face," to create a partner for conscious relationship. God has to play Cupid to our Psyche, it seems.

One way to read the entire Bible is to note the gradual unveiling of our faces, the gradual creating of personhood, from infants, to teenage love, to infatuation, to adult communion. (Do you know that our English word *person* comes from the word selected to describe the "persons" of the Trinity, who were seen as an endless capacity for relationship?) Biblical spirituality has the potential of creating "persons" who can both receive and give out of love, and love that is perfectly free.

The Judeo-Christian tradition really nurtured and brought forth the idea of the individual that was so prevalent among the ancient Greeks. That's probably why we have this strong sense of individuality in the West, which we often think of in negative terms. But there's a very positive sense to it too. Humanity had to be pulled out of tribalism, collectivism and group-think, which is where human consciousness started.

In many ways what we're seeing as we explore the Bible is an observing of the development of human consciousness and human readiness for God. That's why we do see some difference between the earlier and later Scriptures: There's been a development in consciousness.

In short, I see this pattern in the Bible: (1) We start with tribal thinking; (2) we gradually move toward individuation through the dialogue of election, failure and grace; (3) then there is a breakthrough to unitive consciousness by the few who are led and walk fully through those first two stages (Moses, David, many prophets, Job, Mary, the Magdalene, Jesus, Paul). We could describe it also as (1) Simple Consciousness, (2) Complex Consciousness and (3) Non-Dual Consciousness or "the unitive way."

That last stage is utterly mysterious and unknown to people in the first stage, and still rather scary and threatening to people in the second stage. *If you are not trained in a trust of mystery and some degree of tolerance for ambiguity,* frankly you will not proceed very far on the spiritual journey. In fact, you will often run back to stage one when the going gets rough in stage two.

Thus the biblical tradition, and Jesus in particular, both praise faith even more often than love. Why? Because faith is that patience with mystery that allows you to negotiate the stages. As Gerald May points out in *Dark Night of the Soul,* it allows God to lead you through darkness—where God knows and I don't. This is the only way to come to love! *Love is the true goal, but faith is the process of getting there, and hope is the willingness to live without resolution or closure.* They are indeed, "the three things that last" (1 Corinthians 13:13), but there are few practical teachers of the way of faith and the way of hope. Let's see how the Bible tries to get us there.

Let's start with Moses on Mount Sinai. He says to Yahweh, "Show me your glory, I beg you." And Yahweh says, "I will let all my splendor pass in front of you, and I will pronounce before you the name Yahweh. But I have compassion on whom I will. I show pity to whom I please. You are not ready to see my face. For humanity cannot see me and live." And so Yahweh says to him, "There's a place in the cleft of the rock; stand there. When my glory passes by, I will shield you with my hand while I pass by. Then I will take my hand away and you will see the back of me. But my face you cannot see" (Exodus 33:18–20).

At the beginning, mature adult relationship with God is not yet possible. Now hold on to that because, by the end of the Bible, we're going to have perfectly personal interface, but it is going to take us a long time to get there, just as it does with each of us individually (remember, each soul is unique, just as each face is).

We all fear and avoid intimacy, it seems. It is too powerful and demands that we also "have faces," that is, *self-confidence, identity, dignity and a certain courage to accept our own unique face*—and then even worse—that once we have it, to be willing to give it away to another.

At first the individual is not ready for presence. We settle for tribal customs, laws and occupations as our identity, which is still true today. So God starts by giving the whole group a sense of dignity and identity. That's because most individuals cannot contain or sustain trust and love by themselves. Yahweh creates "a chosen people": "You will be my people and I will be your God" (Jeremiah 32:38).

It seems the experience of specialness is almost too awesome to be carried by an individual. One will either disbelieve it or abuse it, either by ego deflation or ego inflation, self-hatred or conceit. We see even now how difficult it is for a person to stand before the face of God in that perfect balance between humility and dignity. So God begins with a people "consecrated as his very own" (Deuteronomy 14:2). The group holds the Mystery together, which becomes the very meaning of "church."

Membership in the group will become a gateway to, but often a substitute for personal encounter and inner experience.

We could say, "In the beginning is the relationship," like the Trinity itself, yet the relationship is between the group and Yahweh. How we relate to God always reveals how we will relate to people, and how we relate to people is an almost infallible indicator of how we relate to God and let God relate to us.

How we relate is how we relate, and how we relate to anything is a good indicator of how we relate to everything. The whole Bible is a school of relationship, revealing both its best qualities and its worst.

That word *trinity*, by the way, is never found in the Bible. It was, and is, simply our way to explain how God gradually comes to be seen as a communion of persons, a perfect giving and a perfect receiving, a total interface, a mutual indwelling, or as Charles Williams called it, "co-inherence." The Bible is slowly making us capable of entering into that co-inherence; it is giving us a face capable of receiving divine dignity, and even daring to think that we could love God back—and that God would care!

We are gradually being drawn inside the very mystery of Divine sharing. Saint Teresa of Avila describes it as "the interior castle." John's whole Gospel could be seen as one great meditation on that momentous realization, especially chapters 13—17, where John is almost drunk with inner realizations of union and divine election.

What's really exciting these days is to see how the science of quantum physics is now changing the way we see things, in a way that recalls what I have just said about Trinity and relationship. The new physics shows that all the elements of the entire known universe, from atomic particles to galaxies, are in orbit and cycle with one another.

This new science, which came in Einstein's footsteps, sees no such thing in the whole universe as autonomy. It seems that any kind of autonomy or self-sufficiency is a total illusion. That's what we really mean by the "general theory of relativity."

All is in flux, physically and psychologically, unless we have an Absolute Center, which is exactly the salvation that the Bible promises.

"you shall have one god before you" (exodus 20:3)

The miracle of monotheism is that, not only is it a gift to spirituality, it is also an utter gift to our mental and emotional health. Somehow monotheism tells us that there is one coherent world. Today some psychologists speak of the "constituting other." At any one moment in our lives we usually seek out a constituting other, a person, to serve as a kind of foil for our own identity. We find our identity through our relationship with another. They mirror us as this or that, and we either accept it or reject it. We either grow from someone loving us or wither from a negative mirroring.

That's probably why all people are first defined in families and why most are called to marriage, because that sets the stage, gives you some grounding for relationship in general. Relationship seems so crucial to the whole plan that God had to risk giving us sexual passion for one another, with all the problems that might bring. That's because outside of relationship we simply "do not know" who we are or what we are created for.

The genius of the first commandment was that by putting "one God before you," you were placed inside of one coherent world, with one center, one pattern, one realm of meaning. If you will allow me to use psychological language related to what we call salvation, let me put it this way: Having *One* who affirms us is a very good start for our ego structure and our growth as persons. God, for the believer, becomes the Ultimate Constituting Other.

No wonder the Hebrews spoke of being "saved" by Yahweh, as did Christians after them! When God names you as good, and "lets his face shine upon you" (Numbers 6:25), you are pretty much home free.

Even humanly, without *some significant other* naming us, we have a very fragile sense of ourselves. "Many gods before us" is like a state of sexual promiscuity; the person remains scattered, dissipated, without focus and like a "reed shaking in the wind." This is particularly true of young people, although it's true for most people in the secular West today. *Without a significant other who* is also *The Significant Other, we are burdened with being our own center and circumference.* That's pretty impossible, and finally futile if you try.

Our center will change literally every few hours or even every few minutes, with every new celebrity, reputation, image, name, TV show, magazine article, billboard or love interest. Constantly the unconstituted (read "unsaved") self changes. Any good therapist can tell you this is what we're dealing with today. It is frightening for our future and its institutions.

I often notice young mothers in stores and supermarkets, and they are invariably some of the happiest people I meet. They often make eye contact and smile at you, and graciously apologize for being in your way. Why? Their constituting other is absolutely clear and constant: their baby. Inside of that they know who they are, and they know exactly what their day's purpose is.

To the Jewish person, and to all of us who have inherited their wisdom, there was one face that we looked to for mirroring, one face that we keep returning to for validation and definition, the face of God. Healthy religion creates very healthy people.

When I was a nineteen-year-old Franciscan novice, I would say that most of my classmates and I were very happy people, joking and peaceful most of the time. Our little world was whittled down to absolute essentials, and inside of that we were quite content. That is the value of stage one, simple consciousness, and why so many want to stay there. The trouble is that it is not yet integrated, mature or even highly conscious. Most of us were living on the cruise control of obeying laws and positive self-image, which had yet to be tried. But it was the best kind of beginning.

being possessed

If a person has a constantly changing reference point, you've got a very insecure person. He or she will take on any persona, negative or positive, and become incapable of much personal integrity. This is the celebrity-obsessed world we are living inside of today in America.

The biblical tradition will eventually use the language of "having a demon," to describe the negative identity. We post-enlightenment, educated people don't like this language too much. But one way to think of "being possessed" is when there is *an unhealthy other* who is defining you, and defining you poorly. It's when a negative projection or agenda has captured you and you have internalized it either consciously or unconsciously.

In that sense, I personally know a lot of possessed people! It's no surprise that Jesus exorcised so many demons who seemed to carry the negative projections of the crowd (epileptic boy), the synagogue (Mark 1:23 ff.), the village (man chained outside in the cemetery), the medical establishment (bent-over woman) or the military ("legion").

The ancients were not as naïve as we might think. In these stories we see exactly what internalization of negative values means. It does need major "exorcism" or healing, we just tend to send them to therapists instead of holy people. In general, the only cure for negative possession is a positive repossession! Jesus is always "repossessing people"— for themselves and for God.

When a holy person or a totally accepting person becomes your chosen and choosing mirror, you are in fact healed! I hope it does not sound too presumptuous, but I think I have exorcised a good number of people in my life, and it was because *they* had the trust and the humility to let me mirror them positively and replace the old mirror of their abusive dad, their toxic church or their racist neighborhood. That's why Jesus says, "*Your* faith has saved you" (Luke 7:50). I am just saying the same.

The Bible is always calling forth a positive "Thou" to which God can be an "I," which wonderfully takes away our own negative "I." That is really the heart of the matter. The I-Thou language of Martin Buber is a way of speaking of the Lover-Beloved relationship, and it is qualitatively quite different than the I-It relationship, where everything is functional, impersonal and earned. Sin could almost be defined as living your whole life inside of I-It and never experiencing the I-Thou relationship of a Beloved.

Another wonderful, but less familiar, Jewish philosopher is Emmanuel Levinas (1906–1995), who kept company with some of the architects of modern thinking, including Edmund Husserl and Martin Heidegger. Levinas illustrates that truth in the biblical tradition is not like the Greek tradition (which is where our Western thinking comes from). The biblical tradition says that truth is found not in abstract concepts, but in *an encounter with otherness.*

It is, in Levinas's vocabulary, "the face of the other" that transforms us, converts us and gives us our deepest identity. The face of Yahweh for Moses, the face of a lover for Jacob, the face of an accuser for David, the face of the enemy for Judith, these change people's "truth." This sets the Jewish moral and mystical coordinates. It's why, to this day, Jewish teachers tell stories or write *midrashim* more than try to create a perfectly systematic theology, as Catholicism does.

In the Greek tradition, where we Western Christians have been educated, truth is formed and found by the private mind and its collections of agreed-upon ideas. Identity can be achieved autonomously, with a certain kind of self-sufficiency. Thus we speak of the "self-made man" and cultural truth. It's the Greek idea of the hero or god, although we never seem to remember that they were normally tragic heroes and nasty gods. Relationships in Greek theater are normally dominating, manipulating and tragic, seldom mutual and loving.

Jesus brings the biblical tradition to a climax when he defines truth itself as personal rather than conceptual. He says "I am the truth" (John 14:6) and then immediately defines himself as one who is in absolute relationship with his "Father" (14:7, 9–10) and the Spirit who is in relationship to both (14:16–18). *This rearranges the world of religion from arguments over ideas and concepts into a world of encounter, relationship and presence to the face of the other. That changes everything.*

respect for mystery allows presence

Let me try to define the mystery of presence if I can, but first of all, the concept of mystery itself. Most of us grew up thinking that mysteries were things we could not understand, so we should not try. But that's not the traditional or true meaning of the word. Mystery is not something that you cannot understand, but it is something that is *endlessly understandable!* It is multilayered and pregnant with meaning and never totally admits to closure or resolution.

Mysterion in the mystery religions of Asia Minor was something that you had to be initiated into through personal experience, not just by reading books or memorizing doctrines. Paul draws upon this frequently in his letters to peoples of that area.

He offered, in his words, "a wisdom to offer those who have reached maturity, not the philosophies of the masters of our age, but the hidden wisdom of God that we teach in our mysteries…things beyond the mind of humanity that God has prepared for those who love him" (1 Corinthians 2:6–7, 9).

A few verses later, he says it is known by a completely different process and mind: "knowing spiritual things spiritually" (2:13). In other words, it could not be communicated to people who had not at least some level of inner experience (read "prayer"). It is that necessity of personal experience that grounds all true religion and is constantly illustrated by story and character in the Bible. The great figures in the Bible do not just "believe," they somehow *know. But they know mysteriously.*

Let's give a concrete example. Christians speak of the "paschal mystery," the process of loss and renewal that was lived and personified in the death and raising up of Jesus. We can affirm that belief in ritual and song, as we do in the Eucharist, but until people have lost their foundation and ground, and then experienced God upholding them so that they come out even more alive on the other side, the expression "paschal mystery" is little understood and not essentially transformative.

Paschal mystery is a doctrine that Christians would probably intellectually assent to, but it is not yet the very cornerstone of one's life philosophy. That is the difference between belief systems and living faith.
*We move from one to the other only through encounter, surrender, trust and
an inner experience of presence and power.*

Healthy religion knows that there are many essential things you can
only know by a different path than cerebral knowing. Atheists do not
know that. The really great truths, like love and inner freedom, are not
fully conceptual, and they can never be understood by reason alone.
They can never be "proven" to others, whether you're a Ph.D. or even
have five degrees in theology. They are known holistically, that is—
when *all* of you is there! (no easy task, by the way). That's why Saint
Bonaventure, scholar and intellectual, said that a cleaning person can
know God much better than can a doctor in theology.

It's critical that we understand that God is not dependent upon
knowledge in the sense that the Western mind understands knowledge.
How could God make such a mistake when 98 percent of the people
who have ever lived could not read or write? Biblical knowing is more
akin to face-to-face presence. It is a full-body knowing, a cellular knowing, and thus the word often used for "knowing" in key biblical texts is
actually the word for "carnal knowledge" or sexual intimacy!

In the biblical tradition you do not see this self-made, autonomous
"getting it right" agenda that you see in later images of Christian holiness. Biblical rightness is primarily right relationship! There are no
Promethean, defiantly original figures idealized in the Bible. With the
possible exception of Jesus' mother, Mary, and Jesus himself, almost
every other biblical character, whether in Hebrew or Christian
Scriptures, is shown as a transformed sinner, as someone who first does
it wrong before he or she ever does it right. The Bible is full of flawed,
wounded individuals.

Those flaws train them, it seems, for mutuality, vulnerability and
honest face-to-face relationship, where you allow the other to influence

you. Our word for that is *presence* or even *faith*. It is rarer than you might think.

presence

Let me describe the effect of presence in this way. The mystery of presence is *that encounter wherein the self-disclosure of one evokes a deeper life in the other*. There is nothing you need to "think" or understand to be present; it is all about giving and receiving right now, and it is not done in the mind. It is actually *a transference and sharing of Being*, and will be experienced as grace, gratuity and inner-groundedness.

Thus there is always a great leap of inner authenticity that is associated with true mutual presence, because in being received graciously, we are able to receive ourselves at an ever-deeper level yet recognize that we are both part of something Greater—Being itself. It gives one great happiness and deep joy.

We really are socially contagious human beings, but we settle for "human doings." It is at the *being* level that life is most vitally transferred. It's no surprise that we Catholics speak of Eucharist as the "Real Presence." It is on that level that life and energy are transferred.

That's what happened to each one of you when you first fell in love—that's why falling in love is so exciting. Suddenly the very eyes of the other receiving me, delighting in me, enjoying me and looking at me—make me feel like *me*, and my best me! For believers, that is also what happens when they apprehend the "Real Presence" in the Eucharist. We move to a deeper level of Being ourselves when we genuinely receive the being and the gaze of the Self-Giving Jesus. It reminds me of what they told me in some Hindu temples in India: "You come here not to gaze at God, but to let God gaze at you."

The lover can say that it's as if I never knew myself until you knew me, or it's as if I never could accept myself until you accepted me. That's how fragile we are and how needy we are of one another's love and affirmation. Thus Jesus said, "When you forgive others, they are unbound;

and those you don't forgive, you keep them bound up" (John 20:22–23).

How much power God has given us for one another! We've been given the capacity to receive one another's love and to receive one another's curse, to affirm one another and to deny one another, and these become the very gateways for Divine affirmation or ignorance of the Divine.

What a risk God took! How sad God must be when there are no truthful and loving mirrors for many newborn children, for rejected groups, gays and lesbians, disabled people, disfigured people or so-called sinners or criminals.

To have naked interface with the Ultimate Other is to know one's self in one's truest and deepest being. When you allow yourself to be perfectly received, totally gazed upon by the One who knows everything and receives everything, you are indestructible.

If you can learn how to receive the perfect gaze of the Other, to be mirrored by the Other, then the voices of the human crowd, even negative ones, have little power to hurt you. Best of all, as Meister Eckhart has been quoted, "the eyes with which you will look back at God will be the same eyes with which God first looked at you."

Standing humbly before God's gaze not only unites the psyche but it does the very thing that I know when I teach contemplative prayer. It unifies desire. It frees us from what Henri de Lubac calls the *vertigo of imagination.* It's the whirlpool of imagination, looking here, there and everywhere. Standing before *one, accepting* God literally allows you to be composed and gathered into one place. You *can* be in one place; you *can* be here, now. You stop always looking over there, for tomorrow's happiness. Then, and always, "now is the favorable time, today is the day of salvation" (2 Corinthians 6:2).

There is a lovely passage in the first chapter of John's Gospel that tracks this passing on of the positive gaze: First John the Baptizer "gazes hard" at Jesus and affirms him (v. 35), then Jesus invites Andrew and another disciple to "come and see" and stay at his house (v. 39). Soon he "gazes hard" at Simon Peter and straightforwardly affirms him (v. 42), then he meets and invites Philip (v. 43). Then Philip invites Nathanael to also "come and see" (v. 46), and Jesus then gazes at Nathanael and reveals a "secret seeing" of something "under the fig tree" (v. 48), which somehow opens the door of full trust and faith affirmation on Nathanael's part (v. 49).

That is an entire chain of lovely male affirmation and validation, which is not easy for men to do. Jesus seems to be calling it Jacob's ladder at the end of the passage, which opens up the heavens in both directions (1:51). It is a perfect text for evangelization by presence, lifestyle and loving relationship, instead of by mere preaching and teaching. As Saint Francis is supposed to have said, "Preach the gospel at all times; when necessary, use words."

A few years ago I was teaching Mother Teresa's sisters at the motherhouse in Calcutta, India, and during that time visited many different Hindu temples and communities. I met many Hindus—they make up most of the people the sisters work with. The sisters kept telling me how tolerant the Hindu people are. They accept everything, perhaps a necessity of survival in India. The sisters know that this level of acceptance and tolerance is very different than in the West, and they told me that Mother Teresa shared in this tolerance.

To their knowledge she never tried to make a single Hindu or a Muslim into a Christian. She told them not to talk *about* Jesus, as much as trying to *be* Jesus! That's how you pass on the gaze. In fact, my definition of a Christian might not seem like one at all: *A true Christian is invariably someone who has met a true Christian.* I even wonder if, in a sense, that is not the real meaning of the passing on of "apostolic succession." The mystery of the Risen Christ is passed on by mutual presence and communion.

If you haven't stood naked before the loving gaze of God, or at least one significant other person, then you're still "unbegotten." You're unborn, spiritually and psychologically. You're dead, as it were. The philosophical word for the same is *nonbeing*. We have no real being "until we have faces" to receive the other, to offer ourselves, and then to pass on our very selves in the same way. It will be experienced as depth, acceptance and forgiveness for being who we are, a quality of being that is shared, compassionate and totally gift.

We see that Saint Paul understands this in a most beautiful paragraph from his Second Letter to the Corinthians. He says, "we with our unveiled faces will gradually reflect like mirrors the brightness of the Lord. All will grow brighter and brighter as we are gradually turned into the image that we reflect" (3:18).

It doesn't have to do with being perfect. It has to do with staying in relationship, holding onto union as tightly as God holds onto you, staying in there. The one who knows all and receives all, as a mirror does, has no trouble forgiving all. It's not a matter of being correct, but of being connected.

On retreat I once wrote in my journal, "How good of you, God, to make truth a relationship instead of an idea. Now there is room between you and me for growth, for conversation, for exception, for the infinite understandings created by intimacy, for the possibility to give back and to give something to You—as if I could give anything back to You. You offer the possibility to undo, to please, to apologize, to change, to surrender. There's room for stages and for suffering, for mutual passion and mutual pity. There's room for mutual everything."

That's the genius of the biblical tradition. Jesus offers himself as "way, truth and life" (John 14:6), and suddenly it has all become the sharing of our person instead of any fighting over ideas. I have no doubt that statement will meet with much resistance and criticism, because *you feel so much more in control when you are right than when you are in right relationship.* I'm afraid we will always resist relational, practical truth in favor of abstractions.

Abstractions offer the ego lots of payoffs: We can remain seemingly in control; we can live in our heads; we can avoid loving in general or loving anyone in particular; we can avoid all humor, paradox and freedom. Even God is not free to act outside of our abstract theological conclusions, yet that is exactly what God does every time God forgives and shows mercy, which is not rational at all.

I served as a jail chaplain near my home in Albuquerque for fourteen years. One Christmas Day I was talking to an old Hispanic man in his cell. I said to him, "Well, it must be pretty lonely today on Christmas Day to be here." He said something that astounded me. He said, "Father, if you agree to be with him, he always agrees to be with you." Now there's a man who learned everything I'm talking about with all my sophisticated theology. He doesn't need to know all this stuff. He knows how to live before the mirror. He has a face, and he allows God a face.

From God's side the gift is total, once and for all, and forever, God's face is turned toward us absolutely. It is we who have to learn, "little by little" as John of the Cross says, to return the gaze. Then we have faces too.

inclusive language for god

As we all know, in the last twenty years we've had a lot of arguments in our culture and in our church about third-person language when speaking of God. Should we say, "he," "she" or "it"? I understand the reason for that questioning and would agree with almost all of it.

We must recognize our extreme overreliance upon masculine images and words. God is clearly beyond gender. For the sake of many people who have been wounded by the masculine, and many who can only trust the feminine because of those wounds, we must also use feminine images for God—or many will never have access to the Divine.

But the important thing to note is that the Bible is amazingly uninterested about third-person language, about he, she or it, although it surely reflects patriarchal worldviews. The much stronger preoccupation of the Bible is the discovery of *second-person language for God!* It is concerned about the direct encounter between two "faces"—God and you, God and the community. What we are aiming for, as this whole chapter asserts, is the possibility of an I-Thou capacity. Sometimes a heady preoccupation with the correct pronoun can actually be an avoidance of such a relationship; sometimes it is a much-needed correction.

Most languages have several words for the second-person *you* like German, Spanish or French, but modern English has only one. That's why we have to use the Old English word *thou* to try to come close to this biblical experience of a special and intimate relationship. It's a relationship in which one feels treasured, not like an object but somehow like a subject, where one feels mutuality, reciprocity and respect.

The second form of *you* in most languages was usually reserved for parents and people in authority, those who deserved respect. We don't have this. You almost wonder if it's a real loss of consciousness in the English-speaking world for the I-Thou relationship. Our language might be telling us that we don't value *thou* relationships enough, those relationships before which we *become* an "I."

In no way would I dismiss or make light of these third-person arguments for inclusive language. We must honor this need whenever and wherever possible (When I fail to do it in this book, it is because I am afraid it might distract from my major point in that sentence.). But I really don't think that the God revealed to us in the Bible cares *what* word you use—as long as it is honest, trustful and somehow an endearment!

The Hebrew text itself offers us a number of choices: Elohim, Yahweh, El Shaddai (warm-breasted One), Lord, Sophia, Lord of Hosts. Clearly, the important thing is that you have the relationship, the encounter, the love and that somewhere you have experienced yourself being addressed as a Beloved.

If the feminine word helps you to address and be addressed, then you *must* use it. If the masculine word helps you to address and be addressed and to enter into intimacy, you *must* use it. There are probably as many different words as there are lovers and ways of loving!

If you've ever been in love, whether between adults or between parents and children, you know you find special little words for each other, little nicknames that you like to call one another that somehow express the specialness that just exists between the two of you. That is the sacred word that you must find, just as we do in prayer! It's far, far oversimplified to simply make it *he, she* or *it.*

You absolutely must find the safe and wondrous "I" before whom you can be a "Thou." Then you will have the face you have always waited for and have always known to be true.

chapter four
the boxing ring

"The Law is only our nursemaid. When the Christ comes, we are legitimated by trust."

—Galatians 3:24

"Do I mean that faith makes the Law pointless? Not at all. In fact, we are giving the Law its true value."

—Romans 3:31

After that last chapter on "mere" mutuality and presence, a lot of you are perhaps worried that I—or the Bible—are leading you into a swamp of relativism. After all, we do need to know where we stand on things, don't we? Surely, we have to eat at least a little of the fruit of the tree of the knowledge of good and evil? This chapter is going to lead you even deeper into what is not a swamp at all, but will feel like it if you are not familiar with biblical themes and directions.

But don't be afraid; I am not a heretic, nor is the Bible leading you astray. Not without good reason did Jesus say that it is a "narrow gate and a hard road that leads to life" (Matthew 7:13). Faith will always be faith, and we are never going to be able to make it into total certitude and clarity, although that is always the temptation of religion.

First of all, I think we must be honest and admit that the only Absolute that the Bible ever promised us is Yahweh, and in relationship to Yahweh all else is indeed relative. No institution, not Israel itself, no priesthood, no kingship, no military might, no conceptual school of thought and no legal system was ever allowed to displace Yahweh as the "rock and only fortress" of Israel (Psalm 71). In fact, one might say that is the major point! Although each one of them tried, and often did, replace Yahweh as the Central Reference Point, it is always called "idolatry" by the prophets.

Paul will say the same. Nothing else can take its place or "come between us and God's love" (Romans 8:38–39), but because morality in particular is a common counterfeit for religion, and often substitutes as a false absolute, we will see that Paul takes law on in a special way; in fact, it absorbs the content of the two books of the Bible quoted at the beginning of this chapter, Romans and Galatians. These two letters are a *tour de force* argument against the idolatry of law and are essential to the entire biblical canon.

The relationship between grace and law ends up being a central issue for almost anyone involved in religion at any depth. Basically, it is the creative tension between religion as requirements and religion as transformation. Is God's favor based on a performance principle, or is it an entirely different economy and equation? As you probably expect, I will come down heavily on the side of a different equation, but I do not want to dismiss or discount the necessary push and pull that is involved here. Thus I call it a boxing match, but a match in which grace *must* and will always win.

law, prophets, wisdom

This creative tension seems to show itself as a necessary staging that we all have to go through. It is amazing to see that the three classic divisions of the Hebrew Scriptures (Law, Prophets, Wisdom) also parallel the normal development of spiritual consciousness and even human growth, which I will call (1) order, (2) criticism and (3) integration.

Clearly the easiest way to start, and the way that most people in history have, in fact, started, is with tradition, custom, law and order: "This is the way we do it." We see that taught very clearly early in the Bible, and would be the best way to start. Torah, or Law, provides ego structure, identity, exclusivity, boundaries, loyalty and necessary discipline to counter the imperial ego. It gives the shapeless self a container, a ground on which to stand, a place from which to move out.

Those elements are largely the concerns of books such as Leviticus, Numbers and Deuteronomy, which most Christians do not read too much, because they are not always "inspiring." But what they do is "keep the edges hot" so that something serious and in-depth can happen inside. There's something about an absolute that compels you, something that pulls you into the boxing ring. Absolutes say, "There's something crucial at stake here." In fact, it's your soul. Do not throw out the very concept of ideals, absolutes, laws, boundaries, goals or you will get nowhere.

If you do not have a solid container, you are not held in one place long enough to go deep. Even if you rebel against the container—*which you will if you keep growing*—you will still have to struggle appropriately with the values espoused by the container! Witness the Adam and Eve conflict, and Paul's inner struggle, especially Romans 7:7–25. Paul takes much of Romans and Galatians to say what the Dalai Lama says in one oft-quoted line: "You must learn the meaning of the law very well, so you will know how to disobey it properly." You must know and respect the rules before you can break the rules.

Now if you think that is rebellious talk, it probably means you have not studied much of the second section of the Hebrew Scriptures, the Prophets or the birth of criticism. Without doubt, the prophetic canon has had the least influence on Catholic and Protestant theology, largely because we only read them insofar as they offered us proof texts for the coming of the Messiah. Yet they take up far too much room in the Bible just to be saying that. Prophesying the Messiah is not even their major concern, except to Christians who need proof texts.

What we do see in the prophetic books is the clear emergence of critical consciousness and interior struggle in Israel. We see them allowing an objective, outer witness, which is the death knell for both the ego and the group ego. They have to leave their false innocence and naïve superiority behind and admit that they do not always live what they say they do at the level of "law" or inside their idealized self-image.

We can call the prophets almost the fathers and mothers of consciousness, because until you move to self-reflexive, self-critical thinking, you don't move to any deep level of consciousness at all. In fact, you largely remain unconscious, falsely innocent and unaware. Thus most people choose to remain in that first stage of consciousness. "First naïveté" is very secure and consoling. It is great to think you are the best and the center of the world. It even passes for holiness, but it isn't at all.

Until an objective inner witness emerges that looks back at us with utter honesty, one cannot speak of being awake or conscious. That is at the heart of what we mean by "waking up"! (If you want to read a fascinating scientific study of this, read Julian Jaynes's, *The Origin of Consciousness in the Breakdown of the Bicameral Mind*.) Until then, most people are on cruise control and cannot see their egocentricity at work.

Very unfortunately, people are so afraid of a negative and judgmental critic, that they never seem to access the "Compassionate Witness" promised us in the gift of the Holy Spirit (see John 14:16 ff.). How wonderful that John calls the Holy Spirit a *paracletos*, or "defense attorney."

It is painful but necessary to be critical of your own system, whatever it is. But do know it will never make you popular. As you know, the prophets are always rejected by their own (see Luke 12:50–51) and usually killed. That sets the stage for understanding Jesus and the rarity of the third stage of "integration."

74

The third section of the Hebrew Scriptures are the Wisdom books, including, among others, many of the Psalms, Ecclesiastes, the Song of Songs, the book of Wisdom and, most especially, the book of Job. Here we see the clear emergence of what I would like to call non-dualistic thinking. They are finally secure enough to deal with mystery and complex issues that cannot be resolved, that allow no closure, that demand trust, surrender and moving to a deeper level that will be called biblical "faith" itself. God, for example, answers none of Job's questions, but rather leads him deeper into mystery.

Look at it this way: (1) The Law is the *thesis;* it lays the ground (2) against which the Prophets develop a positive *antithesis,* but yet a critique. The dialectic begins; people struggle into consciousness. (3) Then, and only then, come the Wisdom books, which are a *synthesis* and integration of the first two. The first two stages are still trapped in a good, but limited, dualistic consciousness; the third breaks through to patience with mystery, paradox, suffering and limitations. Jesus is such a dramatic representation of stage-three wisdom, that he ended up creating a whole new religion—a religion that people trapped in stages one and two always misunderstand.

Remember this: *Transcendence to higher levels of consciousness always means inclusion of the previous levels!* Most reforms and revolutions of history have failed to understand this. This is the genius of the biblical revelation. True wisdom will honor and include both the Law and the Prophets, exactly as Jesus said—"to bring them to completion" (Matthew 5:17).

the actor with a plank in his eye

Allow me some psychological language to explain, partly, this theological staging; it is the language of ego and shadow. The ego is that part of the self that wants to be significant, central, important. It is very defended and self-protective by its very nature. *It must eliminate the negative to succeed*

(Jesus would call it the "actor" in Matthew 23, usually translated from the Greek as "hypocrite").

The shadow is that part of the self that we don't want to see, that we're always afraid of and don't want others to see either. Our tendency is to try to hide it or deny it, even and most especially from ourselves. Jesus, quoting Isaiah, describes it as "listening but not understanding, seeing, but not perceiving" (Matthew 13:14–15). Addicts today just call it "denial."

If our "actor" is defended, the shadow will be denied and repressed, but if our "actor" is over-defended, the shadow is actually hated and projected elsewhere (for example, there are homosexual ministers who hate and attack homosexuals). One point here is crucial: *The shadow self is not of itself evil; it just allows you to do evil without recognizing it as evil!* That is why Jesus criticizes hypocrisy more than anything else. He does not hate sinners at all, but only people who pretend they are not sinners! Check that out, story by story, if you do not believe me.

Archaic religion and most of the history of religion has almost always seen the shadow as the problem. What religion is about is getting rid of the shadow, isn't it? This is the classic example of dealing with the symptom instead of the cause. We cannot really get rid of the shadow; we can only expose its game—which is, in great part, to get rid of its effects. Or as Ephesians puts it, "Anything exposed to the light turns into light itself" (5:14).

Jesus and the prophets deal with the cause, which is the ego. Our problem is not our shadow self nearly as much as our over-defended ego, which always sees and hates its own faults in other people, and thus avoids its own conversion.

Jesus' phrase for the denied shadow is "the plank in your own eye," which you invariably see as the "splinter in your brother's eye" (Matthew 7:4–5). Jesus' advice is absolutely perfect: "Take the plank out of your own eye, and then you will see clearly enough to take the splinter out of your brother's eye." He does not deny that we should deal with evil, but you better do your own housecleaning first—in a most radical way—which he will later even describe as "plucking out your eye" (Matthew 18:9). If we do not see our own "plank," it is inevitable that we will hate it elsewhere.

The genius of Jesus is that he wastes no time on repressing or denying the shadow. In that, he is a classic prophet, one of those who do not merely expose the denied shadow of Israel, but instead attack the real problem, which is the ego and arrogance of Israel and people misusing power. Once you expose the shadow for what it is, its game is over. Its effectiveness entirely depends on disguise and not "seeing the plank in your own eye" (see 2 Corinthians 11:14). Once you see your own plank, the "speck" in your neighbor's eye becomes inconsequential.

Power, perks, prestige symbols and material possessions are the armor of the actor. These are the clear moral concerns of Jesus. Any over-concern for sexual rules or purity codes are almost always repression or punishment of shadow issues, and of other people, and Jesus shows little interest there.

Jesus is not too interested in moral purity because he knows that any preoccupation with repressing the shadow does not lead us into personal transformation, empathy, compassion or patience, but invariably into one of two certain paths: denial or disguise, repression or hypocrisy. Isn't that rather evident? Immature religion creates a high degree of "cognitively rigid" people or very hateful and attacking people—and often both. It is almost our public image today, yet God's goal is exactly the opposite.

the real sin

Jesus, instead, is always trying to undercut the arrogance, the self-validation, the cold calculation of the ego. The entire Sermon on the Mount makes that quite clear (Matthew 5—7). He clearly sees *pride, self-sufficiency and its resultant hypocrisy* as the primary moral problems. "You have neglected the weightier matters of the law—justice, mercy and good faith" (Matthew 23:23) in favor of temple tithes, he says to the scribes and Pharisees.

As such, Jesus is addressing the radical cause of evil and not the mere symptoms. As John the Baptist says of Jesus' work, he "lays his axe to the root *(radix)* of the tree" (Matthew 3:10). Most of us just keep trimming the branches and wonder why the same faults keep regrowing out of the trunk.

Now the definition of sin that many of us were given was "a thought, word or deed contrary to the law of God." The requirements for sin were three: (1) You had to have full knowledge; (2) it had to be a grievous matter; (3) you had to give it full consent.

That all sounds reasonable at first glance, but actually it's not a definition of biblical sin at all; it's a juridical definition of law. We lost touch with the biblical tradition and the *intimately personal struggle* meant by the word *sin*. We made the whole thing juridical where we could easily identify it, shame it and enforce it.

Thus our concerns came with external behavior that could be pointed to, measured, defined and controlled or "brought into court" as it were. You cannot do that with "mercy, justice, and good faith" (Matthew 23:23), which Jesus calls "the weightier matters of the law."

Politicians are seldom voted out for deceit, greed or ambition, which we almost assume, but largely if we catch them in one of the "hot sins." Shaming is much easier to do with body-based issues for some reason. I think the body holds shame quite easily. It easily allows stone-throwing, whereas justice and mercy and good faith do not.

paul's contribution

Although Jesus gives us a clear litany of the creative tensions between law and grace in his six-part litany of "your ancestors said…but I say" (Matthew 5:20–48), the natural ego need for purity codes and group identity markers soon won out again. This is what Paul aggressively attacks in both Romans and Galatians.

These letters are sophisticated studies of the meaning, purpose and limitations of law. They have had little effect on the continued Christian idealization of law, although Paul makes it very clear: *Laws can only give us information, and even helpful information, but they cannot give us transformation* (Romans 3:20; 7:7–13). How have we so consistently missed that point?

Let's begin with a passage from the ninth chapter of Romans. Paul says, "Israel was looking for a righteousness derived from the law and yet it failed to achieve the purposes of the law. Why did they fail? Because they relied on being good instead of trusting in faith! In other words, they stumbled over the stumbling stone" (9:31–32).

He talks as if God almost set up this stumbling stone intentionally. It's a stumbling stone mentioned earlier in Scripture, "See how I lay in Zion, a stone to stumble over, a rock to trip people up. Only those who believe in him, in God, will have no cause for shame" (Romans 9:33).

Law is a necessary stage one, but if you stay there, Paul believes, and I often see, it actually becomes a "stumbling stone." It often frustrates the process of transformation by becoming an end in itself. It inoculates you from the real thing. You might find it hard to stay with Paul's seemingly tortuous logic, but the results are compelling and quite clarifying. They are necessary to distinguish the gospel message from regular moralistic religion.

You're familiar with the English word *foil*. A foil is "a necessary frustration." Now Paul will say that the law is such a foil in Romans 7:7–13 and other places: He will actually say that God gave us the law to show us that we can't obey the law!

God has to get you in the correct arena, involved in the right boxing ring. God has to get you involved with the real issues, the assumption being that if you are in the right container, you have a much better chance of discovering the real contents. The trouble is that most people substitute the container for the contents! It is the common pattern.

Some years ago I was speaking at a conference with theologian Father Richard McBrien. We were being heckled by people calling us liberals and other "bad" names! Richard McBrien, who is much more a theologian than I am, went to the microphone and said, "Brothers and sisters, if you want more people like Richard Rohr and me, just go back to that old church of law and structure because that is what produced us! We were both raised as conservative, law-abiding Catholics, and that very container is what led us to talk the way we do today." Neither of us has left those values; in fact, it is the very values taught to us by the Scriptures and by the church that allow us to critique that church! Is that amazing? *Actually, it is the ordinary pattern.*

The reason we can move toward real freedom is because we started with moral laws and clear expectations from authority figures, which put good and needed limits to our natural egocentricity. I'll bet most of you reading this book began rather conservatively. A good therapist will tell you that predictability, order and tradition are really the only way to create a healthy ego structure in the early years.

Torah, or Law, is the best and most helpful place to begin, but not the place to stay, and surely not the place to end. "Written letters bring death, but the Spirit alone brings life," as Paul said (2 Corinthians 3:6).

One person who understood this is Karl Rahner, the German Jesuit, possibly the single greatest Catholic theologian of the twentieth century. He wrote volume after volume of theology as the church rediscovered itself before, during and after Vatican II. Rahner wrote in his 1972 book, *The Shape of the Church to Come:* "We must show men and women today, at least the beginnings of the path that leads credibly and concretely into the freedom of God. But have no doubt, freedom is the goal. Where men and women have not begun to have the experience of God and of God's spirit who liberates us from the most profound anxieties of life, and from our endless guilt, there is really no point in proclaiming to them the ethical norms of Christianity."[1] But that is exactly what we do. Unfortunately, most do not take the law as a foil, but rather as a fulfillment.

Until people have had some level of inner religious experience, there is no point in asking them to follow the ethical ideals of Jesus. Indeed, they will not be able to understand them. At most they would be only the source of even deeper anxiety. You quite simply don't have the power to obey the law, especially issues like forgiveness of enemies, nonviolence, humble use of power and so on, except in and through union with God. But Paul comes at it from the opposite direction, "Give them the law until it frustrates them to hell!"

Instead of tackling that frustration and moving people toward union with God, what we have by and large done is trivialize the law into small issues that we could obey by willpower, determination and a certain kind of reasonableness, still trying to find salvation through the law. (Two-thirds of the confessions I heard one day recently, in my occasional parish duties, were about "missing Mass on Sunday." Only two penitents showed any significant God-awareness. Most of the confessions were merely laundry lists being brought to the dry cleaner for fear of dirt.)

Morality, which first appears to be the goal and the test of all religion, in time becomes merely the playing field, the theater where the deeper rhythm, the dance of love, shows itself. The moral issues, which are necessary struggles with good and evil, are also necessary struggles with freedom and conditioning. They're struggles between the me and the not-me, the apparent self and the true self. These are the bones on which we sharpen our spiritual teeth. These are the conflicts through which we find the shape of the soul. These are the killing fields in which we surrender to the surgeon.

The smallest of events can teach us everything, if we learn *Who* is doing them with us, through us and for us. But have no doubt: That is the total goal. We want law for the sake of order, obedience and "moral purity"; God and Paul want law for the sake of channeling us toward a realization of divine union, to force the honest person to stumble (see Romans 7:7–13—that's really what it says!), and then "fall into the hands of the living God" (Hebrews 10:31). Juridically, law is an end in itself, absolutely good and necessary for social order.

Spiritually, though, law is a means, not an end at all. This must be made clear, although I sincerely wonder whether it can be, as long as spirituality is exclusively identified with an institution or belonging to a certain group. Please consider this fairly, not as an attack on any institution, but rather as a question of emphasis.

I cannot even understand the purpose of the law except for God in me. It's the Spirit in me that awakens in me the real meaning of the law, which is why Saint John says, "When the Spirit comes, she will show the world how wrong it was about sin, how wrong it was about who was in the right, and how wrong it was in its judgments" (John 16:8). That should give us all some cosmic humility.

Why did Paul come to this so clearly? Because Paul himself was a man of the law. As he tells us in Philippians (3:6–8), he was a perfect Pharisee. "As far as the Law can make you perfect, I was faultless," he says. Yet in the next line he admits that he was a mass-murderer. "How could such perfect religious observance still create hateful and violent men like me?" That was his transformative question, and for him it worked. This still needs to be the question for many religious groups today.

Paul tells us in Romans 7:8 that "sin takes advantage of the law" to achieve its own purposes. What does he mean by that? Our unconverted and natural egocentricity ("sin") uses religion for the purposes of gaining self-respect. If you want to hate somebody, want to be vicious or vengeful or cruel or vindictive, I can tell you a way to do it without feeling an ounce of guilt: Do it for religious reasons! Do it thinking you're obeying a law, thinking you're following some commandment or some verse from the Bible. It works quite well. Your untouched egocentricity can and will use religion to feel superior and "right." It is a common pattern.

Then what is the law really for? It's not to make God love you. That issue is already solved once and forever, and you are powerless to change it one direction or the other. The purpose of spiritual law is simply to sharpen our awareness about who we are and who God is, so that we can name our own insufficiency and, in that same movement, find God's fullness. That's why saints, like Francis, are invariably saying, in effect, "I'm nothing. Everything I've done that's good has come from God. The only things I can claim are my own sins." He is not being overly humble, just truthful. In such people the law has achieved its full purpose.

But because we have not taken Jesus' and Paul's teaching seriously, we have often created a religion of smugness—where people actually think they are not sinners and have obeyed the law. They have "saved" themselves, as it were, and have little need of mercy, compassion and the generosity of God. God is a good Enforcer for them, but not the Saving Love revealed to Israel. They have achieved a certain level of good manners and self-control, but with no real need for divine union, surrender or trust in Anybody Else.

There is so much more you can give to God than obedience. I'm not against obedience, but it's basically the parent-child relationship. It's what you do to create some order with three screaming kids in the house. God did not create the world or the church for the sake of social order and control. Clergy are not policemen, and our job is not enforcement, although many see themselves so, and many want us for the same.

It is always sad for me to hear it, but I am told that after Roman Catholics, the second largest religious group in the United States is former Roman Catholics. Only then can I appreciate Paul's seemingly cheap overstatement: "Through the Law I am dead to the Law, so that finally I can live for God" (Galatians 2:19). When we make black-and-white law our goal and purpose, it comes back to haunt us, because *people leave and attack us with the same black-and-white thinking in which we have trained them.* It always eventually backfires, as we are seeing in those Catholic countries where we once had the total hegemony, like Ireland and Poland, and long ago in Italy, France and Spain.

We, instead, have been given a God who not only allows us to make mistakes, but even uses our mistakes in our favor! That is the gospel economy of grace and is the only thing worthy of being called "good news, and a joy for all the people" (Luke 2:10). If we could have come to God by obedience to laws, there would have been no need for God's love revelation in Jesus. The techniques for order and obedience were already in place.

If we can overcome this stumbling stone, we will have moved to the third section of the Hebrew Scriptures, the wisdom level of consciousness. The quid-pro-quo mind, dualistic thinking, has broken down in the presence of grace and failure, and finally God's mercy is in charge. We can now hold mystery and paradox because God has done the same in us. We will talk about this more in upcoming chapters.

A smaller number of individuals get to the wisdom stage. It was variously symbolized by the *minyan* (the Jewish quorum), the "10 just men" (Genesis 18:32), the remnant (Isaiah 19:20) and the body of Christ. It seems this is more than enough for God to create the yeast and the critical mass that God needs to unfreeze and save the world. "The whole batch is holy if the first handful of dough is holy" as Paul says (Romans 11:16). We rub off on one another, because true spirituality is always contagious.

When you have come out of the boxing ring, the necessary but creative tension of law and grace, you will know that you have won the match, but ironically, you will have won it by losing!

chapter five
good power and bad power

"It is precisely the parts of the body that seem to be
the weakest which are the indispensable ones."

—1 Corinthians 12:22

"How ingeniously you get around the commandment
of God in order to preserve your own traditions."

—Mark 7:9

A prime idea of the Bible is its very straightforward critique of power, from Genesis to Revelation. Watch the news any day, work on a committee, observe a marriage, and you will see that this issue of power has not been well-addressed for most people.

Only very gradually does human consciousness come to a selfless use of power, or the sharing of power, or even a benevolent use of power—in church, politics or even family and marriage. Any critique of power is so counterintuitive that most of Christian history itself has largely avoided it. If you doubt me, just watch the History Channel. It is almost the only story line.

The two epigraphs at the head of this chapter are two subtle Scriptures that I hope illustrate both good power and bad power. In the first Paul encourages his community to protect and honor those without power; in the second Jesus critiques the religious leaders for misusing tradition to enhance their own power.

Good power is what Ken Wilber, in *Sex, Ecology, Spirituality* calls "growth hierarchies," which are needed to protect children, the poor, the entire animal world and all those without power. Bad power is power that is used merely to protect, maintain and promote oneself. Wilber would call those "domination hierarchies." He insists, and I agree, that hierarchy is not inherently bad, nor is power. It is just very dangerous for yourself and others, if you have not done your spiritual work.

Servant leadership is clearly taught, and even commanded by Jesus (see Mark 10:42–45), and when servant leadership is not practiced, we are always set up for a predictable overreaction against all leadership and all authority. It is the perennial pendulum swing of history, which you would think we would see by now. Jesus is clearly the best example of good power—and the strongest critique of bad power that we find in the whole Bible.

A distinction between good and bad power, good and bad authority, is quite important it seems to me. Fortunately both are revealed and judged in the biblical text, although there are many more of the bad kind. (For examples of good authority, see Joseph, Moses and Jesus; for bad authority, see almost everybody else!)

These are quite important clarifications, because in many liberal circles today, the very notion of hierarchy is rejected consciously or unconsciously; in many conservative circles domination hierarchies are often presumed to be the very voice of God. No wonder they so overreact to one another from two such unstable positions.

The development of consciousness charted in the biblical text slowly moves from violence to nonviolence, from imperial power to relational power, from domination hierarchies to growth hierarchies, from the divine right of kings to servant leadership. Without any doubt,

Jesus is the clearest crossover point and is probably why Christianity morphed into a new religion with his teaching and praxis.

This might be the most difficult of all the battles that God seems to have with humanity, although for Christians it should have been resolved in the shared power of the Trinity itself. Here is the dilemma the text creates and does not really resolve: Do a violent people want, create and need a violent God, or has the textual presentation of a sometimes violent God legitimated and even blessed our own violent history? Which comes first?

Both patterns seem to be true and have made it very hard to grow from the scriptural narrative by itself. In other words, nonviolence has been quite slow in coming, just as non-dual thinking has been. Domination hierarchies need both violence and binary thought patterns to survive.

Two thousand years after the revelation of Jesus, many people still seem to prefer a punitive, threatening and violent God, which then produces the same kind of people and the same kind of history. If God does it, then we can—and should—too! Surveys after the U.S. presidential election in 2004 showed that people who had experienced an authoritarian parenting style or God preferred a strong militaristic foreign policy. Voters who had experienced (or learned) a more dialogical parenting style or religion preferred a nonmilitaristic foreign policy. Our parents often become our acceptable God image and government image, for good or for ill.

Psychologically and spiritually, there is no such thing as a triumph by force. Domination is domination, not transformation. How you get there determines where you will finally arrive. The dominated one eventually becomes another dominator, or a sad victim, or both; all of whom are liabilities to society and to themselves. You would think we would see that clear pattern in history. I certainly saw it in my fourteen years as a jail chaplain.

As even Napoleon is supposed to have said, "Only people of the Spirit actually change things, the rest of us just rearrange them;" God alone is patient enough to wait for real change, and powerful enough to know it will happen. The rest of us are content to "rearrange the deck chairs on the Titanic," which is what violence is always doing.

Untransformed people seem to think that problems can be solved by external force, which is to change things from the top down or from the outside in. What the Word of God moves us toward is several kinds of spiritual power. That's where things are not just externally changed but really transformed, and not transformed from the top down but from the bottom up, not from the outside in, but rather from the inside out. Or as Jesus puts it, "Clean the inside of the cup and dish, and the outside will take care of itself" (Matthew 23:26).

Dominative power, or what we usually know as political power, is the ability to influence events or others through coercion, punishment, threat, money, the power of my role or any other external force. It's an illusion that one person can actually change another person; all we can do is externally influence or enforce behavior. (Sometimes, of course, that might be good and necessary, as with children or criminals.)

The trouble with political or dominative power is that even if you attain it by a good process, it invariably has to be maintained by on-going control, which often leads to a multitude of sins—which are no longer called "sin" for some reason. It is very hard for people with power not to become preoccupied with the managing of facts and failure to maintain their power. No one would question that dominative power is probably much more efficient. On the surface, it's even more effective, it gets things done quickly. But it also carries a lot of negative baggage, often in the next generation, which the present generation cannot see in its rush to judgment.

Humans do not have the patience or the humility of God. We want things done tomorrow, today or yesterday to achieve our immediate goals. Spiritual power, however, is the ability to influence events and others through one's very *being.* Evolved people change others interiorly through *who they are,* and through their sharing of wisdom, but not through mere external pressure. It *is* a slower process, but much more long lasting.

In general, the more you try to rely upon external threat, the less you are yourself in touch with your own internal power. They tend to cancel one another out. Conversely, the more you are in touch with your own inner power, the less need you have for any external force, threat or pressure.

I would almost describe spirituality as a concern for one's *being,* one's inner motivation and attitude, one's real inner Source, as opposed to any primary concern for one's "*doing.*" *Doing will always take care of itself when your being is right.* It is our preoccupation with external forms and successes that makes us superficial, judgmental, split off and often just downright wrong—without knowing it.

god sets the tone

We will not trust spiritual power until we have experienced a God who operates in the same way, a God who is willing to wait, allow, forgive, trust and love unconditionally. It is largely a waste of time to tell people to love generously when the God they have been presented with is a taskmaster, loves quite conditionally, is easily offended, very needy and threatens people with eternal torture if they do not "believe" in him.

This is a totally unworkable proposition, and it is largely what we are dealing with today. I don't think most people see this, for some reason, even the clergy who sometimes actually teach such a petty and violent God because they suffer under it themselves.

Fortunately, from the very beginning, the Bible is undercutting this kind of power and teaching us another kind of power. Mark Townsend, in his recent book, *The Gospel of Falling Down,* very creatively and experientially realigns "the beauty of failure in an age of success." He recognizes that God is able to use unlikely figures, and in one way or another they are always unable, inept, unprepared and incapable. The biblical text often shows them to be "powerless" in various ways: Sarah and Abraham, Moses, Rachel and Rebecca, David, Jeremiah, Job and Jesus himself are the upfront examples.

Who is God's choice for the major experiment itself? God didn't pick the Egyptians; God picked the Israelites, an enslaved people in Egypt. In each case, there needs be a discovery of a new kind of power by people who do not have power.

The bottom, the edge, the outsider, as we will see in the Bible, is the privileged spiritual position. In a word, that is why the biblical revelation is revolutionary and even subversive. It is clearly disestablishment literature yet has largely been used by establishments, which is at the heart of our interpretative problem. The so-called "little ones" (Matthew 18:6) or the "poor in spirit" (Matthew 5:3), as Jesus calls them, are the only teachable and "growable" ones according to him. It seems to be God's starting place, sort of like the Twelve-Step programs, because until we admit "that we are powerless," the Real Power will not be recognized, accepted or even sought.

When Moses leads the people to the edge of the Red Sea, Moses says to them, "Have no fear. Stand firm. You will see what Yahweh will do to save you today. *Yahweh will do the fighting for you. You have only to keep still"* (Exodus 14:14). That's the capsulized beginning of what becomes the contemplative mind and the great theme that becomes grace!

Stop trying. Stop forcing reality. Learn the mystery of surrender and trust, and then it will be done unto you, through you, with you, in you and very often, in spite of you. You could say that God's only and forever pattern is *creatio ex nihilo*; Yahweh is always "creating something out of nothing." Christian words for the same eternal pattern are "resurrection" or "grace." All three concepts point to the same thing—that God "brings the dead to life and calls into being what does not exist" (Romans 4:17). You could call it God's primary job description.

barren women & rejected sons

First we have the choice of Israel, the enslaved people on the bottom of the human pile. But then we have the long development of a most fascinating theme, "barren women!" One wonders after a while if there is something wrong with the water in Israel, until we realize that barrenness is a spiritual metaphor for something else.

It's never the fertile, self-sufficient woman who is special, but the woman who is by herself incapable, and then is "graced" from Without. Note how often it happens: Sarah, who finally bears Isaac; Rebecca, who marries Isaac and bears Jacob and Esau; Rachel, the eventual mother of Joseph, Benjamin and Ephraim; Hannah, who finally bears Samuel; the nameless mother of Sampson; Elizabeth, the mother of John the Baptist—all of whom set the stage for the real impact of Mary's virginity ("I am unable by myself; Yahweh can accomplish it through me"). The meaning of Mary's virginity is summed up in Gabriel's dramatic proclamation: "Nothing is impossible with God" (Luke 1:38).

Let's look especially at Hannah (Anna), the mother of the prophet Samuel. Like the others, she comes to God for her fertility, her identity, her deeper personhood. We have a beautiful account of Hannah in the temple asking God to make her able to bear a child (1 Samuel 1:1–18). God gives her a son, Samuel. She goes to the temple and dedicates him to the Lord.

Then she offers this beautiful prayer: "The bow of the mighty has been broken, but the feeble have girded themselves with strength. The well satisfied are hiring themselves out for bread. But the famished cease from all labor. The barren woman bears sevenfold. The mother of many is desolate. Yahweh makes poor and makes rich. Yahweh humbles and he also exalts. He lifts up the poor from the dung heap. And pulls the mighty from their thrones" (1 Samuel 2:4–7).

The great spiritual and political turnaround is beginning! *The theme of themes (grace, free election, bias toward the bottom) is taking shape.* God is turning the world's values upside down (Acts 17:6). You know now where Jesus learned one of his most common and subversive one-liners, "the last will be first and the first will be last" (Matthew 20:16; Luke 13:30; Mark 10:31; Matthew 19:30). He learned this from his own Jewish history. (It is no surprise that the words used for Mary's Magnificat [Luke 1:46–55] are largely taken from Hannah. Not coincidentally, Catholic mythology chose her name, and maybe her spiritual identity, for the mother of Mary and the grandmother of Jesus. We called her "Saint Anne," a form of the name Hannah, although there is no mention of her in the Scriptures.)

That's all God needs to break into the world! It absolutely levels the playing field of history, by making the starting gate a place that none of us would have suspected—an admission not of worthiness but of unworthiness! But it's in a hidden way that only the marginalized ones will recognize, "those who are nothing at all to show up those who are everything," as Paul will eventually call this subversive wisdom (1 Corinthians 1:29).

It seems that until you are excluded from any system, you are not able to recognize the idolatries, lies or shadow side of that system. It is the privileged "knowledge of the victim." It opens up the playing field, granting equal access to all, if they want it, because *it is no longer a winner's script, which the ego prefers to make it, but actually a life script that now includes these so-called losers.*

There seems to be a "structural blindness" for people who are content and satisfied on the inside of groups. They do not realize that it is largely a belonging system that they have created for themselves.

It is important to know that people can be personally well-intentioned and sincere, but structurally they cannot see certain things. Jesus quotes the call of Isaiah to describe this socially blind position: "You will hear and hear again, and not understand, see and see again and not perceive…" (6:9). He uses it, interestingly enough, as his preface to teaching through parables. Insiders are by nature dualistic, because they divide themselves from the so-called outsiders.

Parables never lend themselves to dualistic explanations. In that, they are very similar in purpose to Zen koans or Confucian riddles, which seek to expose our biases and assumptions to ourselves. They all subvert what we think is logic.

The same theme is also expressed in some masculine metaphors, for example, the forgotten son or the rejected son, like Joseph, David and Esau. David's father, Jesse, shows all of his sons to Samuel (read 1 Samuel 16:1–13). And Samuel says, "Don't you have another one?" "Oh, that's right! There's another boy, who remains unnamed, but he's out in the field. We forgot about him," Jesse seems to say. Samuel says, "Send for him, we will not sit down and eat until he comes!" (v. 11).

Samuel immediately anoints him as he enters. "This is the one," he says. Of course this forgotten son becomes the great King David, the archetypal whole man of the Jewish Scriptures. David is also lover, warrior and through Nathan's intervention, even a prophetic wise man. So all four parts of the male soul are finally included. The rejected son knows what sonship is really about—perhaps because he has desired it for so long. Jesus will capitalize on this in his classic story of the Prodigal Son (Luke 15:11–32).

It's always the forgotten one, like the rejected prophet Jeremiah, or the unjustly suffering Job, who understands things more deeply and breaks through to enlightenment. Isaiah probably takes the idea to an art form in what we call the "Four Hymns of the Suffering Servant" found in Isaiah 49 to 53.

Franciscan scholar Ilia Delio, in *The Humility of God,* summarizes this concept profoundly. She recognizes that *before encounter God is perceived as omnipotent power; after encounter God is perceived as humble love. This has always been the Franciscan emphasis: that God, against all expectation, is humble!* After Jesus, God can no longer be perceived as the Pantocrator or Omnipotence Itself, but a member of a self-emptying and humble Trinity. Such is the God that Francis discovered in Jesus.

Again and again in Exodus, Judges, Joshua, Samuel, 1 and 2 Kings, the leaders want to form alliances for their military security. Yet always God tells them they are to have no alliances, no treaties, no horses, no chariots: Trust only in God. Is this utter naïveté? Or is it an attempt to shock and transform conventional wisdom?

As Cynthia Bourgeault and others would say, early-stage consciousness, which is almost entirely win/lose, cannot imagine this is anything but pious dribble. Wisdom is "another way of knowing" and understands things at a higher level of inclusivity, which we are calling here "transformation" or non-dualistic thought.

The human ego hates to change probably more than it hates anything else, and therefore always resists any call to vulnerability or what feels like loss of control. Remember Gideon in Judges 6–7? What a non-commonsense story! God has to whittle his troops down from 22,000 to 300! Yahweh says, "otherwise, Israel might claim the credit for themselves at my expense; they might say, 'My own hand has rescued me' " (7:2).

God has to teach the people that there are alternatives to brute strength. If all you are taught is the art of the hammer, everything in your life is perceived as another nail. Eventually this broader wisdom becomes the virtues of community, patience, forgiveness and frankly "cleverness" (see Luke 16:8 and the preceding parable of the crafty steward).

But why would the Scriptures take on such a strange and utterly countercultural stance? How could you expect any practical person to believe it or live it? Dominative power seems to come along with our testosterone, and hence is more often a spiritual issue for men.

It might be that God cannot risk giving power to anybody except people who have seen through its illusions and placed their identity elsewhere. All others will misuse power and usually misuse religion, too. Thus, even Jesus' three temptations before he begins his public ministry are all temptations to the misuse of power (Matthew 4:1–11). If even Jesus had to face these perennial "demons" head on, surely each one of us should presume that they are in charge in each of us—until major surgery has taken place. Call it conversion, repentance or metanoia.

It is the utterly false self that we bring forward for conversion, and merely joining a new group, or having an emotional God experience, does not usually convert that self at a very deep level, if at all. That is the work of a lifetime of grace, surrender and prayer.

psalms

Most of the Psalms (not all) reveal a rather high level of spiritual consciousness, and also of diverse stages of faith. They reveal both good and bad power in people, and they deserve to be the prayers and songs of believing people.

For me the Psalms illustrate the variety and breadth of spiritual experience that Saint John of the Cross so courageously describes: "God carries each person along a different road, so that you will scarcely find two people following the same route in even half of their journey to God."[1] This is probably why so many are seeking spiritual directors today, because the generic advice from the pulpit cannot call or challenge many, if not most, of our individual soul situations. Often the Psalms do.

Walter Brueggemann, probably my favorite Scripture scholar, finds three major divisions in the Psalms, which I find very helpful: Psalms of Orientation (reaffirming Tradition), Psalms of Disorientation (the prophetic recognition of things not working or not being true) and Psalms of Reorientation (the Wisdom level of a new faith-synthesis). At different times in our lives we need all three orientations, until they eventually operate as one in the spiritually mature person.

It is so helpful that Law (orientation), Prophets (disorientation) and Wisdom (reorientation) levels are all affirmed in the 150 Psalms, and unlike today, one or the other level is not called heretical or faithless. (Although people trapped at stage one will normally call people at the other two levels "sinners" or "heretics," which is what we see happening in the Gospels).

The Psalms in their entirety describe both the necessary three steps forward, and often the two steps backward (see, for example, Psalm 137:9) that our whole life is. For our purposes here, they very often idealize the sufferer, the poor person, the seeming "loser," especially in the Psalms of disorientation and reorientation.

Almost one-third of the Psalms are psalms of lament, yet these are the least-used by the liturgical churches I am told. They both reveal and pave a path for something other than a "winner's script." They allow us to feel, express and publicly own the downside of things. They allow us to complain to God, and trust that God can receive such complaints. The psalms of lament recognize that you cannot heal what you do not acknowledge, and probably express the much-needed meaning of a personal confession or "communal penance service." God alone *forgives*, but sharing with others is needed for *healing*.

Another example would be Psalm 123: "We know you will take pity on us. Pity us, O Lord. Have pity on us. We have had more than our share of scorn. More than our share of jeers from the complacent, and scorn from the crowd." This is clearly a people who have been on the bottom, yet they "lift their eyes to the Lord." Such a refined people are referred to by the prophets as the *anawim*, the remnant, the purified ones (see, for example, Zephaniah 3:11–20). They were on the "outside of things" long enough to relish and understand the beauty of the inside.

Consider another short one, Psalm 131: "Yahweh, my heart has no lofty ambitions. My eyes do not look too high. I am not concerned with great affairs or marvels beyond my scope. Enough for me to keep my soul tranquil and quiet like a child in its mother's arms, as content as a child that has been weaned. Israel relies on this God, now and forever." This is a faith level that can only come *after* being in the belly of the beast!

The Hebrew people are a very different kind of people than most of history has created. You can see the Word of God already is effective. *True transcendence always includes the previous stages* and does not dismiss them or punish them, as most reforms and revolutions have done in history. This is true reconciliation, healing or forgiveness and always characterizes mature believers. They afterward seem to thank God for the pain and the trial.

good power

Power cannot be inherently bad because in the Acts of the Apostles, Luke and Paul it is a name used for the Holy Spirit, who is described as *dynamis*, or power (Acts 10:38; Luke 1:35; 24:49; Romans 15:13; 1 Corinthians 2:5). "You will receive power when the Holy Spirit comes upon you. Then you will be my witnesses…to the very ends of the earth" (Acts 1:8).

Humans, once they contact their Inner Source, become living icons, not so much to a verbal message as to the Divine Image itself (see Isaiah 43:10). By any analysis, that is true, humble and confident power. It is the ultimate meaning of a well-grounded person.

Paul states the divine strategy well in Romans 8:16: "God's Spirit and our spirit bear common witness that we are indeed children of God." The goal is a shared knowing and a common power, and totally initiated and given from God's side, as we see dramatized in the Pentecost event (Acts 2:1–13). Like the very conception in the womb of Mary, it is "done unto us" and all we can do is allow and enjoy and draw life from such a gift of power. One would be foolish to think it is one's own creation.

To span the infinite gap between the Divine and the human, God's agenda is to plant a little bit of God, the Holy Spirit, right inside of us! (Jeremiah 31:31–34; John 14:16 ff.). This is the very meaning of the "new" covenant, and the replacing of our "hearts of stone with a heart of flesh" that Ezekiel promised (36:25–26). Isn't that wonderful!

I would say that the Divine Indwelling is *the nexus that differentiates authentic Christian spirituality from all others*. Yet, as many have said, the Holy Spirit is still the "lost" or undiscovered person of the Blessed Trinity. No wonder we have been seeking power in all the wrong places if we have not made contact with our true power, the Indwelling Spirit (see Romans 8:9, 11; 1 Corinthians 3:16–17).

Power cannot, in itself, be bad. It simply needs to be realigned and redefined as something larger than domination or force. Rather than saying that power is bad, the Bible reveals the paradox of power. If the Holy Spirit is power, then power has to be good, not something that is always the result of ambition or greed. In fact, a truly spiritual woman, a truly whole man, is a very powerful person. In people like Moses, Jesus and Paul, you can assume that it was precisely their powerful egos that God used, built on and transformed, but did not dismiss. If we do not name the good meaning of power, we will invariably be content with the bad, or we will avoid our powerful vocation.

The fully revealed God of the Scriptures is not interested in keeping us children (1 Corinthians 13:11) or "orphans" (John 14:18). God wants adult partners who can handle power and critique themselves (see, for example, Hebrews 5:11—6:1).

Do you know why they can handle it? First of all, because they don't need it, and secondly, they know it is not their own. Until you don't *need* external power, you normally cannot handle power. When you have real power, you do not need to flaunt it. When you know you are being used by a Higher Power, you do not take your small power too seriously.

When do you not need to flaunt it, to show it off? When you have it internally! Then you are most like God, who can wait for fourteen billion years and can allow this universe to unfold on its own as if it were separate from God! People who have such godly power within are often the best in sharing power externally, and can use power for the common good: "Be ambitious for the higher gifts," Paul can dare to say to them

(1 Corinthians 12:31). He knows they will not misuse it because they are participating in the larger power of the Body of Christ, and they do not hold it independently or by reason of their own ambition or neediness.

In the New Testament the twelve apostles are notorious for learning this message very slowly. Right after Jesus teaches them the way of servant leadership, they start arguing about who is the greatest (Mark 9:30–37), and then their silliness is even repeated again (10:32 ff.). You must know that this is meant to be a political cartoon; you're supposed to laugh at it all! He just taught them about the path of descent, and they wonder which one of them is going to be the next archbishop!

Having lived in clergy circles, I can say this has not changed too much—it is the nature of the ego in every age. Clergy are trained, dressed up and largely rewarded for role and function, rather than for relationship, spirituality or even competence. So it is not entirely their fault, but career and ambition are a deep male need that these texts specifically warn us against. The male (or female!) who does not know who he or she is from the inside, will covet all forms of power: titles, costumes, precedence, roles and perks.

Too often the church itself is quick to oblige, even though Jesus roundly mocked and condemned these very things (Luke 20:45–47; Matthew 23:1 ff.). It is such issues as these that reveal every denomination's very selective reading of the Scriptures. Structural blindness might even be more prevalent than personal blindness. The group itself often keeps you from truth and your own sincerity.

Before AD 313, when Constantine made Christianity the establishment, we were on the bottom of society, which was the privileged vantage point for understanding the gospel. Overnight we moved from the bottom position to the top, literally from the catacombs to the basilicas.

The very word *basilica* means the "palaces of the king and queen." The Roman basilicas were large buildings for court or other public assembly, and they became our worship spaces. We became the established religion of the empire and started reading the gospel from the position of power instead of powerlessness. We succeeded in turning Jesus "meek and humble of heart" (Matthew 11:29) into the Righteous Judge we see in the Sistine Chapel or the "Pantocrator" of Byzantine art and modern cathedrals. In a sense, it seems almost a different religion!

The failing Roman Empire needed an emperor, and Jesus was used to fill the gap, making much of his teaching literally incomprehensible and unhearable, even by good people. The relationships of the Trinity were largely lost as the very shape of God: the Father became angry and distant, Jesus became the needed emperor, and for all practical purposes the Holy Spirit was forgotten.

An imperial system needs law and order and clear belonging systems more than it wants mercy or meekness or transformational systems. It was the beginnings of the constant temptation to "Churchianity" that survives strongly to this day, and is probably why we ourselves have so often misused power.

By the grace of God, saints and holy ones of every century and in every group still got the point, but only if they were willing to go through those painful descents that we Catholics called the "way of the cross," which Jesus called "the sign of Jonah," which Augustine called the "paschal mystery," or the Apostles' Creed called "the descent into hell." Without these journeys there's something you simply don't understand about the nature of God or the nature of the soul.

"Can you drink of the cup that I am going to drink?" Jesus said to James and John, who still wanted roles. "We can!" they responded, and he said, to paraphrase, "Indeed, you will and you must, but roles are not my concern" (see Matthew 20:22–23). *Religion is largely populated by people afraid of hell; spirituality begins to make sense to those who have been through hell, that is, who have drunk deeply of life's difficulties.*

Jesus came as the victim of human history because, spiritually speaking, only the victim can reveal both the dark and light sides of that history. The victim knows what the real victory is and what the insiders really stand for. Why else would Jesus say something as ridiculous as, "Happy are you when people abuse you and persecute you and speak all kind of calumny against you!" (Matthew 5:11)?

Not that enlightened people *must* be rejected, but it is true that wounded and rejected people have a much greater chance of seeing clearly and having something to say (they also have a greater chance of being bitter!). But Jesus still sends his followers to that place, because *wisdom emerges from what you do with your pain!* It is a unique and needed perspective, as poets, artists and seers have always understood. In fact, I would find it hard to understand all of the beatitudes in any other way (see Matthew 5:1–12).

It's usually the outsider who can best recognize the real operative belief systems, security systems and illusions of a group. The total insider (read "company man") is too comfortable inside to see the idols and self-serving systems of a country or an institution. This reaches its apogee and even urgency in the teaching of Jesus to love our enemies— not tolerate, but rather "love" and "pray for them"! (Matthew 5:44). Only when we love our critics can we be open to the subversive truth that they often speak, even if it is only 10 percent of the entire truth. A wise person still wants that 10 percent!

The ground is laid for this insight already in the Hebrew Scriptures: "Circumcise your heart…your God is never partial, never to be bribed. Yahweh will see justice done for the orphan, the widow and Yahweh loves the stranger and gives them food and clothing. Love the outsider yourself, therefore, for you were once outsiders yourself in the land of Egypt" (Exodus 22:20 ff.). They are taught to always see things from the structural position of the "other," and one often sees this in the justice-oriented politics of many Jews to this day (also taught in Leviticus 19:34 and Deuteronomy 10:16 ff.).

So it's not, "Preach a deep message and you will be rejected," as we presume. It's, rather, "Be rejected and you will have a deep message." Note that the prophets are almost by definition outside the establishment and always persecuted (Matthew 5:12; 23:34). Jesus is surely an archetype of the same, a seemingly uneducated layman, yet standing on the shoulders of his ancestors Joseph, Jeremiah, Job and John the Baptizer, who were also rejected and persecuted.

Some saints rushed to share this position, like Francis and Clare of Assisi, Vincent de Paul, Benedict Joseph Labre and Simone Weil, to name a few. Saint Thérèse of Lisieux called it her "Little Way"—she is the only person without a formal education ever to be declared a doctor of the church.

rites of passage

This wisdom of the outsider keeps groups from circling the wagons around themselves, a phenomenon that seems to be the very nature of institutionalization. "So happy are you when people abuse you and persecute you and speak all kind of calumny against you on my account. Rejoice and be glad" (Matthew 5:11–12). This wisdom also keeps us open to much needed criticism and course correction. I myself need to pray for one humiliation a day. It is the only way I can recognize my own momentary stance and perspective; whether I am doing God's work or doing Richard's work.

Was Jesus a sadomasochist? Did he delight in victimhood? James Alison, in his book *On Being Liked,* points out that, no, he just knew that there was a very *privileged way of knowing,* and it came to those who were in any way marginalized, expelled, excluded, disabled or in any minority position whatsoever. They all know something that you cannot know in any other way.

Note Jesus' basic training for the apostles. He sends them out away from the group, often in pairs. "Take nothing for your journey. Neither staff nor haversack nor bread nor money. Let none of you take a spare tunic" (Luke 9:3).

It's easy to imagine the apostles balking. Who would want to go on such a journey? He's sending them into a situation of certain failure, rejection, vulnerability, where they have to rely upon other people and upon God. It teaches the way of humble love and trust, and it forces you to look from the outside in. Truthfully, most of us Westerners spend our whole life looking from the inside out. To look in from the "other side" is a marvelous spiritual initiation rite, vision quest or walkabout, as the native peoples call them. I think the Gospel is saying that it is a necessary perspective.

For centuries we've struggled with these texts, especially Franciscans, because Francis took them literally. None of us could ever live up to his radicalism. "We've got to have buildings. We have to have computers and telephones and cars to do this good work," we say. I have all of the above myself. We can't believe that Jesus really meant this teaching. So like much of the Bible, we just ignore it; Evangelical Protestants do too, even those who claim to take the Bible literally.

But this austerity was not a program for the whole of life, but rather it was an initiation rite, a training course in vulnerability and community. Jesus is telling his apostles, as it were, "You've got to go through this or you will never be capable of empathy, compassion and identification with the pain of the world that you are called to serve. You will use ministry as a career move instead of a servant position." Some such rite of passage seems necessary to break our foundational narcissism. Paul says the very same, and it is the only time the word *initiation* is used in the Scriptures, to my knowledge (check out Philippians 4:11–13).

Historically, women have had a spiritual advantage, and did not need initiation, because in almost all patriarchal cultures, they're already in the one-down position. I am not saying that this is just, or that it's God's will, because it isn't. But, spiritually speaking, it's actually a clear head start. It's an "epistemological advantage," to use a philosophical term, an advantage in one's way of knowing.

It's a great leap forward in knowing what needs to be known—to be on the bottom instead of the top. What else did he mean by his most common one-liner: "The last will be first, and the first will be last"?

When I moved to New Mexico in 1986, I lived my first years in downtown Albuquerque, a block from a homeless shelter. One morning I got up early to pick up a paper at the newsstand, where the homeless often sat, along the street. Someone had written these shocking words in chalk on the sidewalk, and since it was early in the morning it was still there. It said, "*I watch how foolishly man guards his nothing, thereby keeping me out. Truly God is hated here.*"

I suspect this was written by an embittered person, but maybe not; maybe she or he was a modern prophet. I knew I was supposed to read it. I knew there was some truth in what the person wrote, especially in a country where most people are quite comfortable churchgoers, and almost all of us do "guard our nothing."

Saint Francis would likely say the same thing. This is a knowing that we folks inside the system are not privy to, whereas the beggars to the system see it clearly. I see why Francis wanted us always to be mendicants, beggars, keeping us structurally outside.

What Jesus and all the prophets are trying to do is to make sure that all of us have had that experience somewhere in our lives, of being on the losing side, knowing how much it hurts to hurt, whether it's having a disabled child, suffering loss, being a racial or sexual minority, or being someone who has been looked down upon for any reason. That place outside of the system is a "liminal space" where transformation and conversion is much more likely.

Isn't it ironic that most of the gospel has probably been preached and taught by people who are very comfortable? That's almost an assurance that these preachers will largely miss the point, that they will not preach the true or full message. Jesus made sure his followers were "pilgrims and strangers" (Hebrews 11:13) to business as usual, so they could be "citizens" of a larger kingdom (Philippians 3:20).

I can see what my father, Saint Francis, was trying to do by keeping us outside the clerical system too. It is not bad, of course, but it is very dangerous. He didn't want us to be priests, who are inherent insiders and even topsiders. He remained a brother himself.

It worries me when we take people to train them for ministry and immediately give them an ascribed role, security and status. We are almost assuring that they will have nothing gospel to say, *unless they learn from their own wounds or those of others, which many do.* Maybe the recent scandals in the church can even be good for us, if they return us to the edge and the bottom.

architectural theology

In Jesus' time the very architecture of the temple revealed in stone what I'm talking about spiritually. The actual design of the building seemed to protect degrees of worthiness. At the center there was the Holy of Holies, which only the high priest could enter, only one day a year. This was surrounded by the court of the priests and the Levites, which only they could enter. Outside that there was the court of the circumcised Jewish men.

The outer court of the temple was the court of the Jewish women, although during their menstruating years, they could get into that court only rarely, because of beliefs about blood and ritual purity (see Leviticus 15:19–30). Outside this entrance there was a sign warning any non-Jew who enters that he or she will be punished by death.

Here we had structured in stone what all religions invariably do, create inside and outside as almost their main purpose. Jews defined us as "gentiles;" we speak of "non-Catholics." Almost everybody seems to need some kind of sinner or heretic against which to compare themselves. Remember that Judaism is an archetypal religion, and what they do right and wrong illustrates the same pattern as almost all religions. On some level we all create meritocracies, worthiness systems and invariably base them on some kind of purity code—racial, national, sexual, moral or cultural.

Now perhaps we are beginning to see what a radical reformer of religion that Jesus was. He showed no interest in maintaining domination systems or closed systems of any kind. He actively undercut them, even against his own followers (see, for example, Luke 9:49–56). He showed no interest in the various debt codes and purity codes of religion (see, for example, Matthew 15:1–14), which are the religious forms of power and exclusion. In fact, he often openly flouted many of the accepted purity codes of his own religion.

Jokingly, I sometimes say that Jesus appears to just relax from Sunday until Thursday, and goes out of his way to do all his work on the Sabbath! It is pretty obvious that he is provoking the religious system that puts customs and human laws before people (see Mark 2:27). He says the same when his disciples are criticized for breaking these human commandments. He defends their official "sinner" status by saying, "The Sabbath was made for humanity, not humanity for the Sabbath" (Mark 2:27).

If you read Leviticus 11—24 in particular, you will find that there are seven distinct groups outside the temple. First of all, and this probably came from health-contagion concerns, there were people with any skin disease. They were declared permanently unworthy and could not come into the temple. This is normally translated as lepers. That's why we have so many lepers in the Bible. Jesus is known for touching them—again the classic provocateur. He becomes unclean himself and cannot enter the temple or even the village for some time (see Mark 1:45).

Second, there are disabled people with any visible physical disabilities, which almost stand as a symbol for what we call "blaming the victim" today.

Third, gentiles, or all non-Jews, would be the biggest group barred from the temple. Most everyone reading this book, unless you're Jewish by background, would have been declared hopelessly lost and unworthy, just as we once thought about non-Catholics, and some still think about us Catholics.

Fourth, there are Jewish women during and after their times of menstruation; fifth, Jewish men after any nonreproductive seminal discharge, and, sixth, those in an occupation that made them permanently unclean or unworthy (like shepherds, any who have contact with blood, tax collectors, leatherworkers, etc.). The final group banned from the temple was the bastard sons and daughters of priests!

If you want to do an interesting exercise to demonstrate this, just go to the four Gospels and make a two-column list. In one, list those people who fight Jesus every step of the way. Almost always they are the people in the inner courts of the temple. In the other column, list those people who consistently respond to Jesus. Who are these? They're almost always in those seven groups above who were declared unworthy and outside the temple.

This is a standing critique of power systems and their capacity for self-serving illusions, yet it has largely been missed while these very texts are constantly being read from the pulpit. That's because we tend to like purity codes. They define groups and give us an identity as superior. Once inside, we cannot hear anything that demotes us.

Now perhaps we see the central significance of Jesus' opening words in his "inaugural address": "Blessed are the poor in spirit, for theirs is the kingdom of God" (Matthew 5:3). *They* have a big head start over the rest of us, because God's privileged and often hidden position is the bottom and edge of things, never the top or the center.

The Bible itself is not establishment literature written from the top—or for the top. "I have come to preach good news to the poor," Jesus says (Luke 4:18), whereas it will often feel like bad news to those who have a lot to protect. The Bible is clearly disestablishment literature written by the outsiders, the weak, the losers and the victims (with the exception of Leviticus, Numbers and Chronicles, written by the priestly class). It is best understood by those who are able to look out at life from that privileged position of disestablishment.

Probably the main structural reason for the misuse of the Bible is that, largely, it has been used and taught by people on the inside and people at the top. It creates an inner and specialized jargon, which has no possibility of outer critique. In fact, you usually have to join the group to even talk to them.

These are not bad people at all. They're just looking out at life from a rather limited and often self-serving viewpoint, with an in-house vocabulary that makes it very hard to talk to others. How different from our preacher *extraordinaire*, Saint Paul, who says that he made himself "a Jew for the Jews," and "to those who have no law, I was free of the law; for the weak I made myself weak." In fact, he says, "I made myself all things to all people in order to save some at any cost" (1 Corinthians 9:20–22). How did we ever lose such greatness and stretching of soul?

Remember, *every viewpoint is a view from a point.* The Bible gives you a new and very free viewpoint from which to read the world. But it will only feel like freedom if you do not have a lot to prove and a lot to protect.

chapter six
the **razor's edge:**
knowing and not knowing

"My thoughts are not your thoughts, my ways are not
your ways.... As high as the heavens are above the
earth, so my ways are beyond your ways, and my
thoughts are beyond your thoughts."

—Isaiah 55:8–9

"You travel over sea and land to make a single convert,
and once you have him, you make him twice as fit
for hell as you are."

—Matthew 23:15

Wow! Why would Jesus talk as he does in that last quote? Isn't he being
a bit unfair and even unkind? In fact, he is saying this to quite "orthodox" believers, teachers and students of the law—people who "know."
To understand, we have to recognize how Jesus and the prophets saw
themselves as radical reformers of religion, as well as how religion knows
what it knows.

The Bible illustrates both healthy and unhealthy religion, right in the text itself, and Jesus offers us a rather simple criterion by which to judge one from the other. It is not a head category at all, but a visual and practical one—"does it bear good fruit or bad fruit?" (Matthew 7:15–20; Luke 6:43–45). Jesus is almost embarrassingly practical.

When religion is not doing its job well, almost every other aspect of society also will be sick. When your God image is true, your self-image also will be true. If your operative God image is toxic, you probably will be toxic too, and it is that toxicity that Jesus is warning about.

Religion is the best thing in the world, but it can also be the worst thing. If your way of relating to God is a life-giving style of relationship (the relationships of the persons of the Trinity being the first and richest pattern!), almost everything else in a society, even the broken parts, are subject to renewal, healing and enlightenment.

That is why true *orthodoxy* ("right ideas") is so very important. Yet we will see in the Bible that orthodoxy is never defined as something that happens only in the head. (In fact, the word is not even in the Bible!) The entire biblical text would emphasize "right relationship" much more than just intellectually being "right." Some call it *orthopraxy* or "right practice." *Jesus consistently declares people to be saved or healed who are in right relationship with him, and he never grills them on their belief or belonging systems.*

Jesus' concern for orthopraxy is at the heart of Jesus' hard saying at this chapter's outset. He has been formed by that first quote from Isaiah, which teaches Jews humility before the mystery of God (see Ecclesiastes 3:11; Job 11:6; Psalm 139; Romans 11:33–35) instead of just trying to get people to join our supposedly saved group, when we ourselves are still more fit for hell than heaven.

When we presume we know fully, we can all be very arrogant and goal-oriented. When we know we don't know fully, we are much more concerned about practical loving behavior. This has become obvious to me as I observe human nature. Those who know God are *always* humble; those who don't are invariably quite sure of themselves.

So we are going to be walking a thin line here. We are saying that it is important to have correct, orthodox teaching about God, but don't for a moment presume you know everything or even most things about God. On that razor's edge we will find the balance that the Bible offers.

I'd like to start our examination of this theme with a quote from the German Heinrich Zimmer (1890–1943), who, among other things, studied sacred images and their relationship to spirituality. He said that "the best things cannot be talked about," and "the second-best things are almost always misunderstood."[1] So we spend our life talking about the "third-best things," which, in our culture, I suppose, are things like sports and the weather and other safe topics. Religion is often tempted to do the same—just to have something clear and clean to talk about!

One of the great difficulties of theology and spirituality is that its subject matter is precisely those "best things that cannot be talked about." So if religion does not have humility about knowing, it ends up being quite smug, silly and superstitious. I think that is what Jesus is criticizing so strongly in our quote at the beginning of this chapter.

When we speak of God and things transcendent, all we can do is use metaphors and pointers. No language is adequate to describe the holy. Like a picture of Saint John of the Cross I once saw, we must place a hushing finger over our lips to remind ourselves that God is finally unspeakable and ineffable. Or like the Jews, we will even refuse to pronounce the name "Yahweh."

Unlike the other sciences, theology cannot validate itself by external "proof," even though we have tried. What Deuteronomy says about prophets certainly applies to all who speak of spiritual things: "But how are we to know that what a prophet says is true?" The only criterion that the Bible gives for a true prophet is this: "If she says it will happen, and it does not happen, then she is not a true prophet" (18:21–22). That does not help a lot, does it? At least not if you want validation or pre-dictability before the fact.

When Dante wrote the three-part *Divine Comedy*, he wrote the "Inferno" and the "Purgatorio" as a younger man, but he waited until the very end of his life to write the "Paradiso." To this day it's the least-read of the three books, because it is so hard to talk about union, about God or about eternity with any clear credibility or any eyewitness accounts. It always feels like the author is grabbing for words, and the reader knows it is merely an approximation. It usually sounds like airy poetry.

The best that spiritual writers can do is somehow imitate the words of the seraphim to Isaiah: "Holy, Holy, Holy" (Isaiah 6:3), or perhaps today we would say, "Awesome, Awesome, Awesome!" The early church just babbled in tongues before such unspeakability (1 Corinthians 14), but that for some reason died out, or was stamped out, and had to be rediscovered from time to time, including in my own hometown of Topeka, Kansas, in the year 1900, at the founding of the modern Pentecostal movement.

That's why preachers and teachers have such a hard time, and prob-ably why we resort to our own "inferno language" of reward and punishment—dualistically clean language. It becomes a substitute and smokescreen for the real goal of religion, which is always divine union. Fire and brimstone, moralistic language, at least feels like something you can hold on to and positions everything in its appropriate place. It gives us a sense of clarity and certitude about who is who, who is where and why. We like that.

The best we can do about heaven, on the other hand, is harps, clouds, white robes and palm branches (see, for example, Revelation 5:8; 7:9; and similar texts), which is always a bit disappointing, at least to me. But that is because the best things cannot be talked about. They can only be experienced—and then if you try to talk, you will know that you saw "through a glass darkly" (1 Corinthians 13:12). Your best attempts will still be merely stammering and stuttering for good enough words.

Now the second-best things, according to Zimmer, which "are almost always misunderstood," are those things that merely point to the first-best things. Those are things like philosophy, theology, psychology, art and poetry, all of which—like sacred Scripture—are so easily misunderstood.

Yet what I am trying to do in this book is to use those second-best things, which point to and clarify the first-best things—"which cannot be talked about." But what else can we do? All our words, beliefs and rituals are merely "fingers pointing to the moon."

I believe Jesus follows the same risky path, which has allowed him to be interpreted in so many different ways (there are now thirty thousand Christian "denominations" worldwide). Apparently he was willing to take that risk, or he would have written things down. (Did that ever occur to you?)

It starts to feel like an impossible task, at least if you think you have a right to certainty or complete clarity. This is the necessary and good poverty of all spiritual language. After all, Jesus never said, "You must be right!" or even that it was important to be right. He largely talked about being honest and being humble (which is probably our only available form of rightness).

Such admitted poverty in words should keep us humble and keep us curious and searching for God, although the history of religion has been quite the contrary. In fact, what we have largely done is talk about "the third-best things" where we can feel that sense of certitude, order and control—things like finances, clothing, edifices, roles, offices and who has the authority. In my experience, I observe that *the people who find God are usually people who are very serious about their quest and their questions, more so than being absolutely certain about their answers.* I offer that as hard-won wisdom.

The Bible, *in its entirety*, finds a fine balance between knowing and not-knowing, between using words and having humility about words, even though the ensuing traditions have not often found that same balance. "Churchianity," by its very definition, needs to speak with absolutes and certainties. It is expected to make total truth claims and feels very fragile when it cannot. It is the same kind of bind that a politician is in, who must pretend he is absolutely sure of himself, even though we all know it is not true. As Marcus Borg and others say in *The Emerging Christian Way* (see my comment in the bibliography), that is the largely impossible task institutional religion has taken upon itself. It is crumbling beneath it, in my opinion.

I understand that structural need for clarity, certitude and identity, especially to get you started when you are young. Religion, though, also needs a balancing agent to unlock itself from inside, which most of us would call the mystical or prayer tradition. ("Mystery," "mystical," to "mutter sounds" all come from the Greek verb *muein,* which means to "hush or close the lips"). Without this unlocking, we will not produce many adult Christians, and certainly not Christians who can build any bridges to anybody else.

Without an in-depth prayer tradition, religion has cried wolf too many times in history and later been proven wrong. Observe earlier authoritative church statements on democracy, war, torture, slavery, women, usury, anti-Semitism, revolution, liturgical forms, native peoples, the Latin language and the earth-centered universe—to name a few big ones. If we had balanced our knowing by some honest not-knowing, we would never have made such egregious mistakes. We proved whatever we wanted from one twisted line of Scripture. The unprayerful heart will always twist reality to its own liking.

the two streams

Now this internal balancing act emerged as two spiritual sidebars in the world of spirituality: what Belden Lane describes as the knowing tradition and the not-knowing tradition. I'm going to try to clarify these in very simple form and then point out how they're already found and taught in the Bible itself.

Perhaps the most universal way to name the two traditions is with the words *darkness* and *light*. The formal theological terms are the *apophatic* or "negative" way, where you move beyond words and images into silence, and the *kataphatic* or "affirmative" way, where you use words, concepts and images. I believe both ways are necessary, and together they create a magnificent form of higher consciousness called biblical faith.

The apophatic way, however, has been underused, undertaught and underdeveloped largely since the Protestant Reformation and the Enlightenment. In fact, we became ashamed of our "not-knowing" and tried to fight our battles rationally. For several centuries religion in the West has been in a defensive mode, a "siege mentality," where we needed certainty and clarity and there was little room for not-knowing or the mystical tradition. We are still often in that regressive position today, but now in defense against secularism, New Age thinking and interfaith dialogue, which all appear, in different ways, to challenge our very sense of identity. It is crucial that we reintegrate these two streams of knowing and not-knowing in our time.

If we are going to talk about light, then we must also talk about darkness, because they only have meaning in relation to one another (see 1 Corinthians 15:40–41), just as we light the Easter fire only after darkness has fallen. In much of the world's art, the sun and the moon are pictured together as sacred symbols. The solar light gives glaring absolute clarity and removes all shadows, but also paradoxically creates very defined shadows. Patriarchal religions almost always preferred "sun" gods and the worship of fire, light and sacred order. There is much to be said for that, but it's not the whole story.

The lunar light was much more subtle, filtered and indirect, and sometimes, in that sense, more clarifying and less threatening. The solar light can sometimes be too bright, and so clear that it actually obscures, or blinds you. Remember that unlike the other acts of creation in Genesis, when God divided light from darkness, he did *not* call it "good"! At the very beginning of the Bible we are warned that we cannot totally separate light from darkness, or the two have no meaning. Genesis brilliantly names *the partial goodness* inside which the whole of creation exists (1:4–5). Remember, *Lucifer* means "Light Bearer" and to think of ourselves as pure light is always demonic.

All things on this earth are a mixture of darkness and light and it is not good to pretend they are totally separate! Or as Jesus positively puts it: "God alone is good" (Mark 10:18). Even the good things of this world are still subject to imperfection, wounding and decay. "Everything under the sun is empty and chasing of the wind," says Qoheleth (Ecclesiastes 1:14). That is the essence of the material state and is always disappointing to admit.

Now I'm all for papal teachings, but I've never met a person who's been converted by a papal encyclical (though I'm sure there are some who have!). It is almost as if the papal teachings are too clear, right, linear, left-brain and brilliant. That's solar energy, and it is often too much; it pleases the mind, especially good minds, more than the soul. Compare that to the parables and aphorisms of Jesus, which are usually indirect, subtle and very capable of misunderstanding and misuse.

Jesus is much more of a "lunar" teacher, patient with darkness and growth. He clearly says himself, "The seed is sprouting and growing, but we do not know how" (Mark 4:27). Jesus seems to be willing to live with such not-knowing, surely representing the cosmic patience and sure control of God. When you know you are finally in charge, you do not have to nail everything down along the way. You can work happily and even effectively with "mustard seeds" (Mark 4:31).

In most of human history, poetry and religion were almost the same thing. Poetry was the only language worthy of religion. Good poetry doesn't try to define an experience as much as it tries to give you the experience itself, just as good liturgy should do. It tries to awaken your own seeing, hearing and knowing. It does not give you the conclusion as much as teach you a process whereby you can know for yourself. It does not "overexplain and destroy astonishment."

Jesus does the same, particularly with the parables, and even says so at both the beginning and end of his parabolic discourse (see Matthew 13:13, 51–52). That's why the long standing language of religion was poetry, aphorism and sacred storytelling, never merely prose or linear doctrines. If I left myself as open to misunderstanding and misinterpretation as Jesus did by teaching in the way he did, I surely would be called a heretic, or at least a very fuzzy and dangerous thinker. Why do we need to be clearer or less capable of misunderstanding than Jesus? Apparently, it was not a problem for him.

desert & mountaintop

For a spirituality of darkness the biblical metaphors would be the cave, the Exodus itself, the exile, the belly of the fish, wilderness and especially desert. A spirituality of light would be represented by mountaintop images, especially Sinai, Horeb, Tabor and even the Mount of the Beatitudes, and to some degree the apocalyptic language found in Daniel, Ezekiel and Revelation, although their attempts to be perfect light (i.e., *apocalypsis* or "revelation") usually end up very confusing for most people, and often leading them back into fear and self-serving conjecture, as we see in most of the rapture and doomsday theories today. (This has been the practical effect of most apocalyptic literature, because it allows the undisciplined mind to project whatever it wants onto the bizarre, dualistic and usually warlike imagery. The best-selling *Left Behind* series would be an example of such an appeal to fear in general, fear of death, God as vengeance and religion as superiority and exclusivity. There's not much love in sight. It's an overwhelming judgment on the immaturity of Western Christianity that it is drawn to such books, which ask almost nothing of the reader except ideas.)

For our purposes we'll juxtapose and honor both desert and mountaintop. Those are the two different metaphors for the great mystery of what cannot be directly talked about in rational language. The tradition of the mountain is about presence; the tradition of the desert is about absence. The tradition of the mountain is about speaking; the tradition of the desert is about silence. It's the mountain of knowing, the desert of not-knowing. "The pillar of flame by night and the pillar of cloud by day" (Exodus 13:21–22) are both good guides, but not one without the other!

We have knowing and not-knowing beautifully integrated in two companion pieces in the Scriptures: Moses on Mount Sinai and Jesus on the Mount of Transfiguration. When Moses is on Sinai, we see in Exodus 20:21 that God is somehow manifest and yet dwelling in thick darkness; in Deuteronomy 4:15 it says, "You saw no shape on that day at Horeb."

In Exodus 33:21 Moses "sees" and "hears" to some degree yet Yahweh does not allow Moses to see his "glory" or his "face." Here we can observe a brilliant and delicate balancing of knowing with "don't dare think you fully know; of seeing with an immediate reminder that you have not fully seen!" The integrating of the two traditions is right in the text. The most that Moses can see is, humorously, Yahweh's backside! (33:23).

Now look at the perfect parallel of Jesus on the Mount of Transfiguration (Luke 9:28–36; Mark 9:2–8; Matthew 17:1–9). Here we have Jesus presented as dazzling light, yet it says that a cloud also overshadowed that same light show. The epiphany is both light and darkness, knowability and unknowability, disclosure and non-disclosure. Jesus then deliberately walks with the disciples back down the mountain, onto the plain and desert of everyday life, and out of this enlightening and inflating experience.

Honeymoon experiences cannot be sustained. You must always leave them and return to the ordinary. What then does he further tell them? "Don't talk about it!" (Matthew 17:9); in Luke's version, at least, it says that they followed his directions (9:36). It was one of the "best things." Jesus knew any talking too soon about it would only weaken the experience. Silence seems necessary to preserve sacrality and mystery, just as in sexual intimacy.

Our later Protestant brothers and sisters have almost no easy access to the apophatic-contemplative-mystical tradition of not-knowing, unless they go back to the Desert Fathers and Mothers, the fifth-century Dionysius the Areopagite, the classic *Cloud of Unknowing* (fourteenth century), or the continually recurring Catholic and Orthodox mystics. Without this tradition they are prone to fundamentalism. Catholics are often out of touch with their own full tradition and frequently overplay light, order and certitude to a sad non-appreciation for darkness, journey and biblical faith. Among the supposed recipients of the whole ("catholic") tradition, you would think they would know better.

today's confusion

As we all know, human history is in a time of great flux, of great cultural and spiritual change. The psyche doesn't know what to do with so much information. I am told that if you take all of the information that human beings had up until 1900, and call that one unit, that unit now has doubled every ten years. That's the confusion and the anxiety that we're dealing with today, especially in our children and in ungrounded people.

In light of today's information overload, people are looking for a few clear certitudes by which to define themselves. We even see fundamentalism in many religious leaders, when it serves their cultural or political worldview. We surely see it at the lowest levels of religion, where God is used to justify violence, hatred, prejudice and "my" way of doing things.

We can almost see this more easily today in Islam than we can see it in ourselves, but it is everywhere. The mind of the fundamentalist is basically the same mind in Judaism, Christianity, Islam and the secular fundamentalists like atheists, militarists and those who think the market economy fell out of heaven.

The fundamentalist mind is a mind that likes answers and explanations so much, that it remains willfully ignorant about how history arrived at those explanations, or how self-serving they usually are. Satisfying untruth is more pleasing to us than unsatisfying truth, and full truth is invariably unsatisfying—at least to the small self.

Great spirituality, on the other hand, is always seeking a balance between opposites, a very subtle but creative balance. As William Johnston, S.J., once said, "Faith is that breakthrough into that deep realm of the soul which accepts paradox with humility."[2] When you go to one side or the other too much, you find yourself either overly righteous or overly skeptical and cynical. There must be a healthy middle, and I hope that is what we are looking for here, as we try to hold both the needed light and the necessary darkness.

My firm belief, however, is that we do not settle today's confusion by pretending to have absolute and certain answers, when the Bible never promised us many anyway. I feel like quoting the ever-popular Dr. Phil, who says to addicted people who keep doing the same destructive thing: "And how has this worked for you?"

Europe was the one continent we thought we had in our Christian pocket. Look at its empty churches today! We settle human confusion not by falsely pretending to settle all the dust, but by teaching people an *honest and humble process for learning and listening for themselves* (prayer, which I will talk about shortly). Then people come to wisdom in a calm and compassionate way. There will not be the angry overreaction against authority and wisdom that we have today, which often comes from trying to force conclusions without also teaching people a process for coming to those conclusions for themselves. Outer authority must be grounded by inner authority.

Remember, as Paul quoted, "The word is near you, in your mouth and in your heart" (Romans 10:8), and Paul precedes that line from Deuteronomy with a challenge that I would repeat today, "Do not tell yourself that you have to bring Christ down!" (10:6). The mystery of the Incarnation is precisely the repositioning of God down here once and forever. Continual top-down religion only creates very passive, passive-dependent and passive-aggressive Christianity.

God overcame that gap by planting an organic source within us: "It is not beyond your strength or beyond your reach. It is not in heaven, so that you will need to wonder, 'Who will go up to heaven for us and bring it down?'... No, the Word is very near to you, it is in your mouth and in your heart for your observance" (30:11–14). The Judeo-Christian tradition was not supposed to be a top-down affair, but *an organic meeting between an Inner Knower, accessed by prayer, and the Outer Knower, which we could call Scripture and Tradition.* So much of our fighting over and about Scripture and Tradition is because we have not taught a parallel and equally serious process of prayer.

prayer as the process

The two paths of knowing and not-knowing are primarily taught through prayer itself! No wonder all spiritual teachers emphasize prayer so much.

In Jesus' teaching we have the prayer of words (what we normally think of as prayer), like saying the Our Father and his encouragement to "ask" (Matthew 7:7 ff.). From this and the Last Supper, we have developed various forms of social, public and liturgical prayer, often centering around intercession, gratitude and worship.

But we also have the much-less-taught prayer beyond words: "praying in secret" (Matthew 6:5–6), "not babbling on as the pagans do" (Matthew 6:7), or the "predawn, lonely prayer" of Jesus (Mark 1:35); these are all pointers toward what many of us today call contemplation. The prayer beyond words is encouraged by Jesus' line that "pagan" prayer thinks that "by using many words they will make themselves be heard, so do not be like them; your Father knows what you need even before you ask" (Matthew 7:8–9).

Given that teaching about "pagan" prayer from Jesus, it is amazing that wordy prayer still took over in the monastic Office, in the Eucharist, and in formulaic prayer like the Catholic rosary. It's all the more important that these be balanced out by prayer beyond words.

(It's an important aside that *the ancient teaching on contemplation, as well as its practice,* was largely lost for centuries until Thomas Merton began to retrieve it in the twentieth century. He pointed out that even formal "contemplative" orders were largely working inside the *kataphatic* [imaged, verbal] tradition, and had little training in the older practice of non-dual consciousness, and non-wordy knowing. Many saints and mystics did become contemplatives, but largely by grace ("infused contemplation") and not by any formal or refined teaching. The exact practice of it is now being taught by such teachers as John Main, Thomas Keating, Cynthia Bourgeault, Ruth Burrows and Lawrence Freeman, sometimes under the rubric of "Centering Prayer.")

"do not talk about it"

This warning from Jesus, after the Transfiguration, not to talk is often called the "messianic secret" by scriptural commentators. It is common for Jesus to demand silence after many of his actions and miracles. He also does not allow demons "who know who he is" to speak (Mark 1:34). So interesting! Why do you think he tells people not to talk? Well, Jesus sometimes adds a very telling phrase after ordering silence: "until after the resurrection" (Mark 9:9).

Here's how I read that: Until you've gone through the mystery of transformation from the false self to the True Self, don't talk about these things, because you will almost always misuse and misinterpret the experience. You will admire Jesus for miracles instead of waiting for *the real meaning of the miracle, which is always inner transformation. Medical cures are different than healings, and Jesus is about healing!* Jesus shows no interest in just being a miracle worker, which largely appeals to peoples' ego needs. He holds out for the real thing.

I give rites of passage at Ghost Ranch in New Mexico and other places, leading men through the historic initiation rites. I always have to tell them on the final day, "Don't talk about this for at least a week and maybe longer." Outside of context they will always be misinterpreted and misunderstood and even ridiculed.

When the initiation experience is over, you move out of sacred, liminal space. Whatever words you use to describe what you've just experienced inside of liminal space will be trivialized outside of that sacred space, or you will concretize and freeze your experience after the first time you communicate it.

Have you noticed that tendency? How you first say it is "how it is" henceforward, even in your own mind. I think that is why Jesus said "Don't talk about it," and maybe why he never *wrote* either! He knew we would make it into verbal dogmas instead of inner experiences, which is what we did anyway.

Quite honestly I think it's much of the attraction of Buddhism for so many people today. Buddhism is absolutely honest about the theology of darkness, about our inability to know. It's much more humble than the monotheistic religions about the possibilities of words. Islam, Judaism and Christianity took a great risk in putting religious experience into words.

So God took an even greater risk in the Incarnation, and allowed word to become flesh (John 1:14). The price we have paid for a certain idolatry of words is that the monotheistic religions became the least tolerant of the world's religions. Both Hinduism and Buddhism tend to be much more accepting of others than we are.

The three monotheistic religions each insist on absolute truth claims *in forms of words,* whereas Jesus' truth claim was his person (John 14:6), his presence (John 6:35 ff.), his ability to participate in God's perfect love

(John 17:21–22). Emphasizing perfect agreement on words and forms (which is never going to happen!) instead of inviting people into an experience of the Formless Presence, has caused much of the violence of human history. Jesus gives us *his risen presence* as "the way, the truth and the life." At that level there is not much to fight about, and in fact fighting becomes uninteresting. *All that forms can do is point to the Formless One, and yet I am not denying the deep need and gift of forms and words.* We do need pointers and "bottle openers."

A fundamentalist friend once told me that you are never to "interpret" the Bible. I hope he now knows that is impossible. You cannot *not* interpret the Bible. Our very reading of the Bible is our interpreting it through our culture, through our temperament, through our personality, through living at this time in history, or wherever. That is *always* an interpretation.

If you refuse informed interpretation, then you are trapped in your own limited cultural interpretation. Truly, you have no choice. You *must* interpret and you *will* interpret. But the best you can do is to own your biases consciously, and try to get your own ego agenda out of the way. Here is where Christianity has been very, very weak in spiritually educating its adherents, and why I keep emphasizing prayer as the necessary process.

Only prayerful, contemplative (not either/or thinking) can draw forth those deeper meanings. The only other major time we tend to move out of dualistic thinking is during times of darkness, sorrow and loss. Thus, I think *prayer and suffering are the two primary paths of transformation.* Only then do we begin to read Scripture with what Deuteronomy (10:16) and Jeremiah (4:4) call "a circumcised heart" and hear it with "circumcised ears" (6:10). For sure, some cutting is required, some pruning of both the ego agenda and cultural agenda.

an idolatry of words

The great shortcoming of biblical literalism is that it presumes it understands, yet in fact it often misses the deep and profound stirrings of the Spirit, the messages that proceed from the unconscious, and what is more often written *between* the lines (just as in human conversation).

Today teachers of communication even insist that as much as two-thirds of what is communicated is by context and nonverbal messages! It's not *what* is said, nearly as much as how, when, where, by whom, and with what inflection and emphasis. Fundamentalism is so dedicated to text that it almost always ignores context. So little depth or breadth is usually communicated.

You must accept the literary forms in which sacred Scripture is written, just as you understand the difference between nonfiction, novels, poetry and research papers when you go to the library. If not, you end up in the fundamentalist dead-end that we are in today—insisting on conclusions that are not there and that are often contradicted in other texts (which are then ignored), condemning things Jesus never once talked about (homosexuality and birth control), and legitimating things that Jesus strongly criticized (wealth and violence). I am not taking a stance here on these issues, but I am pointing out our utter inconsistency. That is my point, and the point of much of the world that criticizes "Churchianity" in its present form. The world has come to recognize our biases of interpretation, and that they are invariably biases in favor of power, and often against the body.

We must approach the Scriptures with humility and patience, with our own agenda out of the way, and allow the Spirit to stir the deeper meaning for us. Otherwise we only hear what we already agree with or what we have decided to look for! Isn't that rather obvious? As Paul will say, "We must teach not in the way philosophy is taught, but in the way the Spirit teaches us: We must teach spiritual things spiritually" (1 Corinthians 2:13). As Tobin Hart says, this mode of teaching is much more about transformation than information. That changes the entire focus and goal.

There is a necessary light that is only available through darkness, the darkness that comes in those liminal spaces of birth, death and suffering. You can't learn it in books alone, not even this one. There are certain truths that can be known only if we are sufficiently emptied, sufficiently ready, sufficiently confused or sufficiently destabilized. That's the genius of the Bible! It doesn't let you resolve all these questions in theology classrooms. In fact, *none* of the Bible appears to be written out of or for academic settings.

It is very clear that Jesus was able to heal, touch, teach and transform people, and there was no prerequisite for any formal education. It was not based on any scholastic philosophy or theology, in spite of our own Catholic fascination with medieval scholasticism. Jesus, as a teacher, largely talked about *what was real and what was unreal,* and how therefore we should live inside of that reality. It required humility and honesty, much more than education. In a thousand ways he was saying that God comes to you disguised as your life! Later we learned to call it the mystery of Incarnation and, as Brueggemann says, the scandal of the particular (see chapter one).

Consider the concrete teaching style of Jesus. He teaches in the temple area several times, but most of his teaching is walking with people on the streets, out into the desert and often into nature. His examples come from the things he sees around him: birds, flowers, animals, clouds, landlords and tenants, little children, women baking and sweeping. It's amazing that we made his teaching into something other than that.

Jesus teaches with anecdote, parable and concrete example much more than creating a systematic theology; it was more the way of "darkness" than the way of light. Yet it was the concrete examples of Jesus that broke people through to the universal light. Particulars seem to most open us up to universals, which is what poets have always understood.

"Thisness" is the actual spiritual doorway to the everywhere and the always, much more than concepts. Storytellers seem to know that better than theologians. Ironically, that was taught to us by a philosopher, Blessed John Duns Scotus, whom you would never expect to say so. This thirteenth-century Franciscan theologian paralleled Dominican Saint Thomas Aquinas's version of scholastic philosophy. Of interest here is particularly his teaching of *haecceity,* that, only individuals, not abstractions, have reality. The derision that his enemies held for Scotus's view resulted in our modern insulting word, *dunce.* Mary Beth Ingham, in *Scotus for Dunces,* tells the story well. (We'll return in detail to Scotus's understanding of the Incarnation in chapter nine.)

Incarnation is always specific and concrete, here and now, like *this* bread and *this* wine, and Jesus in *one* hidden moment of time. Henceforth, we cannot just fall in love with abstractions but only with concrete people and concrete moments and a personal God. I believe that is why "the word became flesh" (John 1:13). *Logos* ("word") became *sarx* ("flesh"), and Greek "logic" met Jewish concrete embodiment. That is indeed a "fullness of grace and truth" (1:14), and we have still not fully adjusted.

the roundabout way of "wilderness"

At the end of the thirteenth chapter of Exodus (vv. 17–18), when Pharaoh had let the people go, the text says, "God did not let them take the direct road, although that was the nearest way…. God led the people by the roundabout way of the wilderness." Isn't that an interesting passage? There was apparently a much quicker way than forty years of wandering around in circles, but the real goal was not getting there, it was the journey itself—through trials, nature, relationships—three steps forward and two steps backward. The medium is always the message, and in this case the message is also to be our medium.

How you get there determines where you will arrive—and what you arrive *as.* There is no path to peace, but peace is itself the path. A journey of faith is going to create a people of faith. You cannot give people the conclusions without walking the journey, or they will substitute the conclusions for the journey itself. Maybe that will always be the downside of religion, for that is what it most often does. The container becomes the substitute for the actual contents of the container.

The Jewish people had no protection from history, all they had was God. They could not take refuge in mythologies or ideologies or answers; God led them into Exodus, into exile. God led them into an ever-attacked kingdom and told the people that it was to be in the middle of politics, economics, culture and suffering that they would meet, serve and worship Yahweh. The only absolute this God ever promised Israel was God's presence itself.

Scholars such as Rainer Albertz and Walter Brueggemann say that there is no consistent pattern of truth, or arriving at truth, in the Old Testament, and that the text itself is "incessantly pluralistic." People who want to say, "The Bible has always taught…" apparently do not have much uniform ground to stand on—no more than the Jews—who only had God's promises and their experience of the same.

The greatest ally of God is reality itself. God's greatest revelation is *what is* (see Romans 1:20) not what we want it to be, and not even what it should be, not abstract theories but concrete encounters. *What is* is what converts us. Birth and death, for example, are the naturally initiating events, yet even these we have medicalized and hidden away in hospitals.

Only people who have first lived and loved, suffered and failed, and lived and loved again, are in a position to read the Scriptures in a humble, needy, inclusive and finally fruitful way. If you put the Scriptures in the hands of a person uninitiated by life, they will always make it into a head trip. It becomes a set of *prescriptions* instead of an actual *description* of what is real and what is unreal.

the best was at the beginning

I want to offer you what I believe is the ultimate caution about presumptuous knowing and speaking. We are all familiar with the second commandment: "You shall not speak the name of God in vain" (Exodus 20:7), as it was often translated, but rarely understood. Most Christians seem to have thought it was a commandment against cussing. Whereas the real meaning of speaking the name of God "in vain" is to speak God's name casually or trivially, with emptiness, with incomprehension, and therefore with a false presumption of understanding—as if we knew what we were talking about!

Soon some Jewish people rightly concluded, lest they be "vain" or irreverent, that the name of God should not be spoken at all! The Sacred Tetragrammaton, *YHWH,* was not even to be pronounced with the lips! Only the four consonants were written, with the educated person knowing how to fill in the necessary vowels—which demanded breath and spirit, of course (more on this in David Abrams's *The Spell of the Sensuous*). Breath and spirit, however, are only given by God and therefore we should not dare to fill in the sacred name with our own breath. Only God can speak God's name, "I AM who I AM" (Exodus 3:14), which when you think of it, is a discreet withholding and a total availability at the same time.

Any glib use of the name of God, therefore, is somehow "in vain" and *always* irreverent. To speak God's name is always somehow to trivialize it. What religious humility was taught the Jewish people at the very beginning! But unfortunately that same humility did not extend to our entire understanding of spiritual things and to the limits of language in general. We would have done well to take this cosmic caution to the whole world of God talk, but we thought it was about cussing!

So let me end this chapter by a first and final movement beyond words, thinking and analyzing, to a place where the dualistic mind has no power, but where God can fill in the gaps. Some Jewish scholars say that the consonants used in the spelling are the very few that do not allow you to close your mouth around them, or even significantly use your lips or tongue; in fact, *they are very likely a brilliant attempt to replicate human breathing: YH on the captured in breath, and WH on the offered out-breath!* (Stop and literally take a breath on that one!)

God's eternal mystery cannot be captured or controlled, but only received and spoken as freely as the breath itself—the one single thing we have done since the moment we were born and will one day cease to do in this body! God is as available and accessible as our breath itself, and no religion is going to be able to portion that out, control it or say who gets it.

Is that not the very meaning of Jesus' dramatic breathing on them after the Resurrection (John 20:22)? The Spirit has been definitively promised by Jesus and is as available as the very air of life! You can stop reading this book now, because nothing else I might say will be any better than that.

God refuses to be an object of knowledge like all other objects of knowledge. God cannot be known the way we know a tree, a scientific fact or a book. God can only be known as a fellow subject. That's a reciprocal knowing, where we "know as fully as we are known" (1 Corinthians 13:12). It will feel like you are being "known through" more than you are knowing something yourself. It will feel like a participative knowing more than an object of your private knowing.

God is not an ordinary datum of experience as much as *the experience that is broad enough and deep enough to allow us to hold all of our other experiences*—safely and richly. Such a spacious place will always feel more like not knowing than anything we have ever called knowing, yet it will have a deeper certitude than anything else that we have known with our minds alone! That is the paradox. That is why it is called faith knowing. It is a different quality of knowing, with even greater inner authority than rational knowing.

This is enough to convince me that there was deep inspiration in the Jewish and Christian Revelation, and it is also enough to keep me humble before Mystery forever. The inspired text knew that the best things could not—should not—be talked about, and *the message comes to its crescendo in the resurrected breath of Jesus, which is precisely Jesus unbound by space or time and yet somehow still in a human body.* All scholarship and study of sacred texts must be done inside of this cosmic humility, radical incarnationalism and Christian wonder. Someone once asked me to sum up my worldview in two words, and without thinking too much, I called it "Incarnational Mysticism." I think the Bible and Jesus gave me that worldview.

Let your breathing in and out, for the rest of your life, be your prayer to—and from—such a living and utterly shared God. You will not need to prove it, nor can you, to anybody else. Just keep breathing with full consciousness and without resistance, and you will know what you need to know.

chapter seven
evil's lie

"Anyone who kills you will think he is doing a holy
 duty for God."

—John 16:2

The Bible, as I will continue to say, is a "text in travail," struggling toward its conclusions, and only getting the point step by step, and frequently stepping backward. The important thing is to stay in the process, stay with the unfolding text and allow it to lead you forward.

You can prove anything you want from a single verse or passage in the Bible. It is a dangerous document, as history has shown, and nowhere has this more been true than its continual usage to legitimate hatred, prejudice, violence, killing, punishing and exclusionary systems, even at the highest levels of church. The very things that Jesus consistently and outrightly opposed we have righteously justified. This alone should tell us that we are not reading the Bible correctly.

The human delusion seems to be this: We seem to think someone else is always the problem, not me. We tend to export our hate and evil elsewhere. In fact, this problem is so central to human nature and human history that its overcoming is at the heart of all spiritual teachings. What mature spirituality tries to do is always keep your own feet to the fire—saying, just as Nathan said, in convicting David, "*You* are the one!" (2 Samuel 12:7).

Human nature always wants either to play the victim or to create victims—and both for the purposes of control. In fact, the second follows from the first. Once you start feeling sorry for yourself, you will soon find someone else to blame, accuse or attack—and with impunity! It settles the dust quickly, and it takes away any immediate shame, guilt or anxiety. In other words, it works—at least for a while. So for untransformed people, there is no reason to stop creating victims or playing the victim.

Most history books could give you the impression that who-killed-whom has been the very story line of history. Even history, however, has been usually written from the side of the victors! In that sense most history is probably "revisionist history," revised so it could be heard by whatever the local people were prepared to hear. Only very recent movies like Tim Robbins's *Dead Man Walking* (about Sister Helen Prejean's fight against the death penalty) and Clint Eastwood's *Flags of Our Fathers* (about the World War II Battle of Iwo Jima) have dared to present Americans a script from the side of the losers. Doesn't that reveal something quite significant? And neither of these films were big hits at the box office.

Read today's paper and you will see the pattern has not changed. Hating, fearing or diminishing someone else holds us together, for some reason. The creating of necessary victims is in our hard wiring. Rene Girard calls "the scapegoat mechanism" the central pattern for the creation and maintenance of cultures worldwide since the beginning.

The sequence, without being too clever, goes something like this: We compare, we copy, we compete, we conflict, we conspire, we condemn and we crucify. If you do not recognize some variation of this pattern within yourself, and nip it in the early stages, it is almost inevitable. That is why spiritual teachers of any depth will always teach simplicity of lifestyle and freedom from the competitive game. It is probably the only way out of the cycle of violence.

It's hard for us religious people to hear, but the most persistent violence in human history has been sacred violence, or more accurately, "sacralized violence." Human beings have found a most effective way to legitimate their instinct toward fear and hatred. They imagine that they are fearing and hating for something holy and noble, like God, religion, truth, morality, their children or love of country. It takes away all guilt, and one can even think of oneself as representing the moral highground or being responsible and prudent, as a result. Good American "soccer moms," along with many other "normal" Americans, seemingly bolstered the charge against terrorism after the September 11, 2001, attacks. It never occurs to most people that they can become what they fear and hate. It is a well-kept secret. Without wisdom, it all appears like a wonderful and moral thing, like "protecting my children."

Scapegoating or sacralized violence is the best possible disguise for evil. We can concentrate on evil "over there" and avoid our own. Evil is never easily recognized as evil by those who do it; or as Paul so wisely says, "Satan disguises itself as an angel of light" (2 Corinthians 11:14). We all choose "apparent goods" inside of our own unrecognized frame of reference. *Your* violence is always bad and evil. *Mine* is always necessary and good.

Notice also that when some murder or other heinous thing happens, sometimes people will say, "Oh, he seemed so normal," or "He was nice to animals." Statements like these show our inability to recognize the real character of evil. The Holocaust happened in a culture that considered itself Christian for centuries. Truthfully, we're not very good at the discernment of true good and real evil, which Paul lists as one of the necessary gifts of the Holy Spirit for the church (1 Corinthians 12:10).

I've met many holy people around the world, but I've also encountered people that I'd have to describe as evil. If I would try to describe the evil people and evil events that I've encountered, they're invariably characterized by a sense of certainty and clarity. They suffer no self-doubt or self-criticism, smirking at people who would dare to question them. They own no shadow from their side, which is always a sign that their evil has been projected elsewhere. Often they are overtly religious. Remember, the very word *satan* means "the accuser." Be careful when you see yourself accusing or as Jesus says "throwing stones" (John 8:8). It is the satanic disguise, a marvelous diversionary tactic.

Like all addictive thinking, scapegoating shows itself as "all or nothing" thinking, totally either/or with no capacity for paradox and little tolerance for ambiguity. I would call them "split" people; Jesus calls them "actors" at least eleven times in Matthew 23:13–29. It is usually translated as "hypocrite." The English word has come to mean "malicious" people, but probably it more often means "deceived" people.

"They know not what they do," as Jesus says (Luke 23:34) of those who kill him, which is probably why he thinks of them as actors more than sinners. They are mostly unconscious—living out of the dominant consciousness—more than directly malicious. Most evil is done by unconscious people, in my opinion. If you were aware and awake you would see right through it all—and never do it!

Do you know that you are never absolutely sure you're right when you're living in faith? That's exactly why it's called "faith"! At the crucial moments in your life's decision making, you are always trusting in God's guidance and mercy and not in your own perfect understanding. You're always "falling into the hands of the living God," as Hebrews (10:31) says, letting God's knowing suffice and God's arms save.

At some level persons of faith are invariably unsure of their own understanding and are asking God, "Is this the right thing to do?" or like Mary, "How can this come about?" (Luke 1:35). The faith stance is humble about its capacity to know the whole picture, as we said in the last chapter. So there we have it, evil is always sure of itself, and goodness is not. I believe that to be true.

Goodness, however, is accompanied by peace and patience, and even "consolation" as Saint Ignatius taught his Jesuits. That is more than enough payoff for sustaining some doubt and ambiguity.

the nature of criticism

The unconverted ego wants one thing and one thing only: control—and it wants it now. It never wants to change, in fact, it hates change. Perhaps that is why Jesus puts *metanoia* (literally, "change your mind" or even "beyond your mind"!) at the very center of his proclamation. It is very unfortunate that this word has been historically translated as "repent" (Mark 1:15; Matthew 4:17). For moderns this word connotes strict moral stances, usually concerning so-called "hot" sins, instead of any actual transformation of consciousness. That's quite a loss, I would say.

The genius of the biblical text is that this capacity for course correction, for self-critique, is actually contained in the book itself! That is necessary and good criticism. In other words, the whole of the Bible unlocks itself from within, by showing us both the capacity to get the point and our endless capacity to miss the point, which it calls *sin* (*hamartia,* "missing the mark").

When you don't have such an unlocking code, you end up with toxic religion. You have a group that cannot tolerate evaluation or criticism and always thinks criticism is coming from enemies. For example, there actually are bishops who think I do not love the church because I criticize it! That is the way a dualistic mind *must and will* think. Yet stay with the Bible, and you will see that it eventually corrects itself, just as I hope I do. The punitive, petty and vengeful lines might be there, but not for long! The Bible shows a very real patience for the bigger picture.

The interesting thing is that until now, rather than generating its own criticism from within, Christianity has most often been criticized from the outside, by its enemies, who often do not know Christianity's inner values. When criticism is allowed and encouraged from within, however, that criticism is subject to Judeo-Christian values and criteria.

In other words, it needs to be accountable to the Tradition and criticized by its own accepted values. This is what Moses, Jesus and Paul do from within the text and in their lifetimes, and why they are true reformers.

This internally generated criticism is the only genuine path of renewal and reform, which even our three-pronged American form of government recognizes. The checks and balances need to be structured inside each system itself. When the church makes room for its own prophets, it is always healthy, which is why Paul called prophecy the second most important gift! (1 Corinthians 12:28). When it "kills its prophets and stones those who are sent" (Matthew 23:37), it is always in a state of decline—a state of fear instead of faith.

The second interesting—and ironic thing—is that many of the supposedly outside critics of Christianity apparently believe the very values and criteria that the Judeo-Christian tradition taught them! Things like justice, love, truth and fairness are preached back to us by our supposed critics.

Sometimes they even live our values more authentically than we do, as Jesus often points out when he praises pagans for their faith (Matthew 8:10). We desperately need such truth speaking from without, and I have always suspected that this is what Jesus meant by his line "the children of this world are more astute in dealing with their own than are the children of light" (Luke 16:8).

In fairness, those outside critics are often looking outside of themselves at someone else's sin. They have usually not benefited from the revelation of the scapegoat mechanism and waste an awful lot of time accusing other people of their faults. That is what I would mean by bad criticism, along with any criticism that is negative in intent, mean-spirited and does not build up anybody or anything. Even negative criticism does not mean, however, that we cannot still use it for our own good and growth, even if it sometimes comes from a bad heart. If it is even partly true, it might be from the Holy Spirit.

the mystery hidden since the foundation of the world

A line from Psalm 78:2, "the mystery hidden since the foundation of the world," is used by Matthew to describe why Jesus teaches in parables. Rene Girard uses it to describe the hidden nature of the scapegoat mechanism. He believes it is precisely the Bible that blows the cover of the accusing instinct once and for all. "The Accuser has been brought down" (Revelation 12:10).

If ignorant killing or warranted violence is the basic moral problem of human history, we become the religion that worships one who was ignorantly killed! The game of smoke and mirrors should be over, at least for us. But the pattern runs deep and is well-hidden from a small self, even a Christian small self.

This accusing and blaming pattern begins to be revealed in the very first chapters of the Bible. Genesis shows Adam blaming Eve (3:12), Eve blaming the serpent (3:13) and then very soon we have Cain envying and then killing Abel (4:6–8). It's always someone else who has to be punished, accused, eliminated, tortured or killed, until it eventually takes over and "the thoughts in their hearts fashioned nothing but wickedness all the day long" (6:5). That leads to the story of Noah's flood and God's seeming destruction of the whole world.

Unfortunately, this picturesque and ancient story that explains God's salvation of a few, ends up presenting Yahweh as accusing, petty and even one who kills the unworthy and the innocent (Genesis 6—9). God's love has not yet been received at a deep or reflective level by this biblical author. It is still a very conditional and deserved love, and God is free to drown a whole world of animals and children, even if we can assume all the other adults on the rest of the earth were sinful and "violent" (Genesis 6:11–13). Here God is created in our own punitive image and is made worse than we would hopefully be! But it is a good start, because Yahweh is at least revealed as a "savior" of some (6:19–20).

God loves it seems, but at this stage God's love is still exclusive and determined by the worthiness of the receiver. We are not yet ready for a love that is determined by the abundance of the Giver. It is going to take us a long time to get to the point where God's love is self-determined, instead of being determined by our behavior. This is an important story to use to reveal what I mean by a text in travail: *getting part of the point, but not all of it yet, and partly in direct opposition to the tangent that will develop.*

In the book of Deuteronomy we will see at least some evolution of thought. It says, the "Hittites, Girgashites, Amorites, Canaanites, Perizzites, Hivites and Jebusites" all fall before the Hebrews. The text says, "You must lay them under the ban...show them no pity...deal with them like this: Tear down their altars, smash their standing stones, cut down their sacred poles and set fire to their idols" (7:2, 5). This is certainly not interreligious dialogue, yet within a few verses we will see this dynamic of legitimated violence move toward humility and a lovely recognition of God's nonviolence, which is translated as "graciousness."

The text reveals and creates a problem for us, and then at least partially unlocks it: "Do you think it was because you were greater than the other nations, that Yahweh set his heart on you? No, you were the least of all the peoples.... Yahweh was being true to his own graciousness in loving you" (Deuteronomy 7:7, 9). So we still have God justifying violence, it seems, but at least Yahweh is telling them that they are not any better than anyone else, and their election is absolutely free from God's side and undeserved from theirs. Yahweh reveals the Godself as "gracious," and now the hope is that this will rub off on them!

They would never have come naturally to such a notion of a God who is so utterly unlike they are; so a passage like this has all the earmarks of authentic breakthrough and authentic "revelation." It is the three-steps-forward kind of passage. Whereas killing those they fear is their natural pattern, we can rightly assume this killing is *not* revelation at all. It is a two-steps-backward kind of passage. I would like to offer this as a classic self-balancing text, and one that gives us criteria for determining what is a revelatory breakthrough and what is a mere repetition of the worst levels of ego consciousness.

Remember, what makes you holy can also make you evil. After any real religious encounter, people are normally dangerous for a few weeks or months, because religious experience necessarily makes you think you're the center of the world. God, it seems, has to take that risk every time God chooses us and loves us. We can utterly misuse that ego inflation for self-advancement instead of generative love. *Self-centered people misuse human love, and they will do the same with divine love.* I used to say "Beware of new converts for two years after their altar call or their baptism in the Spirit."

So why do people do such unloving and even hateful things, and worse, why does the Bible appear to teach it, and why does God appear to condone it? *That* is our problem. Unless we resolve that textual conflict, I think the Bible will continue to be one of the most dangerous and, for those who misuse it, unhelpful books in the world. So I will repeat it one more time, because it is at the heart of my message here: The text reveals both the problem and the solution. The statement of the problem is not to be interpreted as spiritual guidance or teaching, although it has been used that way for most of Christian history.

We must learn from those texts that move us beyond our natural desire for ego security, status needs and group idolatry. Only then can we trust that it is God who is breaking into human consciousness—and into the text. But how can we trust that we are following the correct tangent? By noting the trim of the sails! Where is the tack of the text directing us? This is precisely the meaning of the Christian affirmation that Jesus is the fulfillment of the Scriptures. The sails are set for a God of suffering and humble love, as we finally see in Jesus. Only because of him are we totally assured that God is beyond tribalism, violence, hatred and validating the vanities of the small self.

the scapegoat ritual

In Leviticus 16:21–22 we see an abbreviated account of the ancient scapegoat ritual. The word itself came from an early English mistranslation of "the escaping goat."

On the Day of the Atonement, a goat was brought into the sanctuary. The high priest would lay his hands on the goat and all the sins and failures of the people were ceremonially laid on the goat, and the goat was sent out into the desert to die. It was a classic displacement ritual, and what some have called "participation mystique" of the many with the symbolic One. It was quite effective.

Apparently it was one of the more ingenious liturgical rites ever created. If you really believed that every bad thing you ever did was on a goat and forgotten forever, you'd be beating that goat into the desert, too! What immediately follows from the scapegoat story of Leviticus 16 is what is called "The Law of Holiness" (Leviticus 17—27), which largely defines holiness as *separation from evil*—which is exactly what they had just ritualized.

Three thousand years later human consciousness hasn't moved a great deal beyond that, despite the message of the cross. *Jesus does not define holiness as separation from evil as much as absorption and transformation of it, wherein I pay the price instead of always asking others to pay the price.* It moves history from the persistent myth of redemptive violence to the divine plan of redemptive suffering.

I would say only a small minority of Christianity ever got the point. Maybe because when it asked us to do the same, we backed away from it as a life agenda and made it into a cosmic transaction between Jesus and the Father. Traditional atonement theories asked a lot of Jesus but little of us, except lots of thank-yous. (We will look at this more deeply in chapter nine.)

Even education does not necessarily expose our deep need to scapegoat. Education is not the same as transformation. You'd think that, if you'd educate people, they'd stop scapegoating. Yet all I see is that scapegoating becomes more sophisticated among intellectuals.

Being of German heritage myself, I feel somewhat free to look at the example of my own people. When I go to Germany to teach, I'm always struck by how well-educated Germans are. There are bookstores on every corner. They seem like the best-educated people in the world, but without a contemplative mind, education just gives you better reasons for your dualistic rationalizations. They, like us Americans, can be extremely "defended" people.

In this most educated country of Germany, half Catholic and half Lutheran—the *Holocaust* happened. Christianity must deal with that. How has the gospel been so utterly ineffective in transforming people's lives and consciousness?

We, who worship the scapegoat, Jesus, became many times in history the primary scapegoaters ourselves: Jews, heretics, sinners, witches, homosexuals, the poor, other denominations, other religions. The pattern of exporting our evil elsewhere, and righteously hating it there, is in the hardwiring of all peoples. After all, our task is to *separate* from evil, isn't it? That is the lie! *Any exclusionary process of thinking, any exclusively dualistic thinking, will always create violent people on some level.*

That I state as an absolute, and precisely because the cross revealed it to me. The crucifixion scene is our standing icon stating both the problem and the solution for all of history.

So we will pose the great spiritual problem in this way, "How do you stand against hate without becoming hate yourself?" We would all agree that evil is to be rejected and overcome; the only question is, how? How can we stand against evil without becoming a mirror—but denied—image of the same? That is often the heart of the matter, and in my experience, is resolved successfully by a very small portion of people, even though it is quite clearly resolved in the life, death and teaching of Jesus.

There are three clear scapegoats in the Christian Scripture: John the Baptist, Jesus and Stephen. Yet John the Baptist's words are very different than Stephen's words before he dies. Why? Because Jesus' ministry, his death and resurrection, have happened in between. John the Baptist is still a rather all-or-nothing thinker, an oppositional mind in most ways. That's why Jesus says, in effect, "I love my cousin but he hasn't got it all together yet. His zeal is just a good starting place, but it is not what I am going to offer you," or, to quote Jesus himself, "The least in the kingdom of God is greater than he is."

By the time you get to the death of Stephen, in Acts 7:58–60, Stephen accepts his death and forgives his enemies. Even the Sanhedrin said that "his face shone like the face of an angel" (6:15). He apparently faces his persecution and death with joy. He names the problem strongly in the speech that takes up most of chapter seven but he doesn't hate his attackers. His energy is not oppositional or hateful, and he even says, "Receive my spirit" at the end.

Stephen, the proto-martyr of Christianity, has become a new Jesus, which is henceforth the only and neverending goal. The first martyr did it right. (Some of the later ones I have doubts about, who seemed to beg and maneuver for the role, turning their persecutors into inferiors so they can have the moral high ground.)

Jesus and Stephen state the truth, then forgive, let go and are released into a transformed state, that we call "risen." I suspect that it is Saul's presence at such a death (Acts 8:1) that is the beginning of his own transformation. A chapter later (Acts 9) he is becoming Paul.

The fantastic image of Jesus as the "lamb of God" first mentioned by the Baptist (John 1:36) takes on a heroic meaning that is central to history. The Lamb (which is certainly not a natural or logical God image) is enthroned at the center and judgment seat of all things (Revelation 5:6—8:1). The Lamb is presented as the one who opens "the seven seals," as if he were the code to understanding history; he stands perpetually slain (5:6, 12) and perpetually victorious (7:10)—at the same time. Both sides of this paradox are presented as inseparable—there is no life without death, there is no death without life. We call it the paschal or Passover mystery.

Some have called this part of Revelation "The Lamb's War," which is a totally different way of dealing with evil—absorbing it in God (which is the real meaning of the suffering body of Jesus) instead of attacking it outside. It is undoubtedly the most counterintuitive theme of the entire Bible, although much of the bellicose and violent imagery in the rest of the book of Revelation probably undoes any Lamb's War message, at least in that book. The book of Revelation is indeed a text in *great* travail! Immature people will almost always misuse it.

hebrew preparation for the lamb's war

After Moses' insistence that Israel's role in the Exodus is simply to "keep still!" and "Yahweh will do the fighting for you" (Exodus 14:14), there is not much more direct nonviolent teaching. But the theme does continue to develop. Under siege, however, it is the win/lose mind that by and large controls Israel's history, just as it has controlled Christian history. The Lamb's War, which becomes the final crescendo point, is still a minority position in most of the text, "hidden since the foundation of the world."

There is at least one further example of our theme in the historical books and that is the marvelous story of Gideon in Judges 6—8. Yahweh keeps cutting down Gideon's army, saying "There are too many people with you for me to put Midian into your power, or you might claim the credit at my expense. You might say, 'My own hand has rescued me' " (7:2).

Slowly Yahweh whittles Gideon down from 33,000 to 300! But the direction is clear; the text is moving us from a total trust in violence to an ever-so-slow trust in nonviolence and spiritual transformation.

The message continues and broadens largely through the prophetic books; it is admittedly a largely lost position inside of the historic books of Joshua, Judges, Kings, Samuel and Maccabees. Yet the subtext emerges on the side, and that is among the Hebrew prophets. They are continually railing against all military alliances, and Israel's desire "to trust in horses, chariots and armies" (see, for example, the "Testament" of Isaiah in 30:15–18 or Hosea 1:7). Perhaps this is why the prophetic books are the least used in church, prayer and liturgical settings.

Isaiah, especially that part of Isaiah called Second Isaiah (chapters 40—55), is already moving toward inclusivity and away from tribalism. Israel's vocation is for the sake of the whole earth. The Four "Servant Songs" (42:1–9; 49:1–6; 50:4–10; 52:13—53:12) lay a strong foundation for a nonviolent spirituality. They lay a solid basis for an understanding of redemptive suffering in particular, which is why these readings are used so much in Holy Week.

In some ways that's why they killed most of the prophets. Their message was not that of an empire or a security state, nor was it based on militarism or worldly power. Only if we recognize this are we ready for Jesus' entering the city on a donkey (see Zechariah 9:9) and a totally new kind of Messiah, with a new kind of kingdom. Jesus makes that very point clearly in his words to Pilate, "If my kingdom were of this world, my men would have fought" (John 18:36). It's rather amazing that we missed that line.

Universalism (non-groupthink) is the point of the whole book of Jonah. Jonah doesn't want to go and preach to the Ninevites because, like a member of any group, he does not like his God caring about other people! God has to shipwreck him and, through the marvelous imagery of the big fish, spit him up on the very shore he is fleeing from. Jonah moves into a jealous and resentful rage (4:1, 4, 9) when the Ninevites actually believe his message! (3:5). So Yahweh says to Jonah in the last verse of the book, "Am I not free to feel sorry for Nineveh?" (4:11). The foundation is being laid for a universal compassion, and not just a small superiority system, which is what Jonah, the unwilling prophet, seems to want.

I think the story of Jonah is *the much needed journey from ministry as mere careerism to ministry as actual vocation*, from doing *my* work for God, to letting God do God's work in and through me.

Common opinion to the contrary, the God of the so-called Old Testament is *not* violent! It is the same God who becomes the Father of Jesus in the New Testament, and certainly Jesus does not see his father as violent at all. We'll find texts of violence and nonviolence in both Hebrew and Christian Scriptures, but the deepest and utterly new revelation in both Testaments is that God is not violent, in spite of the violence of the people whom God dwells among. As Jesus puts it, "God's sun rises on the good and the bad, God's rain falls on the just and the unjust" (Matthew 5:45).

paul, the first catholic

Although Paul is not a systematic teacher of nonviolence, he does lay the solid theological foundation for it by his insistence on the "folly" of the cross, "when I am weak, I am strong" theology and his constant calls to forgiveness, long suffering and grace. But here I want to emphasize his foundation for universalism, which does not tend to set in place any violence of group against group.

We must see in Paul's ministry to the gentiles (all non-Jews) that he is creating a tangent that we are still riding today. But the so-called first pope, Peter, probably intuited where this would lead: "Hey, this is just for the Jews, you know. We don't believe this is for the outsiders," he seems to say (see Galatians 2:11–13). But while in Jaffa, he falls into a trance and a voice from heaven says to him, "What God has made clean, you have no right to call profane" (Acts 10:16), and soon afterward Peter also says, "The truth I have now come to realize is that God does not have favorites, but that anybody who fears God and does what is right is acceptable to him" (Acts 10:34). Why doesn't anyone point that out as the first infallible sermon of a pope!

It always takes us a while to move beyond groupthink and to join the God of all the earth in universal compassion, even for popes. Paul is the bearer of the big message at this point, and "opposed [Peter] to his face since he was manifestly in the wrong!" (Galatians 2:11). I wonder how many bishops would have such courage today. Fortunately, Peter eventually does come around (Acts 10:34–35; 15:11) and almost sounds like Paul: "Remember, we believe that we are saved in the same way as they are: through grace" (Acts 15:11).

When the Holy Spirit actually shows itself in pagans, Peter says, "Who am I to stand in God's way?" (Acts 11:17) and changes his own policy, even though he hides it for fear of the conservative Judaizers, and for this Paul calls him a "pagan" and a "pretender" (see Galatians 2:13–14). Wow!

Remember, both Peter and Paul still understood Jesus' very adamant teaching on servant leadership (Luke 22:24–27; John 13:14–16, etc.). Our later fascination with dominative power finds no basis in Jesus and has only set loose a spiral of violence throughout Christian history, as groups and individuals reacted against church authority. One does not need or desire to react against servants, whereas kings usually call forth "an equal and opposite reaction," to borrow Newton's description of nature.   One wonders if we can ever regain the trust that Jesus placed in us.

Paul, of course, in the New Testament, is presented as a trans-formed accuser, a converted persecutor, maybe even a mass-murderer, whom we now call a saint. No one had been more pious, Jewish and law-abiding than Paul (Philippians 3:5–16). He was a perfect Pharisee, as he said, and suddenly he realized that in the name of love he had become hate, in the name of religion he had become a murderer, in the name of goodness he had become evil.

Paul was set up to recognize the dark side of religion, the scapegoat-ing mechanism, the self-serving laws of small religion. He went global and that changed everything, and is probably why most of us are reading the Bible today. It is extraordinary that such an iconoclast would end up producing, directly or indirectly, such a large part of the Christian Scriptures. More and more scholars today would only insist on Romans, 1 and 2 Corinthians (without additions), Galatians, Philippians, 1 Thessalonians and Philemon as authentically from Paul. But his life generated much of Acts (written by Luke) and significantly influenced whoever wrote Ephesians, Colossians, 2 Thessalonians and the letters to Timothy and Titus.

jesus, forgiver

Jesus has no part in any "myth of redemptive violence," as some have called it, even though redemptive violence is the primary story line of history, and even of much of the Bible (conquering of the Promised Land, imposing of the ban, wars of the Kings of Israel, Saul, David, Herod and the like). Jesus' story, instead, becomes a pattern of redemptive *forgiveness*.

Jesus' life and teaching is starkly opposed to that perennial, universal mistake that is happening probably every three minutes in most human minds and hearts—the instinct to destroy what we perceive as the source of the problem. In that sense, he really is the "Savior of the World" (John 4:42) because that is the world's primary agenda, which he unmasks and then resolves with a quite different agenda. If we do not learn it, it is hard to believe there is much future for our world.

To oppose violence, he has to diminish the very things that people tend to absolutize, because our absolutes are normally what we use to justify our violence. He has to relativize at least three things that almost all peoples idealize: (1) my group identity, (2) my security system or occupation and (3) the nuclear family and so-called "family values," which are often used as a defense mechanism against the larger spiritual family.

Let's see how he does all three: First, when the disciples want to stop another group that is using Jesus' name, he says, "You must not stop

149

them, anyone who is not against you is for you" (Luke 9:50). They clearly do not get the point because in the next verse they want to "call down fire from heaven to burn them up" (Luke 9:51–55). He "turns and rebukes them," probably sighing inside. Jesus will speak critically against his own group, whenever they try to use his message for oppositional thinking or group arrogance or to justify violence. How different Christian history would have been had we listened to him!

The only thing more dangerous than the individual ego is the group ego. That's why, when Jesus calls the apostles, he immediately calls into question the two sacred institutions inside of a Semitic culture, or most cultures for that matter, job and family.

He told them to "leave their nets" (Mark 1:18), their only occupation, which is your extended self-interest group, and in many ways your very identity. He also tells Matthew to leave his job as a tax collector (Luke 5:28).

Finally, even more nonsensically, they leave their father "and the men he employed" (Mark 1:19–20). He repeats this demand in shocking form by speaking of "hating" (radical detachment) all blood relatives (Luke 14:26) and even illustrates it in relationship to his own mother (Matthew 12:48 ff.). These are clear indications that we are talking about some form of radical discipleship, change of lifestyle, countercultural world view and not just religion as attendance at worship services. All three absolutes that keep people small and paranoid have been undone by Jesus: my identity or power group, my job, and my family.

Jesus is moving his Jewish disciples beyond any kind of narrow worldview. Not surprisingly, we often find outsiders understanding him and responding to him more than the insiders. Take the Roman centurion who called him the "Son of God" (Mark 15:39). Or take the Syro-Phoenician woman (Matthew 15:21–28), the centurion's servant (Luke 7:1–10), the Gerasene demoniac (Luke 8:26–39), the Good Samaritan

(Luke 10:29–37), the "foreign" leper (Luke 17:19), Zacchaeus (Luke 19:1–10) and other non-Jews who respond strongly to Jesus.

What does he usually tell them? "You have great faith" (Matthew 15:28), or "Nowhere in Israel have I found faith like this" (Matthew 8:10). You'd think he'd call them to Jerusalem to join his group, or to accept John's baptism. But, no, even to public sinners he says, "Go in peace. Your faith has made you whole" (Luke 7:50). No wonder the religious zealots killed him!

This is Jesus' simple message: Holiness is no longer to be found through separation from or exclusion of, but in fact, the radical inclusion (read "forgiveness") of the supposedly contaminating element. Any exclusionary system only lays the solid foundation for violence in thought, word and deed. So he has to lead us on a new path: "He will give the people knowledge of salvation through the forgiveness of their sins" (Luke 1:77) and inclusion of the enemy (Matthew 5:44), and even departure from what we think is ourself (Mark 8:34–38).

My lifetime of studying Jesus would lead me to summarize all of his teaching inside of two prime ideas: *forgiveness and inclusion.* Don't believe me; just go through the Gospels, story by story. It is rather self-evident. Forgiveness and inclusion are Jesus' "great themes." They are the practical name of love, and without forgiveness and inclusivity love is largely a sentimental valentine. They are also the two practices that most undercut human violence.

Let me unpack that even further: What Leviticus 16—27 had described as the "law of holiness," separation from sinful people, the rejection of certain actions and things, is turned around in Jesus so that it is instead the very act of separation, superiority and rejecting that is in fact the sin!

James Alison, in *The Joy of Being Wrong,* points out this dynamic in the punch line of the marvelous story of the man born blind: "Blind? If you were, you would not be guilty, but because you say, 'We see,' your guilt remains" (John 9:41). "All humans are blind," Alison says, "but where the blindness is compounded by active participation in the mechanisms of exclusion pretending to sight, this blindness is culpable."[1]

I believe Jesus is teaching us that *if we put our energy into choosing the good—instead of the negative and largely illusionary energy of rejecting the bad—we will overcome evil in a much better way, and will not become evil ourselves!* This is exactly what he does on the cross, and that is what gives me the courage to believe this is at the heart of his message. At our center in New Mexico, we have taken it as one of our central axioms that *"the best criticism of the bad is the practice of the better."*

More than anything else, this is how Jesus reformed the laws of religion and undercut the basis for all violent, exclusionary and punitive behavior. He became the forgiving victim, so we would stop creating victims ourselves. He became the falsely accused one, so we would be careful whom we accuse.

The New Testament passion accounts go out of their way to point out that it was precisely the "high priests, elders and leaders of the people," Caiaphas, Herod and Pilate, both church and state, who judged Jesus to be the problem; every authority in sight is trotted out to judge him unworthy. Then, to add insult to injury, they release a clearly violent man like Barabbas (Matthew 27:26).

Any worldly system actually prefers violent partners to nonviolent ones; it gives them a clear target and a credible enemy. Empires are actually relieved to have terrorists to shoot at and Barabbasses loose on the streets. Types like Jesus, Martin Luther King and Gandhi make difficult enemies for empires. They cannot be used or co-opted.

The powers that be know that nonviolent prophets are a much deeper problem, but you cannot gather public hatred toward them. They are a much deeper problem because they refuse to buy into the very illusions that the whole empire is built on, especially the myth of redemptive violence.

The passion account reveals that it is an utterly upside-down world, from the top down (see Acts 17:6–7). The system of power and violence is judged to be wrong. It's not Jews, priests, scribal lawyers or Rome who are wrong, as such, but rather it is the way power is exercised and violence is justified in all of these institutions.

It is all the more amazing that Christians ever blamed Jews for the death of Jesus. That is smoke and mirrors! The killing of Jesus is a judgment on how blind we *all* can be when we are enjoying the perks and privileges of power. Bad power, which *always* eliminates its opponents, killed Jesus. In Jesus' lifetime that bad power was exercised by both Roman Empire and Jewish high priests, but you can change the names in every age and every culture.

That's how deep, unconscious and irrational the scapegoat mechanism seems to be. This scapegoating issue is so central to the Bible, and to the unlocking of history, that chapter nine will see how Jesus uniquely overcame it.

chapter eight
the resented banquet

"It is by grace that you are saved, through faith, not by anything of your own, but by a pure gift from God, and not by anything you have achieved. Nobody can claim the credit. You are God's work of art."

—Ephesians 2:8

"By grace you notice, nothing to do with good deeds, or grace would not be grace at all."

—Romans 11:6

"Happy are those servants whom the master finds awake. I tell you he will put on an apron, sit them down at table and wait on them."

—Luke 12:37

At this point I want to name what I think is the central positive theme of the Bible. It is the Divine Unmerited Generosity that is everywhere available, totally given, usually undetected as such, and often even undesired. It is called grace and has been rightly defined as "that which confers on our souls a new life, that is, a sharing in the life of God

Himself" (that's from *The New Baltimore Catechism* of yesteryear—the more recent catechisms say essentially the same thing).[1]

In the parable of the watchful servants (Luke 12:35–40), God is actually presented as *waiting on us*—in the middle of the night! In fact, God is presented as both our personal servant inside of our house, and a "burglar" who "breaks through the walls of that house." That's really quite extraordinary and not our usual image of God at all. That is how much God wants to get to us, and how unrelenting is the work of grace.

Unless and until you understand the biblical concept of God's unmerited favor, God's unaccountable love, Francis Thompson's "Hound of Heaven," most of the biblical text cannot be interpreted or tied together in any positive way. It is, without doubt, the key and the code to everything transformative in the Bible. In fact, people who have not experienced the radical character of grace will always misinterpret the meanings and the direction of the Bible. The Bible will become a burden and obligation more than a gift.

Grace cannot be understood by any ledger of merits and demerits. It cannot be held to any patterns of buying, losing, earning, achieving or manipulating, which is where, unfortunately, most of us live our lives. Grace is, quite literally, "for the taking." It is God eternally giving away God—for nothing—except the giving itself. I believe grace is the life energy that makes flowers bloom, animals lovingly raise their young, babies smile and the planets remain in their orbits—for no good reason whatsoever—except love alone.

Abundance, largesse, excess is the spiritual name of the game, "full measure, pressed down, shaken together, running over and pouring into your lap" (Luke 6:38). Grace will always be experienced as *more than enough* instead of a mere survival mode. If there is not grace to a situation, it does not really satisfy or give any deep joy.

The ego does not know how to receive things freely or without logic. It prefers a worldview of scarcity, or at least quid pro quo, where only the clever win. It likes to be worthy and needs to understand in order to be able to accept things. That problem, and its overcoming, is at the very center of the gospel plot line. It has always been overcome from God's side. The only problem is getting us in on the process! That very inclusion of us is God's humility, graciousness and love. That God wants free partners becomes very clear in the economy of grace (Romans 8:28). "Not servants, but friends" (John 15:15) is God's plan.

The early flag words that become the awesome theme of grace are *banquet* and *food.* It starts with the gratuitous manna and quails in the desert and the water gushing from a rock (Exodus 16—17); it continues with Abraham and Sarah's meal with the three visitors (Genesis 18:1–8). It becomes an entire ritual system of eating sacred foods, like Passover meals, and communion sacrifices, which were consumed by the priests (for example, Leviticus 8:31).

Jesus opens up a new tradition of common and open table fellowship, including both a bread-and-fish tradition that seems to have fallen into disuse ("potluck suppers" for all, as alluded to in 1 Corinthians 11:17 ff. and the multiplication stories in the Gospels) and a bread-and-wine tradition (which was preserved as the Eucharist we now enjoy, but was largely used to define membership and worthy membership). After the resurrection Jesus repeats the fish tradition with the Eleven (Luke 24:42–43), the bread and fish with seven of them by the seashore (John 21:9–12) and the bread tradition with the two disciples on the way to Emmaus (Luke 24:30 ff.).

A common meal—perhaps a meal with sinners, or Pharisees or often a wedding banquet—becomes Jesus' most common audiovisual aid for his message. It has all the elements of community, equality, joy, nurturance, delight, generous host and open invitation to the "good and bad alike" (Matthew 22:10; Luke 14:21). What better metaphor for eternity and salvation! He makes that connection clear when he says at his Last Supper that this wine drinking and "feasting" is a foretaste and promise of what they will do forever (Mark 14:25; Luke 22:16) and "together in the kingdom of my Father" (Matthew 26:29). I can't wait!

But that is to jump ahead. Let's build up to it, for it takes us a long time to be willing to "come to the banquet" (Luke 14:23; Matthew 22:8). *Strangely enough, in real life, people have tended to resent it, fear it, deny it and make it impossible or difficult to attend. We are either afraid or unwilling to just celebrate the feast of divine union.*

Christopher Fry, in his not-so-well-known play, *Thor, With Angels*, observes Christianity in its early attempts to plant itself in northern Europe. (I am grateful to Gil Bailie for pointing this play out to me.) In the play Christianity cannot decide whether its message has to do with "Monday washing day" or "Thursday baking day." The choice it made was largely for Monday washing day, for mopping-up exercises: purity codes, debt codes, atonement theories to a God who had to be paid off.

Yet the glory of the "good news"—why it's good and why it's new—is that our story is not the old hackneyed story of mopping up, of purity codes that supposedly placate a distant God. It's about liberating and undercutting the problem *before the fact* by offering Thursday baking day! The gospel needs to present humankind with a worldview of abundance instead of one of scarcity, a vision of grace instead of one of fear, of Holy Thursday baking day instead of Monday laundry day. But, so very sadly for the vast majority of Christians, a laundry day of purity codes has seemed to suffice.

Even much of the European Reformation strikes one as guilt-based and not joy-encountered. Like nothing else, it perhaps explains the dour, dutiful and often resentful character of so much civil religion. Such a passive-aggressive stance toward reality will never invite or change the world.

A friend of mine recently shared this story with me: An angel was walking down the street carrying a torch in one hand and a pail of water in the other. A woman asked the angel, "What are you going to do with the torch and with the pail?" The angel said, "With the torch, I'm going to burn down the mansions of heaven, and with the pail I'm going to put out the fires of hell. Then we shall see who really loves God."

That's what grace does; it empowers those who really love and trust God, and frankly leaves all others in the realm of missed opportunity. Our image for that missed opportunity has been a later-hell, but it is primarily and clearly a now-emptiness.

Only the theme of grace is prepared to move religion beyond this bad and tired novel of reward and punishment. We need such an angel; we need grace to reform religion and to recapture the gospel. As Marcus Borg says, in *Meeting Jesus Again for the First Time,* only the theme of grace can move us into religion beyond a list of "requirements" to a religion of real transformation of consciousness (Ephesians 4:23–24).

As long as we remain inside of a win-lose script, Christianity will continue to appeal to low-level and self-interested morality and never rise to the mystical banquet that Jesus really offered us. It will be duty instead of delight, "jars of purification" (John 2:6) instead of 150 gallons of intoxicating wine at the end of the party! (2:7–10). How did we avoid missing the clear message on that one?

We kept the basic storyline of all human history in place and simply laid the gospel on top of it, frosting on top of a non-cake, as it were. Jesus offered us a whole new cake—which by itself is its own frosting. Yet, except for those who experienced grace, Christianity has not been "a new mind" (Romans 12:2) or a "new self" (Ephesians 4:23–24) significantly different than the surrounding cultures it inhabited. It is the old, tired win/lose scenario which seems to be in our hard drive, whereas the scenario of grace is much more imaginative and installs totally new programs, which most of the world has yet to recognize, like win/win!

We have largely mirrored culture instead of transforming it. Reward/punishment is the plot line of almost all novels, plays, operas, movies and the wars that define cultures. It is the only way that a dualistic mind, unrenewed by prayer, can read reality.

We've taken this win/lose scenario to an art form in contemporary Western capitalism. Our conversations always get around to the price of things, or not being able to afford things, or how to make more money to buy things. You cannot easily change that mindset by attending church services, you just transfer that mindset to the world of religion. Non-gospel Catholics try to calculate indulgences and days in purgatory; immature Protestants and many Catholics make it into either a "prosperity gospel" or a moral achievement contest. That's the only language we really get in most sermons, a binary system of good guys and bad guys, in which we all lose, if the truth be told.

The game that I call "meritocracy" is really found in almost all cultures, insofar as I can tell. Maybe culture could even be defined as attempts to "earn worthiness" or to validate the self by some extrinsic measure. This is the dead-ended mentality that made Jesus, as John's Gospel puts it (2:15), "create a whip of cords" and go to the temple to destroy "the system of buying and selling." Why? Because until that mind is somehow changed, you *cannot* understand the gospel.

The symbolism is not accidental: Buying and selling invariably takes over the temple itself. It defeats the essential work of religion, or at least as Jesus understood religion. It obviously made Jesus quite angry, and if there is any violence in Jesus' life, this is it, but he directs it toward any attempts to "buy" God. His violence is not against people, but at self-serving religion and its frequent alliance with power and money.

Also, I am sure, Jesus is quite angry at any attempt to "buy" God's love or to make religion into an exclusive club, which is shown by the overtly inclusive quote that he takes from Isaiah, "My house is to be a house of prayer for *all the peoples*" (56:7).

One parable that everyone is familiar with is the story of the man coming to work at the last hour, who gets paid as much as the one that comes at the first hour (Matthew 20:1–16). Let's be honest, none of us worker-bees appreciate that story. We're good, well-trained Americans. We all say, "Thanks be to God" at Mass when we hear this Gospel read, but we don't really like it or believe it. It's not the way we think; it's not the way you and I have organized the world. Such a parable as this should be a clear signal that Jesus is presenting a very different world-view than the achievement contest of Western capitalism.

A parable is a unique form of literature that is always trying to subvert business as usual, much like a Zen koan or a Confucian riddle, both of which use paradox to undo our reliance on what we think is logic. Yet we typically do not let parables do that for us. Our dominant consciousness is so in control that we try to figure them out inside of our existing consciousness—or more commonly we just ignore them or consider them out of date. Yet as Einstein was reported to have said, "*No problem can be solved by the same consciousness that caused it in the first place.*" Parables aim to subvert our old consciousness and offer us a way through by utterly reframing our worldview.

So often the biblical text is not a transformative document and does not bring about a "new creation," because we pull it inside of our own security systems and what we call "common sense." At that point, no divine breakthrough is possible. Frankly speaking, much of Scripture, then, has become largely harmless and forgettable.

Our understanding of forgiveness has changed over time and culture, it seems. A history of forgiveness I once read pointed out that after Constantine, the Roman emperor who in 313 made Christianity the established religion of the Empire, you will see two concepts start changing at a radical pace. With Constantine's Edict of Milan in 313, both grace and forgiveness became basically politicized and controlled by formula and technique. *They became juridical concepts instead of spiritual realizations.*

That was pretty obvious in the Catholicism that I grew up with in 1950s Kansas: prescribed penances and methods that made sacramental absolution licit and valid, exact periods of punishment in purgatory for precise sins and for timed release, the quantification of Masses themselves, liturgical errors that made Masses invalid or illicit, various formulas for "meriting" heaven (nine of anything was especially miraculous), and even "buying" the salvation of pagan babies! Sin management became the work of the priesthood much more than the marvelous work of transformation and inner realization that we see in Jesus' ministry.

Church had largely become a "worthiness and attainment system" managed from without, instead of a transformational system awakening us from within. As little altar boys in Kansas, my friends and I set out the black vestments for "requiem Masses" more than 50 percent of the time! Our church had become a funereal society, obviously much more concerned about saving the dead than healing the living, despite Jesus' two explicit warnings against that very thing (Mark 12:27; Luke 9:60). A new generation of priests seems to know nothing about these heresies, and even want to go back to such unbiblical Christianity!

When forgiveness becomes largely a juridical process, then we who are in charge can measure it out, define who's in and who's out, find ways to earn it and exclude the unworthy. *It makes for good religion, but not at all for good spirituality.* We have destroyed the likelihood that most people will ever experience the pure gift of God's forgiveness. We have pushed people away from God, whose forgiveness cannot be earned by any technique whatsoever. It is only and always received as a pure gift—and that is *precisely* the experience that changes us so deeply. Otherwise, it is not grace!

For most of us, the world of reward and punishment is the frame that we all began with as children. I've always said if I had three screaming kids, I'd be into crime and punishment, too! "You only get the lollipop when you're a good boy," or "Mommy punishes me when I'm a bad boy so, that must be the way God is, too." Right? No, that is the very program that God has to change by inserting some new software.

At the beginning of spiritual direction at least 80 percent of peoples' operative God image is a subtle combination of their mom and their dad or any other significant authority figures. Once they begin an inner life of prayer and in-depth study of sacred texts, that slowly begins to change, and from then on it only gets better and better. Grace does its work and creates a "work of art" (Ephesians 2:10).

To illustrate how deep this pattern is in all of us, an analysis of the 2004 U.S. election patterns showed that people with punitive parenting backgrounds were much more likely to vote for warlike candidates, people who had experienced more permissive parenting were more likely to vote for nonviolent approaches to national and international disputes.

Our unconscious and early patterns determine much of what we imagine to be our fully conscious and deliberate behavior and even influence our politics and surely our religion.

"God talk" without self-knowledge and inner journey is largely a smokescreen, even to the person who believes the language (see the teachings of Socrates, Teresa of Avila, Carl Jung). The miracle of grace and true prayer is that it invades the unconscious mind and heart! It invades them so much that the love of God and the love of self invariably proceed forward together. On the practical level, they are experienced as the same thing! Think about that, and see if it is not true.

free, gratuitous election

The idea of grace grows through the concepts of election or personal chosenness. That's what is finally and daringly called covenant love, or love between "equals" in some sense. Remember, the whole movement of the Bible is toward the possibility of intimacy, divine union, full personhood, and there has to be some degree of "sameness" for that to happen. I will keep repeating that, so you will know the tangent and will be ready for God's solution.

In Deuteronomy God says to Israel, "If Yahweh set his heart on you and chose you, it was not because you were greater than other peoples. In fact, you were the least of all the peoples. It was for love of you and to keep the oath that he swore to your fathers that Yahweh has brought you out with his mighty hand and redeemed you from the house of slavery" (7:7–8).

This quote, and its continual, constant pattern, is the foundation stone of our entire theology of grace! God did not choose or love the

Israelites because they were good, but out of free and arbitrary choice. From the very beginning, Divine election is utterly free, gratuitous and indifferent to any criterion of worthiness or earnedness. It never has been a "worthiness contest," and God's favor never will be. This is very hard for almost everybody to accept. It just does not compute.

I remember a bumper sticker from many years ago, made by some of our New Jerusalem Community members, quoting something I told them again and again: *"God does not love you because you are good, but you are good because God loves you."* I was so happy they chose that quote, but I think we have improved on it thirty years later. Now I say, *"God does not love you because you are good, God loves you because God is good."* Both sayings are true—in fact, the older I get the more I am sure that God does all the giving and we do all of the receiving.

God is always and forever the initiator, and we are always the respondents. That is not to say that our mustard seed of response does not matter, but it is still "the tiniest of all the seeds" (Matthew 13:32). God seems both very humble and very patient, if everything we see about the universe is true. God makes use of everything that we offer, and seems most grateful for the tiniest bit of connection from our side. This is the faith desire that is needed, and even important, from us. Otherwise it would not be a covenant, but rather a coercion. There is no evidence that Jesus heals worthy people. He does heal desirous people, but even God creates that desire!

Divine election starts with the utterly unpredictable choice of the enslaved people Israel, but continues in God's continual choice of quite ordinary people for extraordinary tasks. Always their résumé and their skill-set are totally inadequate, but it is *the very experience of being chosen that somehow empowers them.*

Perhaps no example is clearer than God's use of a single, unprepared person like David. God's utterly free and undeserved election is somewhat "scandalous" and even nonsensical. Walter Brueggemann rightly calls it "the scandal of particularity." Why here? Why now? Why this? Why him? Why her? There is no answer, except God's freedom.

David is the archetypal whole person of the Hebrew Scriptures, even psychologically speaking yet his "holiness" is totally created by God's involvement with him. He's the violent warrior (2 Samuel 8—10); he's the adulterer who impregnates a married woman, Bathsheba (11:2 ff.), he's the egocentric person who allows Uriah to be killed to protect his own name (11:5). Some say that his relationship with Jonathan might well have had a homosexual character to it (1 Samuel 18:1; 2 Samuel 1:26), yet he's chosen.

He's loved by God, who continually reaches out to him. "I will be a father to him and he a son to me. Even if he does evil...I will still not withdraw my favor from him" (1 Samuel 18:1). David relies on this promise forever (23:5), and not coincidentally it becomes "The House of David" (Luke 1:28, 33) from which Jesus (who will become the Christian whole man) is born. David has learned that God's choice is absolutely free, and by our standards, arbitrary, having nothing to do with his worthiness, and if he did write many of the Psalms, now it makes sense why they are still the songs and prayers of true biblical faith.

David, like all of us on the spiritual path, eventually realizes that whatever worthiness he has is entirely a gift. God implants a bit of the Godself in us, called the Holy Spirit (Romans 5:5; 8:9–10; 1 Corinthians 3:16–17), and God *cannot not* love what God sees there. Paul even calls our very bodies "temples" (1 Corinthians 6:19). God has created just enough equality to make a "covenant" of love possible! This is called "the new covenant in my blood," where the same blood is shared, implying union between equals (1 Corinthians 11:25; Luke 22:14). This is almost embarrassingly ritualized at the Eucharist and is probably why the eucharistic churches have so much easier access to non-dual or mystical Christianity.

Our lovability is not a moral achievement on our part, but God's pure gift on God's part. To paraphrase Meister Eckhart, "The love by which we think we are loving God is actually the love by which God first loved us." All we are doing is completing the circuit, and allowing the flow (see John 15:16). You cannot really get there; you can only be there. God does all the loving.

Such an understanding and experience is the heart of what we call the gospel, and why it is such good news. It only fully unfolds once we understand the Trinitarian mystery and how we fit into that flow. Salvation has always been an objective gift, which we must still allow and access, but we unfortunately have largely made it into a subjective achievement. As I will continue to say, that mystery of union cannot be accessed by the "calculative mind." The dualistic mind cannot access union, wholeness, eternity or holiness. Only God in me can know God, only love can recognize love, only union can enjoy union.

There is a very telling passage in 2 Samuel in which David's sin is publicly exposed by the prophet Nathan. This is the only time in the whole Bible where a king is confronted by a prophet and the king admits that he is wrong and that the prophet is right (12:13–14).

That encounter is why I call David the archetypal whole man. As I explain in *From Wild Man to Wise Man*, when the man who is king-warrior-lover accepts the truth of his rejected self, "the wise man" or prophet, he fills out the four quadrants of his full male soul. There always seems to be one part of us that begs for recognition and integration, and often holds the key to our maturity.

The moment you become whole and holy is when you can accept your shadow self, or, to put it in moral language, that is when you can admit your sin. *Basically we move from unconsciousness to consciousness by a deliberate struggle with our shadow self.* Jesus himself only begins to speak after he has been "led by the Spirit…to be tempted by the devil" (Matthew 4:1). The reason that the devils always know who Jesus is (e.g., Mark 1:24), is because he has engaged them! Only then do we "awaken." Unconscious people have invariably never struggled with their own poverty and woundedness, and are falsely "innocent" (which translates *unwounded*).

Most of the world's great literature, poetry and theater make that compelling and obvious. *The problem isn't sinning, nearly as much as our unwillingness to admit that we have sinned,* or at least as Jesus does, to engage honestly with darkness and our capacity for evil. To put it simply, it was not accidental or unimportant that Jesus was "tempted." Those who pretend to be above it all are the ones to worry about.

These are the ones who destroy history and relationships, and Jesus calls them "whitewashed tombs" and "blind guides" (Matthew 23:24, 27). God seems quite practiced in using peoples' sin for good, but those who refuse to see their dark side God cannot use! *Jesus himself is never upset at sinners. He's only upset with people who don't think they're sinners.* Righteous folks are much more problematic for Jesus, because they are only half there, at best.

In 2 Samuel 7 David wants to build Yahweh a house to prove to Yahweh that he's a good boy. Through Nathan, Yahweh says to David, "I don't want you to build me a house. *I* will build *you* a house. I will give you rest from all your enemies. Yahweh will make you great. Yahweh will build you a house and when your days are ended and you are laid to rest with your ancestors, I will preserve your offspring until eternity."

This passage could be called the Great Turnaround, and I might add, the necessary turnaround. We all start by thinking we are going to do something for God, and by the end of our lives we know God has done it all for us. We start with a willingness to enter into this bilateral covenant with God, and eventually we know that it is mostly unilateral, and grace has filled in all the gaps!

At that turnaround point, we have David offering a beautiful prayer back to Yahweh, that I call the " 'But Who Am I?' prayer." (This is the prayer of all of us when grace has been bestowed upon us. It's the prayer of Mary at her annunciation, and it is the all-night prayer of

Saint Francis in the cave.) "Who am I, Lord Yahweh, and what is my house that you have led me as far as this?" (v. 18 ff.), says David.

To allow yourself to be God's beloved is to be God's beloved. To allow yourself to be chosen is to be chosen. To allow yourself to be blessed is to be blessed. It is so hard to accept being accepted, especially from God. It takes a certain kind of humility to surrender to it, and even more to persist in believing it. Any used persons know this to be true: God chooses and then uses whom God chooses, and their usability comes from their willingness to allow themselves to be chosen in the first place. What a paradox!

God's love is constant and irrevocable; our part is to be open to it and let it transform us. There is absolutely nothing we can do to make God love us more than God already does; and there is absolutely nothing we can do to make God love us less. We are stuck with it! The only difference is between those who allow that and those who don't, but they are both equally and objectively the beloved. One just enjoys it and draws ever-new life from that realization.

Even though it's been the story of my whole life, I don't fully believe it yet myself, because it still seems too much, too good, beyond my wildest hopes, maybe whistling in the dark, maybe wishful thinking, maybe "cheap grace," maybe my faulty theology. But then I read the accounts of the scriptural saints, and I meet saints in jails and hospitals, and their very lives tell me this is true. They are always *sinners in recovery*, and they know that God does not love them because they are good, but God loves them because God is good.

"credo of adjectives"

"Yahweh, Yahweh, a God of tenderness and compassion, slow to anger, rich in kindness, and abounding in faithfulness. For the thousandth generation, Yahweh maintains his kindness, forgiving all our faults, transgressions and sins" (Exodus 34:6–7).

In this marvelous early affirmation we have in one short text, in the words of Walter Brueggemann, "a formulation so studied that it may be reckoned to be something of a classic, normative statement to which Israel regularly returned, meriting the label 'credo.'"[2] In it are found five generous and glorious adjectives that describe the heart and soul of Israel's belief. Somehow, against all odds and neighbors, they were able to experience a God who was merciful (in Hebrew, *rhm*), compassionate/gracious *(hnn)*, steadfast in love *(hsd)*, tenaciously faithful *('emeth)* and forgiving *(ns')*.

This is the dynamic center of their entire belief system, and like all spiritual mystery, seems to be endlessly generative and fruitful, ending up in the full-blown—and literally unthinkable—concept of grace. If a passage like this is not divine breakthrough, five steps forward, I do not know what revelation is!

Let's illustrate just a bit of this fruitfulness; I strongly encourage you to go to your Bible and read these passages in their entirety, because my short summaries will not do them justice. Try Ezekiel chapters 36—37. There Yahweh really chews Israel out, telling them, in effect, through the prophet, "You haven't done anything right, you've missed the whole point."

You can see them all sitting with their tails between their legs. He completely disqualifies them as a worthy people, almost as if to tell them to throw the whole thing out and start over. Then seemingly out of nowhere, a new creation out of nothing is offered. Yahweh promises to rebuild the project from the bottom up, and says in verse 36:22, "I am not doing this for your sake, House of Israel, but for the sake of my holy name." God is God's own reference point. God is being true to the Godself in loving. God's faithfulness has never been dependent on our worthiness or readiness.

Then the whole of chapter 37 is the presentation of what God does with "dry bones." Like new Adams and Eves, God will breathe new life into old earth and make it live! Yahweh says several times in these passages that his reputation is at stake, and God is not going to let his well-deserved public reputation for love and faithfulness be undone by our silliness and laziness. Great stuff!

The word that is translated as "steadfast love" is often rendered "covenant love" or "faithful love." Today we often call it unconditional love. It's "one-sided love," if you will, because Israel never, never keeps its side of the covenant, just as we never keep our side of the relationship to this day. Yahweh has learned to do it all from God's side, and that is the constant and relentless message of much of the Hebrew Scriptures.

The early Mosaic covenant is clearly presented as bilateral between the people and Yahweh (Exodus 24), which is repeated by Joshua (Joshua 24:1 ff.), and by Ezra (Nehemiah 8:12 ff.) every time after continuous failures, "adultery," on Israel's part. One doubts whether there was ever a time when the covenant was observed from humanity's side, which is what Paul seems to say (Romans 3:9; 5:12 ff.).

Then the Noah story goes further, God again taking the initiative. Noah's covenant is extended to "every living creature of every kind that is found on the earth" (Genesis 9:16). *It is quite amazing that we have not seen that as a very strong mandate for ecology, earth and animal care!*

By the time we get to David, however, the covenant has become almost entirely unilateral, with God always buying more and more shares in the company, until he seems to be the major shareholder while we are always the beneficiaries. This becomes "the new covenant" promised by Jeremiah (31:31). It's "not a covenant like the one I made with their ancestors…they broke it, so now I will show them who is the Master!" (31:32) Yahweh shows that he is the Master by outdoing them in love, and now writing the law within their hearts (31:33), giving them a "new heart and new spirit" (Ezekiel 36:25–27) all from God's side.

Isaiah repeats the same theme. After reaming them out for phony, half-hearted religion (29:13), God's response, as paraphrased in *The Message,* is, "Very well, I am going to step in and shock them awake, astonish them and stand them on their ears. The wise ones who had it all figured out will be exposed as fools" (29:14).

Those two lines are about as good a description of both *the intent and the effects of grace*, as any I have found in all the Scriptures, and as always they follow upon significant failure by Israel. Yahweh's response to failure is *"I will love you at even deeper levels, because I am determined to win. Your pettiness is not going to determine or limit my greatness."* What other kind of victory could God have? I know humans who have loved me at least this well, and this beautifully, so how could human love possibly be greater than God's capacity to love?

ecstasy or garbage dump?

Some saint is supposed have said, "If you'd ask the people in hell if they are happy, almost all of them would say, 'yes!' " Hell is a description for people who have become comfortable with nothingness, with non-life, even a dead existence, while even being content with it. It is all they ever knew or ever expected. I know many people like that right now. Hell is later only because it was allowed and chosen now.

Perhaps I would put it this way: The gate of hell is always a door swinging both ways. No one is there unless they want to be, and anyone who wants more can always decide differently. But when I see how people resist and avoid change here, I can see why the Scriptures used the metaphor of a tragic and "eternal fire." The logical possibility of an eternal hell must be allowed, even though, interestingly, the church has never declared a single person to be there.

No one is going to be in heaven who doesn't want to be there; no one is going to be in hell who doesn't want to be there. You're choosing it right now, and God apparently gives us exactly what we want. Do you want life, to live inside the city of Jerusalem, "where you will be suckled, filled from her consoling breasts, where you will savor with delight her glorious breasts" (Isaiah 66:11). Or do you want "Gehenna," the garbage dump still outside the walls of Jerusalem, "where the worm never dies nor the fire ever goes out" (Isaiah 66:24). That is always the choice, and in these concluding verses of the prophet Isaiah the choices are dramatically portrayed.

They became archetypal metaphors that were used in the Jewish tradition down to Jesus himself. They were used so dramatically, however, that they become literalized and localized. This has had an unfortunate effect for generations of Christians, who were often not consciously realizing that to take it literally would make the loving God into an eternal torturer. It's an absurd notion, because then God would be less loving than we are. And don't forget the very material notions of fire and burning, when the physical body is, in fact, dead. That should have been a giveaway that we were dealing with a metaphor, albeit a potent one.

A good spiritual teacher always puts a deliberate choice before her or his students, to call them to decision. Moses did so in his last days: "I set before you life or death, blessing or curse. Choose life!" (Deuteronomy 30:20).

This will be continued in many of the prophets in one form or another, including Jesus, who stated his radical alternatives as "God or money" (Matthew 6:24; Luke 16:13). For centuries this was normally translated as "Mammon" presumably because his direct use of the word *money* was too embarrassing and convicting for most of us, as it still is, just as is the word *hell.* Prophetic choices are made quite black-and-white, intentionally dualistic, to force you to the weighing of consequences, to choicefulness and consciousness.

What was meant to be such a call became frozen in the imagination into geographical places, which even Pope John Paul II, in a newsmaking General Audience of July 28, 1999, said was incorrect. When hell became falsely read as a geographical place, it stopped serving its decisive and descriptive function, and instead became the largely useless threats of exasperated church parents.

Metaphors such as this one and others have had incalculable influence on the religion, psyche and art of the Western world. Instead of images for states of life, they became both threats and carrots on a stick. Most religions seem to have some similar metaphors symbolizing the ultimate imperatives; it is an important way of saying that our decisions do have consequences and meaning in eternity. As J.A.T. Robinson said in the '60s, they provide a life on cruise control with a necessary existential shock.

Unfortunately, we made them into *physical* places instead of descriptions of states of mind and heart and calls to decision *in this world*. That was precisely John Paul II's point. We pushed the whole thing off into the future, and took it out of the now. Inasmuch as we did so, we lost the in-depth transformative power of the Christian religion. Threat and fear is not transformation. It became a soul-saving society for the next world, instead of a healing of body, soul and society now—and therefore—forever!

All of Jesus' healings, touchings and "salvations" (Luke 7:50; 17:19; 19:9) were clearly *now*. He never once said, "Be good now, and I will give you a reward later." Show me one prerequisite that Jesus ever has for a single one of his healings. The healing now seems to be an end in itself and has nothing to do with earning it.

For Jesus *all rewards are inherent to the action itself, and all punishments are inherent to the action itself,* but we largely pushed all rewards and punishments into the future. I sometimes wonder if we clergy and preachers do not have an unconscious but vested interest in keeping people codependent on us, by holding that carrot always out in front of them. It is clearly "Now *and* forever" talk in Jesus, but we made it into "Not now, but perhaps forever if you play the game right."

What you choose now, you will have then. God is giving everyone exactly what they want. Mature religion creates an affinity, a connaturality, a kinship between this world and the next. One is not a testing ground for the next, but a "practicing" and choosing for the next. Christianity is quite simply "practicing for heaven." If you want it later, do it now, and God seems to be saying, "I will give you whatever you want."

You do not transform people by threatening them with hellfire, because then the whole thing is grounded in fear and not love, and heaven is not fear. Remember, *how you get there determines where you finally arrive.* You cannot prepare for love by practicing fear. Means determines the end: Fear creates hell; love creates heaven. No one will be in heaven who does not want to be there. No one will be in hell who does not want to be there.

In Catholic spirituality, we called the three classic stages of growth: the purgative, the illuminative and the unitive paths. Yet the irony is that the last stage empowers the first two. We cannot threaten people into love with hellfire or fear. It's like trying to move a train forward from the caboose. The actual engine that pulls the whole train is the third stage—union itself—not moral concerns, which are much more the caboose that follows afterward.

If we could just allow the engine of Experienced Love to stay up front, much of this would take care of itself. You have to experience a certain degree of union to even have the desire to *start* the early purgative path or to *stay* on the illuminative path. Most people allow the purgative path to be an end in itself. This has caused major distortion of the entire Christian life; we end up with this preoccupation with hell, threat and punishment, and it never moves much beyond that. Grace becomes unknown and unnecessary. As Alan Watts so well argues in *Behold the Spirit,* the Bible's primary concern is mystical, not moral.

banquets as audiovisual aid

In the New Testament, and particularly in Jesus, the most common image for what God is offering us is a banquet. It's not a trophy, not a prize, not a reward later, but a participative and joyous party now. A banquet has everything to do with invitation and acceptance; it is never a command performance. One needs only to see the clear pattern in the evolving text itself, then it will be obvious. I will only give you a few further flag markers, culminating in the Eucharist itself.

For example, we have the lovely "Parable of the Wedding Banquet" (Matthew 22:1–14). Here the king is sending out people to get everybody to come to the banquet. The invited make very good excuses not to come. They're about being married, being busy, having a job or occupation. These are not bad things, but just "busyness with many things" that keep them from "the one thing important" (Luke 10:42), which is the banquet of conscious divine union.

It is not the "hot sins" that keep people from the banquet, as much as our daily obsession with small things that do not matter, and not being able to see beyond "the shadow and the disguise." It's not seeing the "deep down of things," as Gerard Manley Hopkins put it. Spirituality basically teaches us that *the inside of things is bigger than the outside.*

At the end of the parable (Matthew 22:9) the king says, "Go out and invite everyone to the wedding feast, the good and the bad alike." That phrase has been shocking to Christians from the very beginning. They didn't know how to compute it, precisely because they assumed that Jesus' message was primarily a moral matter at which "bad" people would clearly not belong. Once you know it is primarily a mystical matter, a realization of union, it reframes the entire journey, and almost by accident you find yourself becoming "moral." But your morality did not earn you a ticket to the banquet.

Luke 14 has three different stories of banquets. People are either avoiding them, trying to create hierarchies at them or simply refusing to come. Just as in Matthew 22, the host has to almost "force" people to come and even offers a bit of nonsensical advice: "When you give a lunch or a dinner, don't ask your friends, brothers, relations or rich neighbors" (Luke 14:12).

He picks the logical people that you'd invite and says, don't invite them "for fear they might repay you in return." (Remember, all rewards for Jesus are inherent, not expecting something later.) But it is also a warning against ego systems of reciprocity, and an invitation to pure gratuity. How have we been able to miss this for so long? I suspect the mercantile mind is so hardwired that we just can't think outside of it. Grace is too revolutionary.

Jesus is always undercutting what we think is common sense. I don't think this passage is a call to love the poor as much as a call to think non-dualistically, to change our entire form of consciousness. "When you have a party, invite the poor, the crippled, the lame, the blind, *that they cannot pay you back will mean you are fortunate*" (14:13). Because now you are inside of a different mind that will allow you to read all of your life from a worldview of abundance instead of a world-view of scarcity. That, by the way, *will* cause you to start loving the poor—almost naturally.

I recently saw a Hubble telescope picture of the Sombrero Galaxy, just one of the galaxies that human eyes have never seen before, and this one galaxy alone, out of what we now know are billions of galaxies, has eight hundred *billion* suns! Read that again, if it did not blow you over. God is clearly into abundance and excess, and his genuine followers share in that largesse, first in receiving it, resting in it, and then allowing it to flow through them toward the world. When we realize God's abundance, we might respond like one of those gathered around the table did: "Happy the person who will be at this banquet in the kingdom of God" (v. 15).

We will continue to see the banquet theme re-imaged at the wedding feast of Cana, at the numerous meals with both sinners and disciples. We finally see it at what we call the Last Supper itself, which became for many of us the wonderful, ongoing eucharistic meal.

Yet even the Eucharist has usually been presented as a reward system for good behavior, a worthiness contest, a sacrificial system. We see it often more as an agreed-upon belief system, than the simple, gratuitous table fellowship that it was for Jesus and his first unworthy ones.

He first of all included those who could not possibly have understood what he was saying (there seems to be no needed belief in exactly "how" this is his body), two betrayers (Judas and Peter), and in fact, what would have been scandalized and confused Jewish men who could never have drank "blood" (Leviticus 17:12). By drinking blood they would become sinners themselves and impure by the law. The Last Supper was a gathering of the unworthy, not to speak of John laying his head on the breast of Jesus, which would have made most men quite uncomfortable.

Maybe they had already begun to understand that Jesus' message was always healing, risky, new and inclusive of the so-called "contaminating element." That's the way he transformed the contaminating element! His final meal was a repeat of the very thing he had been accused of doing—"eating with sinners" (Mark 2:16). The Apostles remembered his common practice and were not afraid, at least in the early church (see 1 Corinthians 11:18–20).

God is still trying, as I said earlier, to give away God. Yet no one seems to want God; what we want is a worthiness system. We like superiority contests. I want something that I can say that I have earned. Totally free gifts say nothing about me. So God chose Mary of Nazareth, a "perfect receiver station," to be the archetype of salvation.

mary, the "perfectly personified process"

Most of the central chosen figures in the Bible up to this point have been men, yet some have said that the soul is always "feminine" in relation to God. Maybe it took a woman to symbolize the interaction most perfectly. The name *Miriam* in Hebrew probably means "most excellent one" or "the excellent one."

We're going to see that Mary is the archetype, the personification of the one who represents and sums up the entire mystery of *received salvation,* one that has many dimensions: (1) the "immaculate conception" before she had done anything right or anything wrong (perhaps implied in Romans 8:30), (2) free election at the Annunciation with no mention of merit (Luke 1:38), (3) her virgin motherhood is shrouded in mystery even for her (Luke 2:19, 52), (4) a quiet, ordinary life (no statements for thirty years), (5) her heroic "standing" in dignity and solidarity with the pain and despair at the end (John 19:25) and (6) her receptivity to the shared life of the Holy Spirit along with everybody else at Pentecost (Acts 1:14).

All of these dimensions point to the full meaning of how God is born into the world! It is never about us, and always about God. We, like she, are merely "handmaids" (Luke 1:38) and instruments, and it took such a woman as this to make the whole pattern clear.

I want to point out the greeting of the angel Gabriel in Luke 1:29, "Hail, favored one." In Greek it's more revealing. The word we translate "highly favored one," scholars will tell you, is a very unusual tense. It means, "you who are as favored as you can possibly be favored," or "you supercharged one," or "you who have got it all." There's almost no way we can translate it fully. "Most favored one" is probably about as well as we can do in English.

Now notice that the word *favor* doesn't mean anything about you. Favor says something about the one who is doing the favoring. So it's really not saying anything about Mary. It's saying something about God's election of Mary. She is one who is the absolutely perfect receiver, and refuses to play the "Lord, I am not worthy" card that had become normative in most biblical theophanies. She just says, "Let it be done unto me" (Luke 1:33). It is passages like that which convince me the Bible is inspired, despite all the two-steps backward texts.

We have in Mary's story what some call the second creation story in the Bible. Again it is a creation "out of nothing." Mary is the one quite willing to be "nothing." God does not need worthiness ahead of time; God creates worthiness by the choice itself.

As we said earlier, "God does not love you because you are good; you are good because God loves you." It seems God will not come into the world unreceived, uninvited. God does not come into the world unless you want God. God offers the Divine Presence, "the banquet," but presence itself is a reciprocal concept.

God is the eternal "I" waiting for those willing to be a "Thou." It's no surprise that it would be two Jewish teachers, Martin Buber and Emmanuel Levinas, who would come to this insight as entire philosophical worldviews. Buber makes the I-Thou encounter the essence of reality, and says "all real living is meeting." Emmanuel Levinas says that we are not converted by ideas but "by the face of the other." They both understood the reciprocity of presence. Why? Because they were both steeped in the biblical tradition—just as Jesus was.

It is no surprise that Mary became the icon of prayer for so many in Orthodox and Catholic Christianity, and in many religious orders, even though the Bible never once mentions her "praying." The closest is that lovely line in Luke: "She treasured all these things and pondered them in her heart" (Luke 2:19, 52).

Why? Because every time you pray, it's God in you telling you to pray. You wouldn't even desire to pray except for God in you. It's God in you that loves God, that desires God, that seeks God (see Romans 8:14–27). Every time you choose God on some level, God has in the previous nanosecond just chosen you, and you have somehow allowed yourself to be chosen—and responded back! (John 15:16).

We don't know how to say yes by ourselves. We just "second the motion"! *There is a part of you that has always said yes to God, it is the Holy Spirit within you.* God first says "yes" inside of us and we say, "Oh yeah," thinking it comes from us! In other words, God rewards us for letting God reward us. Think about that, maybe even for the rest of your life.

Are we ever ready for that? Probably not, but by the end of the Bible we see the New Jerusalem, descending, unearned, undesired and unprepared for (Revelation 21:2). It's totally a gift from God. After an entire Bible of warring, arguing, protecting, earning, competing, buying and selling of God, finally the gift is simply given and handed over to us. The New Jerusalem descends from the heavens freely and without warrant.

Yet I am convinced that the struggle is good and even necessary. Struggle carves out the space within us for deep desire. God both creates the desire and fulfills it. Our job is to be the desiring. God is never going to give you anything that you don't really want. Your *fiat*, like Mary's "Let it be done unto me, according to your word" (Luke 1:38), is still essential.

We all find ourselves with this surprising ability to love God and to desire love from God, often for no reason in particular. That doesn't happen every day, truly, but hopefully more often as you learn to trust and rest in life. Moments of unconditional love sort of slip out of you and no one is more surprised than you when it happens! But when it does, you always know you are living inside of a Larger Life than your own. You know, henceforth, that your life is not about you but you are about God.

"babette's feast"

I want to end this chapter with a nonbiblical text, because sometimes we can understand biblical text more by hearing different words from outside the biblical revelation. I want to read from Isak Dinesen's marvelous short story, "Babette's Feast," which was made into an award-winning foreign film. She also wrote *Out of Africa,* under the Dinesen pen name. Her real name was Karen Blixen. (I visited her lovely home in Africa some years ago.)

Let me give you a little background about "Babette's Feast." It is set in a little village on the west coast of Norway, which is sort of sparse and sour. The people there are good people, but they're living inside an isolated and lonely town.

It's a tiny world of laws and pettiness and religious rigor where the protagonists, two elderly, spinster daughters of a deceased Lutheran minister, live a pretty Spartan lifestyle. They eat the same food every day, the same bowl of soup and the same codfish. They dutifully share their food with the disadvantaged, carrying on a ministry of their father. In fact, joyless duty might be the key theme in their lives.

The movie version depicts a sort of dark and cloudy, not-so-inviting environment. The place is bland, the food is bland, it's all in service of some sense of obligation. Undoubtedly it's the state of their consciousness. They're not bad people at all, but surely they live a not-so-desirable life.

Into this village comes Babette, a French woman, a cook, it turns out, who has lost her family in the revolutionary war in France. She runs away from France to save her own life, and is sent by a friend to these sisters. She offers to be the sisters' cook in return for room and board. For fourteen years she dutifully cooks ale-bread soup and codfish, every day, just as the sisters wish. That's what they like—they never knew there was anything else. Remember "Monday washing day" earlier in the book!

Then, Babette wins the lottery, ten thousand francs! After some negotiation, she talks the sisters into allowing her to prepare a fine French banquet to celebrate their deceased father's one hundredth anniversary. First they ask what kind of food she would serve. She replies that she wants to give them a French dinner, the way they eat in France.

They have a major meeting, among the remnants of their father's Puritanical flock, to see whether they even want a French dinner. There's a lot of talk about whether or not they can allow alcohol, and the sisters, to humor their faithful Babette, go along with it. But they resolve to themselves only to feign enjoyment. "It will be as if we did not taste it," they promise.

Now there is a general who comes to this feast, one who is visiting his aunt, a member of the congregation. He's a man who has seen the larger world. He has been hurt, has gone through success and failure.

He, who has eaten at the finest tables, knows better than anyone present the quality of the feast that he is experiencing. Course after course, Babette lays on the table an enormous, beautiful, sumptuous feast. The guests' eyes just widen, but as they drink a little more and more of the wine, they loosen up, too. They learn, finally, to enjoy this banquet that they never thought they could possibly enjoy. It was a world into which no one had ever invited them. (You can see why the story fits here!)

Before I quote the general's after-dinner speech, I'd like to describe him. Dinesen, the author, says he had obtained everything that he had striven for in life at this point. He was admired and envied by everyone. But "only he himself knew of a queer fact that jarred with his prosperous existence: "that he was not perfectly happy. Something was wrong somewhere. He carefully felt his mental self all over as one feels a finger to determine the place of a deep-seated, invisible thorn."

He was a moral person, a good person, loyal to the king, loyal to his wife and his friends. He was a good example to everyone in his village. But "there were moments when it seemed to him that the world was not a moral concern but a mystical concern."[3] I think Dinesen is trying to describe religion without grace, and of course, Lutherans were supposed to be the very ones who championed grace—but even they could forget, because grace is always too much.

Now after the sixth course all are starting around the table to sort of forgive one another—in the years since the pastor's death they have degraded into petty rivalries. Into the fourth glass of wine, they actually start enjoying it all. Up to now, their Christianity has been a *resented* banquet, where as Christians they were more afraid of the Risen Christ than even the crucified one. A fairly common pattern, I am afraid.

The general stands up and he quotes that lovely verse from Psalm 85:10, "Mercy and truth have met." Remember, mercy and truth are supposed to be opposites. "Righteousness and bliss have kissed." Again, righteousness and bliss are supposed to be opposites. What we have in Psalm 85 is two great opposites overcoming their opposition and kissing one another, embracing one another. It's now one world made safe by an all-encompassing love. Love alone can overcome paradoxes and other contradictions and lead us toward non-dual consciousness, which is always the character of mystical thought, as I keep saying in this book.

"Humanity, my friends, is frail and foolish. We have all of us been told that grace is to be found in the universe but in our human foolishness and shortsightedness we imagine that divine grace is finite and for this reason we tremble. The moment comes when our eyes are opened, and we see and realize that grace is infinite.

"Grace...demands nothing from us but that we shall await it with confidence and acknowledge it in gratitude. Grace... makes no conditions and singles out none of us in particular; grace takes us all...to its bosom and proclaims general amnesty.

"That which we have chosen is given to us, and that which we have refused is...granted us. Ay, that which we have rejected is poured upon us abundantly."

And although the brothers and sisters had not altogether understood the General's speech...they only knew that the rooms had been filled with a heavenly light...taciturn old people received the gift of tongues, ears that for years had been almost deaf are open to it. Time itself had merged into eternity and long after midnight the windows of the house shone like gold.... It never occurred to any of them that they might have been exalted by their own merit. They realized that the infinite grace of which the general spoke had been allotted to them.... The vain illusions of this earth had dissolved before their eyes like smoke and they had seen the universe as it really is.[4]

If the Bible doesn't lead you to that experience, I don't believe you are allowing it to do its greatest work.

chapter nine
the mystery of the cross

> "It is a wisdom that none of the masters of this age
> have ever known, or they would not have crucified
> the Lord of Glory."

> —1 Corinthians 2:8

The doctrine of the cross is the great interpretative key that makes many things clear, at least for Christians, but perhaps also for history. It's no accident that we have made the cross the Christian logo, because in the revelation of the cross, many great truths become obvious and even overwhelming, yet not so obvious beforehand. I guess that is what we mean by the "revelation of a mystery" that Paul speaks of in the quote above.

Crux probat omnia was a statement used by some early systematic theologians. Translated, it says, "the cross proves everything." This might seem like an overstatement or like more Christian triumphalism. But once you see the crucifixion event as an iconic symbol clarifying the very nature of God, the core human dilemma, and the essential religious agenda, one can see how true the statement is. Let's try to see why we would claim so much wisdom from one event. Trust me on this one, and stay with me, if you will.

There was a book, out of print now, written by Sebastian Moore. It was entitled *The Crucified Jesus Is No Stranger.* I was haunted by that title because I realized, certainly for me and for many people I have worked with, the crucified Jesus was no stranger to their souls at all. It had little to do with the traditional atonement theories and everything to do with their inner lives, and their attempts to make sense out of the tragic history of the world. The mystery of Jesus crucified *names* and *releases* the lives and even the deaths of many who live on our planet.

Those who "gaze upon" (John 19:37) the crucified long enough—with contemplative eyes—are always healed at deep levels of pain, unforgiveness, aggressivity and victimhood. It demands no theological education at all, just an "inner exchange" by receiving the image within and offering one's soul back in safe return. No surprise that C.G. Jung is supposed to have said that a naked man nailed to a cross is perhaps the deepest archetypal symbol in the Western psyche.

The crucified Jesus certainly is no stranger to human history either. It offers, at a largely unconscious level, a *very compassionate meaning system for history.* The mystery of the rejection, suffering, passion, death and raising up of Jesus is *the interpretative key* for what history means and where it is all going. Without such cosmic meaning and soul significance, the agonies and tragedies of humanity feel like Shakespeare's "sound and fury signifying nothing." The body can live without food easier than the soul can live without such meaning.

If all these human crucifixions are leading to some possible resurrection, and are not dead-end tragedies, this changes everything. If God is somehow participating in human suffering, instead of just passively tolerating it and observing it, that also changes everything—at least for those who are willing to "gaze" contemplatively.

We Christians are given the privilege to *name* the mystery rightly and to know it directly and consciously, but in many ways we have not lived it much better than many other religions and cultures. *All humble, suffering souls learn this from God*, but the Christian Scriptures named it and revealed it to us publicly and dramatically in Jesus. It all depends on whether you have "gazed" long enough and deep enough. Call it prayer.

Our patterns of violence and alienation pretty much match and often surpass those of non-Christian peoples. In fact, Rene Girard says that because our justifications for war and hatred were taken away from us by the Gospel, *we are actually more culturally unstable than others.* We are caught in the double bind of approach and avoidance. We kill just as much as others, but do feel a bit guilty about it. I guess that is a good start, anyway. But such guilt has not kept Christian nations from our own rather consistent patterns of scapegoating and violence.

But before we leap to Jesus, let's look at some earlier biblical figures to see how the stage is both prepared and set for the Jesus "saga" that we now take as normative. Jacob's son, Joseph, is thrown into the well by his own brothers, and then rescued (Genesis 37:20–28). The prophet Jeremiah is thrown into a cistern by the civil leaders after he preaches retreat and defeat, and rescued by a eunuch (Jeremiah 38:6–13). Jonah of course is swallowed by the whale and then spit up on the right shore (Jonah 2:1–11). The whole people are sent into exile in Babylon and then released and allowed to return by Cyrus, the King of Persia (2 Chronicles 36:22–23). Enslavement and exodus is the great Jewish lens through which history is read.

Add to that the story of Job as one unjustly but trustfully suffering and restored (Job 42:9–17), and the four "Servant Songs" of Isaiah 42—53, of one who suffers in a way that is vicarious, redemptive and life-giving for others. The Jewish psyche and expectation is gradually formed by these stories and images. Clearly they were known by Jesus, and he evidently sees himself as representing this pattern in his talks to his disciples.

Three times, for example, in Mark's Gospel he makes it clear that this is his destiny, although it is always either misunderstood or outrightly rejected by the apostles themselves (Mark 8:31 ff., 9:30 ff., 10:32 ff.), just as you and I reject and fear any language of descent.

The pattern of down and up, loss and renewal, enslavement and liberation, exile and return, transformation through darkness and suffering has become quite clear in the Hebrew Scriptures, and you do not need to wait for the New Testament. Jesus will use his Jonah symbol and say, "it is the only sign he is going to give" (Luke 11:29). It almost seems like Jonah in the belly of the whale was Jesus' own metaphor for what would later become the doctrine of the cross.

The theological term for this classic pattern of descent and ascent was coined by Saint Augustine as "the paschal mystery." We now proclaim it publicly at every Eucharist as "*the* mystery of faith"!

So how does this happen? How does the victim transform us? How does the Lamb of God "take away" our sin (John 1:29), to use the common metaphor? How does Jesus "overcome death and darkness," as we often say? Is it just a heavenly transaction on God's side, or is it more an *agenda that God gives us for our side?*

Did Jesus not reveal for all humanity the very pattern of redemption itself? Could that not be what we mean by calling him "The Savior of the World"? (John 4:42). Jesus is, in effect, saying, "*This is how evil is transformed into good! I am going to take the worst thing and turn it into the best thing, so you will never be victimized, destroyed or helpless again! I am giving YOU the victory over all death!*"

Jesus takes away the sin of the world by dramatically exposing what is the real sin of the world (ignorant attacking and killing, not purity codes), by refusing the usual pattern of attacking and killing back, and, in fact, "returning their curses with blessings" (Luke 6:27), then finally by teaching us that we can "follow him" in doing the same.

At that point, the human tragedy is over, at least in "yeast" form, which is exactly what he offers. He has set the inevitable in motion. Both the lie and the strategy have been revealed in one compelling action on God's part. It is not that Jesus is working some magic in the sky that "saves the world from sin and death." Jesus is working some magic in history that redefines its direction forever. Jesus is not changing his Father's mind about us; he is changing our mind about what is real and what is not.

When I was a little boy, my family had one of those common statuettes of the three monkeys, and Mother told me it meant, "See no evil, hear no evil and speak no evil" with each monkey covering the appropriate body part. It felt right to me, and I tried to do just that.

But this is not God's plan for overcoming evil, not at all. He did not come to merely offer us willpower and an upstanding moral education. That is more Confucianism than Christianity. There is nothing wrong with intellect and will, but I want you to compare the three monkeys image with the image of Jesus crucified, and feel the huge difference. The monkeys are good conventional wisdom; the cross is absolutely subversive wisdom that came from God.

Jesus on the cross identifies with the human problem, the sin, the darkness. He refuses to stand above or outside the human dilemma. Further, he refuses to be the scapegoater, and instead becomes the scapegoat personified. In Paul's language, "Christ redeemed us from the curse...by being cursed himself" (Galatians 3:13); or "God made the sinless one into sin, so that in him [together with him!] we might become the very goodness of God" (2 Corinthians 5:21). Wow! Just gaze upon that mystery for a few years!

Like most spiritual things, it cannot be understood with any dualistic or rational mind, but only at the level of soul. It is a transformational image and message that utterly rearranges one's reality and idea of the very nature of God. *Evil is not overcome by attack or even avoidance, but by union at a higher level. It is overcome not by fight or flight, but rather by "fusion"!*

In Jesus we have a confluence of three sacred healing images: the Passover lamb, which is the presentation of the innocent victim (Exodus 12); the "Lifted-up One," which is the homeopathic curing of the victim (Numbers 21:6–9); and, finally, the scapegoat ritual, wherein we have the presentation of the rejected victim (Leviticus 16) whom we beat into the desert, with our sins, to die.

The victim state has been the plight of most people who have ever lived on this earth, so in all three cases we see Jesus identifying with humanity at its most critical and vulnerable level. It is God in solidarity with the pain of the world, it seems, much more than the Omnipotent One who, with a flick of the hand, overcomes all pain. Let's look at all of them to unpack these rich images of compassion and transformation.

During the Holy Thursday celebration each year we read from Exodus 12:1–14. It tells each family that every year, on the tenth day of Nisan, they should pick out a perfect little lamb without any spot or blemish and take it to their home and then, on the fourteenth day, kill it!

Now if any of you have children, you would know what's happened in four days time with a cute little lamb in the house. Your children have fallen in love with it, and probably have even named it. This little lamb becomes part of the family. So, in the Passover commemoration we have an image of the death of something good, innocent and even loved.

What could that symbolize? I personally think it is an image of the ego, or the false self, which always feels good, adequate and even innocent. It is not something that looks evil that has to die but, in fact, something that feels like "me"! It is exactly who I think I am; it is what I deem necessary for my identity; it is what I cannot live without. *It is these seemingly essential and good things—when let go of—that break us through into much deeper levels of life!*

Jesus on the cross is not an image of the death of the bad self but, in fact, the self that feels essential, right and necessary—but isn't necessary at all! It's the image of Jesus who was only thirty-three years old and had not even gotten started on his mission, the misunderstood and misinterpreted Jesus, the oppressed Jesus. There were all kinds of good justice arguments he could have made. He had every good reason to play the victim card or the blaming card, but he was not attached to this petty, false self. You will know this to be true at your greatest moments of conversion. It is invariably our deep attachment to this false and passing self that leads us into our greatest illusions and even sins. It is precisely this "lamb" that has to be killed, our self-image as innocent, right and sufficient.

To understand Jesus in a whole new way, you must first know that *Christ* is not his last name, but his transformed identity after the Resurrection—which takes humanity and all of creation along in its sweet path. Jesus *became* the Christ, and included us in this identity.

That's why Paul will create the new term "the body of Christ," which clearly includes all of us. So think of the good Jesus, who has to die to what seems like him—so that he can rise as the Christ. *It is not a "bad" man who must die on the cross, but a good man ("false self")—so that he can be a much larger man ("True Self").* Jesus dies, Christ rises. The false self is not the bad self; it is just *not* the true self. It is inadequate, and thus needy and small, symbolized by Jesus' human body, which he let go of.

The second image of the "Lifted-Up One" is the image from Moses and the bronze serpent in the desert that became the symbol for doctors and healers. In the book of Numbers, Yahweh tells Moses to raise up a serpent on a standard, and "anyone who has been bitten by a serpent and looks upon it will be healed" (21:8). The very thing that was killing them is the thing that will heal them!

I would ask you to consider the crucifix as a *homeopathic* image, like those medicines that give you just enough of the disease so you could develop a resistance and be healed from it. *The cross dramatically reveals the problem of ignorant killing, to inoculate us against doing the same thing.*

Salvation history seems to lead people into the very darkness that they seek to overcome. There they learn its real character, and how to unlock it from inside. John sees it as what Jesus is doing on the cross (John 3:13; 8:28; 12:31; 19:37).

Jesus becomes the seeming problem and the homeopathic cure for the same—by dramatically exposing it for what it is, "parading it in public" (Colossians 2:15) for those who have eyes to see, and inviting us to gaze upon it with sympathetic understanding. This, I believe, is "the wisdom that none of the masters of the age have ever known—or they would never have crucified the Lord of Glory" (1 Corinthians 1:8). Amazing that we still are so ready to trust the masters of this age instead of him crucified.

This deep gazing upon the mystery of divine and human suffering is found in the prophet Zechariah in a very telling text that became a prophecy for the transformative power of the victims of history. He calls Israel to "Look upon the pierced one and to mourn over him as for an only son," and "weep for him as for a firstborn child," and then "from that mourning" (five times repeated) will flow "a spirit of kindness and prayer" (12:10) and "a fountain of water" (13:1; 14:8).

Today this is perhaps what we would call "grief work," holding the mystery of pain and looking right at it and learning deeply from it, which normally leads to an uncanny and newfound compassion and understanding. The hospice movement and the exponential growth in bereavement ministries throughout many of the churches are showing this to be true, but look how long it has taken us to rediscover such wisdom.

I believe we are invited to gaze upon the image of the crucified *to soften our hearts toward God, and to know that God's heart has always been softened toward us, even and most especially in our suffering.* This softens us toward ourselves and all others who suffer.

John's Gospel seems to see it this way, since he quotes this verse from Zechariah at the crucifixion scene (John 19:37) and seems to refer to it in the "breast from which flows fountains of living water" (7:38). They pierce the crucified Jesus' side and from it flows forth blood and water (19:34). Remember, those are two bookmark images, the blood being the price of letting go and the water being the invitation to union and divine feeding. Such images as these have been central to many, if not most, of our Catholic mystics. They cannot be unimportant for the soul.

I very much agree with Carl Jung, who said that transformation at the deeper levels happens in the presence of images much more than through concepts. This is a difficulty for both Protestantism and Islam, in my opinion. Good art seems absolutely essential to healthy religion. Jews use the "art" of storytelling and midrash.

jesus as scapegoat

The third image deserves a bit more treatment, because it is central to understanding the very engines of history, and how Jesus resets that engine.

What has happened in human history is this. We have always needed to find a way to deal with human anxiety and evil by some means—and it was invariably some "technology" other than forgiveness.

We usually dealt with human anxiety and evil by sacrificial systems, and that has largely continued to this day. Something has to be sacrificed. Blood has to be shed. Somebody has to be killed. Someone has to be blamed, accused, attacked, tortured or imprisoned—or there has to be capital punishment—because we just don't know how to deal with evil without sacrificial systems. It always creates religions of exclusion and violence, because we think it is our job to destroy the evil element. Remember, both communism and fascism thought the same, from inside their logic.

Historically, we at least moved from human sacrifice to animal sacrifice, to various modes of seeming self-sacrifice. Unfortunately it was not usually the ego self that we sacrificed, but most often the body self as its vicarious substitute. In forgiveness, it is precisely my ego self that has to die, my need to be right, to be in control, to be superior. Very few want to go there, but that is exactly what Jesus emphasized and taught. I am told that forgiveness is at least implied in two-thirds of his teaching!

As long as you can deal with evil by some other means than forgiveness, you will never experience the real meaning of evil and sin. You will keep projecting it over there, fearing it over there and attacking it over there, instead of "gazing" on it within and "weeping" over it within all of us.

The longer you gaze, the more you will see your own complicity *in* and profitability *from* the sin of others, even if it is the satisfaction of feeling you are on higher moral ground. Forgiveness is probably the only human action that demands three new "seeings" at the same time: I must see God in the other, I must access God in myself, and I must see God in a new way that is larger than "an Enforcer." That is a whole new world on three levels at once.

We are the only religion in the world that worships the scapegoat as God. In worshiping the scapegoat, we should gradually learn to stop scapegoating, because we also could be utterly wrong, just as "church" and state, high priest and king, Jerusalem and Rome, the highest levels of discernment were utterly wrong in the death of Jesus. He was the very one that many of us call the most perfect man who ever lived! If power itself can be that wrong, then be careful whom you decide to hate, kill and execute. Power and authority itself is not a good guide, if we are to judge by history. For many, if not most people, authority takes away all of their anxiety, and often their own responsibility to form a mature conscience.

Much of history has been determined by powerful people telling us whom to fear and hate. Millions of soldiers have given their only lives by believing the lies of Genghis Khan, Napoleon, Stalin, Pol Pot and Hitler, to name a few. If only they had not believed "the masters of the age" and had gazed upon the victim whom first-century Palestine was also taught to fear and hate. He offered us what some call "the intelligence of the victim," a unique intelligence from the bottom and the side and the edge of history. That's God's hiding place, the Scriptures seem to be saying.

Jesus took away the sin of the world, by exposing it first of all as different than we imagined, and letting us know that our pattern of ignorant killing, attacking and blaming is in fact history's primary illusion, its primary lie. Then he shared with us a Great Participative Love, which would make it possible for us not to hate at all. The game was over after Jesus, at least for those who gazed long enough.

We all had to face the embarassing truth that *we ourselves* are our primary problem. Our greatest temptation is to try to change other people instead of ourselves. Jesus allowed *himself* to be transformed and *thus* transformed others!

Here are what the Three Transformative Images can achieve in the soul, and which come together in the image of a crucified man/God:

1.   The Scapegoat—Shocking revelation of the essential human lie that underlies most fear, hatred and violence. As long as we project our evil elsewhere, we cannot heal it here—*or* there.

2.   The Passover Lamb—Surprising revelation that it is not the so-called bad things that we have to let go of, nearly as much as the things that appear good and make us feel strong, secure and superior. This is the "lamb" that must be sacrificed, an apparent good.

3.   "The Pierced One" that must be gazed upon—

     a.   The accessing and forgiving of our own humanity as wounded and yet resurrected at the same time.

     b.   The reshaping of God from an omnipotent dictator to a participating Lover.

     c.   The effective understanding of both the Scapegoat mechanism and the Passover Lamb.

     d.   The release of immense reserves of compassion, solidarity and forgiveness of ourselves, others, history and even God.

atonement: did jesus need to "die for our sins"?

Most Christians—Catholic, Orthodox or Protestant—do not realize that what is commonly accepted as the mainline opinion—on Jesus' death as an atonement or heroic "sacrifice" of some type—was not the only Christian opinion in earlier centuries. Most assumed that a debt or sacrifice had to be paid to someone for some reason. Some said to the devil, Saint Anselm said to God the Father, while others like Peter Abelard were not sure why either was necessary.

This "Atonement Theory" was a subject open to debate as the universities appeared on the scene. The Franciscan spokesman and scholar was a Scotsman whom we now know as Blessed John Duns Scotus (1266–1308). He held the early theology chairs at Oxford and Cologne, after studying at the University of Paris.

He is known as the "subtle doctor" of the church. Such subtlety is surely exemplified in his teaching on Saint Anselm's (1033–1109) famous writing, *Cur Deus Homo*? ("Why Did God Become a Human Being?"). Duns Scotus did not question God's redemptive work in Jesus, but only the precise "how?" and "what?" of it. *How* did God transfer transformative love to humanity? Not *if*, but *what* is the precise nature of Jesus' redemption? And why the strange metaphors of "debt" and "payment of price"?

Our Franciscan interpretation was never condemned or denied by the orthodox Catholic tradition and was considered a legitimate "minority position." When the Reformation occurred, the Protestant reformers largely accepted and even furthered the "majority position" (necessary blood sacrifice, or atonement), rather uncritically. This opinion was, of course, developed by early church fathers, and later by Saint Anselm, Saint Thomas Aquinas and the mainline Catholic tradition.

This very issue is an example of two telling patterns: Catholicism was once more broad-minded. It allowed for alternative interpretations of doctrine more often before the Reformation than it does today. Second, the Protestant Reformation often either *reacted to*—or *continued with*—popular Catholicism much more than it realized.

In short and simple form, John Duns Scotus was not swayed or limited by the numerous metaphors of ransom, debt, redemption as "buying," blood sacrifice, payment of price (the Hebrew *goel*), "purchased in blood" vocabulary that we frequently find in the Bible, in both the New and the Old Testaments.

Recognizing he was primarily a philosopher, I would assume that Scotus saw them for the metaphors that they were: images that would have spoken powerfully to a people formed by temple sacrifice, animal offerings, a quid-pro-quo kind of mind. The biblical text, after all, did use frequent sacrificial imagery, and even images of divine vengeance, from Genesis to Revelation.

Duns Scotus saw these metaphors as limited because they made God's redemptive action a "reaction" based on human sin *instead of God's perfect and utterly free initiative of love.* This he could not tolerate. God is in charge of history, Scotus knew; not us and surely not our sinfulness.

These sacrificial and atonement metaphors would have appealed, or even seemed necessary, to a judicial mind uncomfortable with the concept of forgiveness. They would have made sense to any dualistic mind that prefers tit-for-tat explanations. Jesus came to change all of that, of course. That's where we get our central concept of grace, discussed in chapter eight. Duns Scotus's systematic philosophy and theology was utterly committed *to protecting the perfect freedom of God, and also the necessary inner-freedom of each creature.*

The freedom of the will (to love!) was a higher attribute than knowledge for the "Subtle Doctor" and his followers. This differentiated the Franciscan from the Dominican school, which Aquinas, the Dominican, represented. The Franciscan and Dominican schools were almost the official "debating society" of that time.

I would like to think Duns Scotus got his concept of free will from the concepts of biblical election and chosenness, those concepts discussed above. Choice is absolutely free and arbitrary on God's part, and not in any way rational or determined.

John Duns Scotus, however, was more in harmony with Colossians and Ephesians. Those would have appealed to his philosophical and aesthetic sense of the whole and of history, more than would any of the literal symbols of sacrificial payment found elsewhere in the Bible. These letters saw Jesus as the "first image in the mind of God" (Ephesians 1:3–6, 10–11), which is even further described in the hymn in Colossians 1:15–20.

Jesus, Scotus said, was not "necessary" to solve any problem whatsoever—he was no mopping-up exercise after the fact—but a pure and gracious declaration of the primordial truth from the very beginning which was called the doctrine of "the primacy of Christ."

The Incarnation of God, in Jesus, gives us the living "icon of the invisible God" (Colossians 1:15), who is the template for all else (1:16), who reconciles all things in himself (1:17), who is the headmaster in a cosmic body that follows after him (1:18). If I may use a contemporary image: Jesus is the "hologram" for all that is happening in a holographic, constant and repetitive universe (1:19). He is the pattern for all. He does what we also must do, which is why he says, "follow me."

The human Jesus, in other words, is God's preemptive statement to humanity about history and the soul. This "Word of God"—all distilled and focused in one visible life—which is "secretly" Divine but overtly human. Sort of like us!

Let me summarize: *Whatever happens to Jesus is what must and will happen to the soul:* incarnation, an embodied life of ordinariness and hiddenness, initiation, trial, faith, death, surrender, resurrection and return to God. Such is the Christ pattern that we all share in, either joyfully and trustfully (heaven), or unwillingly and resentfully (hell).

Christ's *primacy* and *pattern* is ironically undone and even made unnecessary when all that really matters is the last week of his life. One could get that impression from such movies as Mel Gibson's *The Passion of the Christ.*

Instead, "Through *his goodness revealed* to us in Christ Jesus, he *showed us* how infinitely rich God is in grace, saving us by pure gift...so that we are God's work of art, created in Christ Jesus to live the good life as from the beginning he had meant us to live it" (Ephesians 2:7–10). *Jesus is not the afterthought here, but the forethought, the first thought, the distilled icon of all that God is doing in creation.* It says that what God is doing, in the words of Genesis, "is good, very good!"

Jesus Christ is both the medium and the message, therefore (read, "way, truth and life")—all combined in one compelling and convincing human body (Jesus) and cosmic body (Christ)! Jesus is not a necessity. Rather, Jesus is pure gift, grace and glory! And why would a gift be less good than a necessity? "From his fullness *(pleroma)* we have all received, grace in return for grace.... No one has ever seen God; it is the only Son, who is nearest to the Father's heart, who has made him known" (John 16:18).

Jesus, of course, communicates this Godself most graphically and dramatically on the cross itself. There *we see and learn to trust* the free offer of God's love in a brutal yet utterly compelling image. It's one that assaults the defended psyche, mind and heart. Self-giving "love calls forth love in return," my Father Francis would say.

The trouble is that we emphasized paying a cosmic debt more than communicating a credible love, which is the utterly central issue. The cross became more an image of a Divine *transaction* than an image of human transformation.

We ended up with a God who appears—*at least unconsciously*—to be vindictive, violent and petty, not at all free, subject to supposed laws of offended justice—and a Son who is mainly sent to solve a problem instead of revealing the heart of God. As J. Denny Weaver points out in *The Nonviolent Atonement,* sin becomes the very motive for redemption instead of love, and the very central act of the redemption of the world appears to be based on an act of violence!

The Son of God is presented as *reacting*, whereas a free and loving God would always *act* from God's own primordial and eternal truth. *Divine love is not determined by the worthiness of the object but by the goodness of the subject.* Such problem-based, sin-based Christianity makes for a very uninviting and even unsafe universe to the Franciscan mind.

No wonder mainline Christianity has produced so few mystics and so many detractors. True Christianity beguiles, seduces, invites, cajoles, creates spiritual yearning and draws humanity into ever more desirable mystery, healing and grace.

When Christianity is not rightly mystical (read "experiential"), it always settles for mere moralisms, belief systems and explanations, which invariably reflect a dualistic mind. God instead wants us to become "an altogether new creation" (Galatians 6:16), "with the mind of Christ" (1 Corinthians 2:16), "friends, not servants" (John 15:15).

whose mind needs changing?

In Franciscan parlance, once again, *Jesus did not come to change the mind of God about humanity; Jesus came to change the mind of humanity about God.* This grounds Christianity in love and freedom from the very beginning; it creates a very coherent and utterly attractive religion, which draws people toward lives of inner depth, prayer, reconciliation, healing and even universal "at-one-ment," instead of mere sacrificial atonement. Nothing "changed" on Calvary, but *everything* was revealed so *we* could change!

Soon we have an energetic basis for a joy-filled and mystical Christianity, as Franciscanism always preferred. God is not someone we need to fear or mistrust, a nonviolent atonement theory says. ("What will God ask of me if he demands violent blood sacrifice from his only Son?") Our only desire is "to fall into the hands of [such a] living and loving God" (Hebrews 10:31). But like any trust fall, first we have to trust the one we are going to fall toward.

Jesus, for us, is the mediator of a Christianity that is much more about divine union than a demanded payoff or a solution to a cosmic problem. Such "ungracious" religion has only led to a kind of false idealization of egotistic self-sacrifice, a quid-pro-quo universe that Jesus himself never taught and even rejected: "Go, learn the meaning of the words, what I want is mercy not sacrifice. I did not come for the virtuous, but for the sick" (Matthew 9:13). After all, suicide bombers are living a much more sacrificial life than most of us, but there is no love! (see 1 Corinthians 13:3).

Jesus was precisely the "once and for all" sacrifice given to reveal the lie and the absurdity of the very notion and necessity of "sacrificial" religion itself. That's much of the point of Hebrews 10 if you are willing to read it with new eyes. But we perpetuated such regressive and sacrificial patterns by making God the Father into the Chief Sacrificer, and basing the very notion of divine redemption on a kind of "necessary violence."

Can God do no better than that? Or were we attracted to such a violent redemption theory to legitimate our own conscious or unconscious desire to be violent? Is dominative power not *our humanly* preferred way of dealing with our problems? (We *must* ask that question!) A violent theory of redemption legitimated punitive and violent problem solving all the way down—from papacy to parenting! There eventually emerged a huge disconnect between the founding story and the message of Jesus itself!

If even God uses and needs violence, maybe Jesus did not really mean what he said in the Sermon the Mount, and we don't have to follow it. Remember, *how* you get there determines where you finally arrive!

Our bellicose Christian history has made this core problem rather clear. If God solves problems by domination, coercion and violent demand, then we can too. Grace, mercy and eternal generosity are no longer the very shape of God, as the Trinitarian nature of God seemed to say. Free will, grace and love became less admirable than some theoretical cosmic justice, law and blind obedience. We end up making God very small and draw the Godhead into our own ego-driven need for retribution, judicial resolution and punishment. Yet that's exactly what Jesus came to undo!

If God can forgive, then God can forgive! We do not need one major exception where we need atonement and payment of price. But theoretical religion has always been more comfortable with cosmic problem solving than with personal surrender to the healing and transformative mystery of divine love. Healing and forgiveness have not been in the forefront of Christian history, even though these are almost the only things Jesus does.

Sacrificial thinking is in the human hardwiring and has been so glorified in myth, ego and war, that most people are unable to live without some form of blood expiation and vengeance toward problems. Now if the Godself even needs appeasement, atonement and necessary victims—we are in an utterly closed system of supposed *redemptive violence.* That's exactly the "useless" offerings that most of the prophets, and many of the Psalms (40, 51, 69) railed against.

It has always surprised me that many Catholics, and those who know through story, inner image, prayer and art, are not so invested in any sacrificial atonement theory as those who begin and end with books and texts. In fact, Catholics will say, "What is the atonement theory?" Most do not even get upset if you deny it!

I have a strong opinion why this is true. Although the Dominicans might have formally won the debate back in the thirteenth century, and the Protestants largely followed them, God actually won—through the many who learned how to pray, look and listen. They just gazed upon the crucifix long enough—and they *knew.* They knew it was all OK. They knew "Jesus died for our sins," but not through any needed heavenly transaction or convincing Bible quotes. *They knew it by gazing upon the one that we have pierced,* praying from a place of needed mercy and allowing Love which changed them from the bottom up.

They needed no top-down theory. God gazed at them through the suffering and sad eyes of Jesus, and they looked back—and up. Redemption again happened. To stand-under is still the best way to *under-stand.* You do not need to believe a theory to know God's love.

cross as agenda

It all hinges on the cross of Jesus Christ. The cross is about how to fight and not become a casualty yourself. The cross is about being the victory instead of just winning a victory. It is a way of winning that tries to bring along your opponents with you.

The cross is about refusing the simplistic win-lose scenario and holding out for a possible win-win scenario. The cross is refusing to hate or needing to defeat the other because that would be to only continue the same pattern and reciprocate the violence and to stay inside of the inexorable wheel that the world has always called normal.

The cross is very clearly saying that evil is to be opposed but I am willing to hold the tension, the ambiguity, the pain of it, instead of insisting that others do the same. "Resist evil and overcome it with good," as Paul says (Romans 12:21). The cross moves us from the rather universal myth of redemptive violence to a new scenario of redemptive suffering.

On the cross of life we accept our own complicity and cooperation with evil, instead of imagining that we are standing on some pedestal of moral superiority. Jesus identified with what Paul taught: "everyone has sinned" (Romans 5:12) and the Lamb of God had the humility to "become sin" (2 Corinthians 5:21) with us, whereas we pretend to be above it all.

What the mystery of the cross teaches us is how to *stand against* hate without *becoming* hate, how to oppose evil without becoming evil ourselves. Can you feel yourself stretching in both directions—toward God's goodness and also toward recognition of your complicity in evil? If you look at yourself at that moment, you will feel crucified. You *hang in between*, without resolution, your very life a paradox, held in *hope* by God (see Romans 8:23–25).

The goal of nonviolence is always winning the true understanding of the supposed opponent, not his or her humiliation or defeat. It is to facilitate reconciliation, but also to realize, probably sadly, that I, like Jesus, must pay the price for this reconciliation, that "the two might become one," as Ephesians so poetically states (2:13–18). All religion is, in its best moments, making one out of two!

What the mystery of the cross reveals is that *the opponent is not so much evil as a symbol of a greater evil of which he or she also is a victim!* Please think about that. The mystery of the cross takes a great capacity for empathy and forgiveness, and probably is a sign of "fusion" with God. On the cross we agree to carry that victim status together with Jesus. We agree to bear the burden of human evil, of which we *all* are victims and all are complicit. It is the ultimate act of solidarity with humanity.

We can't do it alone at all, but only by a deep identification with the Crucified One and crucified humanity. Jesus then does it in us, through us, with us and for us. Then we have become his "new creation" (Galatians 5:14–16) and definitely a very different kind of human being.

This is Christianity's unique revelation. We share many things with many religions, but no other world religion has the revelation of the cross. It's called a revelation because it's not something the rational and calculating mind will ever come to it by itself. It's given almost from outside of history because our logical mind doesn't come to it by any rational or dualistic process. The best it can do is to go halfway.

The mystery of the cross is saying that human existence is neither perfectly consistent (though that's what educated, ideological and control-needy people want), nor is it total chaos (our philosophical words for that are *post-modernism, nihilism* or even *atheism*). *Human existence, though, is filled with contradictions.* To hold the contradictions with God, with Jesus, is to be a Christian and to share and participate in the redemption of the world (Colossians 1:24). It feels like a "forgiving" of reality for being what it is.

If the choices are either perfect consistency or utter chaos, don't go there. The cross is holding the middle. The world is neither perfectly consistent nor total chaos; it's a coincidence of opposites, and even geometrically that forms the cross. The price you pay for holding together the contradictions within yourself, others and the world is always some form of crucifixion, *but the gift you receive and the gift you offer is that— at least in you—"everything belongs."*

chapter ten
mutual indwelling

"You must therefore be perfect just as your heavenly
Father is perfect."

"Live generously and graciously toward others, the
way God has lived toward you."

—two translations of Matthew 5:48

The oft-retranslated passage above is an almost perfect indicator today of the two minds that have tried to understand the Bible. The first reads it in terms of Platonic idealism and ego-based moralism. It uses a mathematical or divine concept ("perfection") and mandates it for the human person. This leads readers to impossible head-based abstractions that only results in denial, splitting and pretending. It appeals to the binary ("yes/no") system of the ordinary mind, wherein we all lose, since none of us is perfect and never will be.

The second translation still sets the ideal very high, but now the goal has become divine union instead of personal perfection. This translation emerges from the non-dualistic mind that has already experienced divine union at some level. As Ken Wilber so brilliantly teaches, "It is not what a person says, but the level from which they say it that determines the truth of a spiritual statement." A spiritually mature person could use the word *perfection* and know they are talking about God's perfection abiding in us. An immature person will think of it as a moral achievement that they can attain by trying harder.

The higher level is well-illustrated in that transitional statement from Paul, "I no longer seek any perfection from my own efforts...but only the perfection that comes from faith and is from God.... We who are called perfect must all think in this way" (Philippians 3:9, 15). Paul rightly redefines perfection as union rather than achievement.

Our goal is not personal or private wholeness, which is clearly impossible, anyway, and yet has been offered as an achievable goal for Western individualists for some centuries now. This is at the heart of our problem, and in my opinion, has fostered massive withdrawal from Christianity.

Where the text finally points, leads and calls is to the total mystery of divine union—and nothing less. Only those who have begun to experience election, grace, forgiveness, love, union, relationship, will use the Bible fittingly. Without these, the Bible is and has been much more a problem for humanity, than any kind of gift. It remains the mere wineskin, but not yet the wine. It becomes ego enhancement and ego ammunition instead of a description of the backward-and-forward movement that was the original Hebrew journey through the desert, what Saint Bonaventure called "the soul's journey into God."

But if divine union is the sure goal, let's try to chart how the end was already found at the beginning, and try to map the path in-between.

There's a story I have often told that I'd like to use here. It's apparently a true story of a newborn baby's homecoming. The family's other child, a precocious four-year-old, said, "I want to talk to my new little brother." We think of ages three to four as the magical years, where you haven't moved into left-brain consciousness. For the young child, it's still an enchanted universe; it's still possible to comprehend mystery (probably why Jesus praised their ability to "receive"). Anyway, the little one then says, "I want to talk to him alone."

Now that surprised the parents, but they let the four-year-old go in the nursery alone with the new baby and put their own ears to the door. They wanted to protect the infant from any harm that any sibling rivalry might inflict, but they also wanted to hear what he was going to say. Now this is the gist of what the four-year-old reportedly said: "Quick, tell me who made you. Tell me where you came from. I'm beginning to forget!"

True or not, this story illustrates what I would like to say here. The newborn babe represents the "little ones" that Jesus praises so much. The four-year-old represents all of us, caught in between knowing and forgetting and wanting to know again! My assumption in this entire book is the same as that of John in his First Letter: "It is not because you do not know the truth that I am writing to you but because you know it already" (2:21). "There is an Inner Knower called the Holy Spirit" (John 14:17).

I am assuming and totally relying upon the Divine Indwelling to "teach you and remind you of all things" (John 14:26). All you need is to offer the Spirit a little desire, although you will learn after the fact that even the desire came from God. But what a burden that is off of my own back. I do not need to prove anything or convince you of anything. *My only job is to proclaim and offer the symbols and promises of divine union.* Those of you who know will know even more, "thirty, sixty and a hundredfold" (Mark 4:20).

Those of you who do not know, those of you who have lost contact with spiritual desire, will go away contentious, disappointed or empty, but maybe intrigued! Jesus is making this very point in his marvelous parable of the sower, and the different responses to the same seed.

"Anyone who has will be given more, and they will have more than enough; but from anyone who does not have, even what he has will be taken away" (Matthew 13:12). *A deep consciousness multiplies insight and feeds on holy yearning; narrow consciousness actually destroys both.* It is so important to have the "beginner's mind," which, ironically, the child has more than the adult (Matthew 18:2–4). We have to "change," he says, to get *back* there.

The Bible has us begin in "the garden" where Adam and Eve walk in easy proximity with God, and where they "know no shame" (2:25). But soon they split ("subject-object split"), "their eyes are opened, and they realize that they are naked and sew fig leaves to cover themselves" (3:8). Even though God refuses to see them as an object, and says, "Who told you that you were naked?" (3:11), they have begun to hide from God (3:8–9). They start scapegoating (3:12; 4:8), fearing (3:10) and seeking "to be like gods" (3:5) with "desirable knowledge" (3:6). All this sets the plot for the entire Bible. It is very hard to doubt that the creation stories from Genesis are not deeply inspired texts. The essential clues are all there in the first four chapters.

You could say that from then on the whole Bible is trying to return us to the Garden. By the end (Revelation 21—22) it becomes the New Jerusalem, where there is no temple, but only the River of Life and the Trees of Life, where even "the leaves are for the cure of the pagans" (22:2) and where "God lives among humans" (21:3).

Finally, Ezekiel's vision (37:27) has been fulfilled and humanity has become God's people and God has become their God. There is no need for a religious building, because the Garden itself is the temple. Life is now one sacred reality.

The Garden, you see, is the symbol of unitive consciousness. We cannot objectively be separate from God; we all walk in the garden whether we know it or not. We came from God and we will return to God. Everything in-between is a school of conscious loving. The English Romantic poet William Wordsworth wrote so well: "the Child is father of the Man; and I could wish my days to be bound each to each by natural piety...." We live the rest of our lives "trailing clouds of glory,"[1] as he put it.

Authentic spiritual cognition always has the character of *re*-cognition! It is returning to where we started and as T.S. Eliot says, "knowing the place for the first time." Or as Jacob put it when he awoke from his sleep: "Truly, Yahweh was always in this place all the time, and I never knew it" (Genesis 28:16). That is, without doubt, the common knowing of mystics, saints and all recovered sinners.

Many of the journeys before that point are journeys away from the center, where we literally become "ec-centric." These are the recurring biblical texts of fall and recovery, hiddenness and discovery, loss and renewal, failure and forgiveness, exile and return.

Fortunately, we are always being led back to the real Center to find who we really are, to find ourselves in God. God seems both very patient and very productive with the journeys back and forth. Such is the pattern of the soul, of history and of the Bible, a progress of sorts, two steps backward and three forward.

Note for yourselves that the parables of the treasure, the pearl, the dragnet, the weeds and the wheat, the lost coin, the lost son and the lost sheep all have this as a foundational theme, and in most cases, the final stage is a party or celebration. That's a rather clear pattern of Jesus' teaching!

That humble productivity and slow efficiency on God's part is called "the economy of grace" or the good news. Here God fills in all the gaps, everything is used, and nothing is wasted, not even sin. It leads to a worldview of abundance and enoughness. Why would anyone want to live in any other world? Buying and selling is a cheap substitute, and always leads to a worldview of scarcity, judgmentalism, fear and stinginess. Why would anyone want to live there? And yet many, if not most, do.

The whole movement of the Bible is toward ever-greater Incarnation and embodiment, until the mystery of mutual indwelling is finally experienced and enjoyed even here in this world and this life. It then becomes the banquet that we call eternal life or heaven. For

Christians, *Jesus, the Christ, is the ultimate symbol of this divine goal, pattern and embodiment:* "When Christ is revealed, and he is your life, you will be revealed in all your glory with him" (Colossians 3:4). Henceforth we know our true and lasting life in the new "force field" that Paul calls the Body of Christ and not in individual or private perfection. It becomes more important to be *connected* than to be privately *correct.*

Paul's notion of the body of Christ has a material and cosmic character to it, and begins in this world (which is why we believe in the resurrection of the body and not just the soul). Yes, there is "a new heaven" but there is also "a new earth" (Revelation 21:1). What more fitting meaning could the "Second Coming of Christ" have except that humanity becomes "a beautiful bride all dressed for her husband?" (Revelation 21:3). Union is finally enjoyed, and God's win-win story line has achieved its full purpose. What a hopeful end to history! What an *apokatastasis,* or "universal restoration" (Revelation 3:21)! What a victory for God—and for humanity!

What the full biblical revelation has given us is the history within the history, the coherence inside of the seeming incoherence. If you don't get this inner pattern, then religion becomes simply aimless anecdotes—just little stories here and there, with no pattern or direction. They come from no place and there is no place they are going. You have to know where the text is heading, or you do not know how to "thin slice" and look through the appropriate lenses.

What we are saying is that the clear goal and direction is mutual indwelling, where "the mystery is Christ within you, your hope of glory" (Colossians 1:27). In this mutual indwelling you no longer live as just you, but you live in a larger force field called the body of Christ (Galatians 2:20). As Charles Williams said, the "master idea" of Christianity is *co-inherence.* But it takes a long time to allow, believe, trust and enjoy such wonder.

Only in the final chapter of the Bible can it say, "Now God lives among humans, they have become God's people, and he has become their God" (Revelation 21:3). Only at the end does the New Jerusalem descend from heaven to earth.

"Quick, tell me, who made you? Where'd you come from?" In the complexity of life's journeys we all begin to forget, just like the little child who opened this chapter. As we get older, the patterns become too complex and eventually we don't even expect any pattern anymore. That is probably the loss of faith we see among so many today.

There is no one telling them "the big patterns that are always true," so they leave, wandering in circles in the desert. It is post-modernism, deconstruction or nihilism, and is not a happy world to live in. Many of our children grow up inside of such a meaningless world, and are thus drawn to easy and glib fundamentalism. Anything, even silliness, is better than meaninglessness.

What we're facing today is a crisis of meaning that becomes very quickly a crisis of hope and a scrambling for external power, perks and possessions. The world will be destroyed by two things, it seems to me: greed and violence. Perhaps it seems obvious. That's why great spiritual teachers will always teach you, first, to live a simple life, to not take more than your share, so that communion and community, brotherhood and sisterhood, are possible.

Then a good spiritual teacher will teach you some kind of inner disciplines to reveal and heal inner fears and aggression, which are transformed, quite simply, into happiness. I call it contemplation or nondual consciousness, which is achieved by abiding in God, who already abides in us. It is the Holy Spirit.

Yet the things Jesus talked about constantly, like living a simple and nonviolent life in this world, like forgiveness and inclusivity, are still considered fringe thinking by many Christians. How strange that we have the capacity to not see what is taught so clearly by the one we consider our teacher. It must be what saddened Isaiah and Jesus too: "This people will hear and hear again, but not understand, see and see again but not perceive" (Isaiah 6:9; Matthew 13:14).

What I hope I am saying here is that it is not primarily bad will that keeps people spiritually blind, but that *they were never taught how to see!* I hope this book gives you a *way* of seeing, more than just *what* to see.

In a sense, the Christ is always too much for us. He's always "going ahead of us into Galilee" (Matthew 28:7). The Risen Christ is leading us into a future for which we're never, ever, ready. Only little by little do we become capable of mutuality, of communion, of pure presence. Remember, presence does not happen in the mind. We return to what Eckhart Tolle said at this book's outset, that *all the mind can do is before and after, but does not know how to be present in the now.* That is the mind's great limitation, and why all teachers of prayer give you methods for moving beyond the mind (*meta-noia,* "beyond the mind").

God is creating Real Presence, just as eucharistic practice always said, which is probably why the images of bride and bridegroom are used by the prophets, by John the Baptist, by Jesus himself and gloriously in the last verses of the Bible (Revelation 19:7; 21:2, 9; 22:17), where the marriage is symbolically consummated. Mutual presence, even intimacy, is clearly the ultimate goal.

To be capable of mutual indwelling, or coinherence, means that religion has achieved its full and final purpose. Bride and bridegroom are together just for the sake of being together! Presence is the naked language of union, of being lost and found in the face of the other, or in Jesus, the very breath of the Other (John 20:22). If that is the core meaning of eternal life, then why wouldn't we practice it now, enjoy it now, choose it now? Once more let me say it: How you get there is where you will arrive.

You don't have to figure it all out or get it all right ahead of time. You just have to stay on the journey. All you can do is stay connected. We don't know how to be perfect, but we can stay in union. "If you remain in me and I remain you," says Jesus, "you can ask for whatever you want and you're going to get it" (see John 15:7). When you're connected, there are no coincidences anymore.

Synchronicities, coincidences, accidents and "providences" just keep happening. Union realigns you with everything, and things just start happening. I cannot explain the "chemistry" of it all. Some people call it "the secret." All I know is that "the branch cut off from the vine is useless" (John 15:5), yet on the vine it bears much fruit (15:5, 7). The True Self is endlessly generative, in touch with its Source; the false self is fragile, needy and insecure.

eucharist

Catholics are right when they talk about "going to Communion." So many people have left the church, but invariably they long for one thing after they've left. They will say that much of the church was easy to leave but it was so hard to give up "going to Communion." Their intuition and loss is absolutely correct.

Let's end with something personal, practical and immediate. Some call it a Communion service, some the Mass and some the Eucharist, but the important thing is that the method is also the message. In the eucharistic meal, Jesus gave us a very ingenious "mime," as Gil Bailie rightly calls it, whereby we could continue to experience union at a cellular level, instead of just arguing about whether Incarnation, election and "divinization" (*theosis*, as the Orthodox call it) can really happen.

He gave us something that he did not say we needed to "think about" or "agree upon," "look at" or even "worship," but he just said, "Do this!" It was an action, an audiovisual aid, a sacred ritual for a community, built on Jewish roots, that would summarize his whole lasting message for the world.

After I leave, said Jesus, just keep doing this mime until I come back again and you'll get it right, you will know what it means to be a Christian, and the bride will be ready to meet the bridegroom:

1. Take your whole life in your hands, as I am about to do tonight and tomorrow. (In very physical and scandalous Jewish language, table bread is "my body" and alcoholic wine is "my blood.")

2. Thank God *(eucharisteo),* who is the origin of your own goodness. Make a choice for gratitude, abundance and appreciation beyond the self, which always de-centers the self. Your life is pure gift, and it must be based in an attitude of gratitude.

3. Break it, let it be broken, give it away and don't protect it. The sharing of the small self will be the discovery of the True Self in God. "Unless the grain of wheat dies, it remains just a grain of wheat" (John 12:24). The broken grain becomes the broken bread.

4. Now chew on that, drink that! "Take this," "eat and drink together until I return," and you will have the heart of the message, a "new covenant" based on love and divine union. Your drinking and eating is your agreement to "do what I can to make up in my own body all that still has to be undergone by Christ for the sake of his body the church" (Colossians 1:24). You now know that you *are* a participation in the very life of God. Now you have the "who" right!

The Eucharist is actually a homeopathic medicine, whereby we eat and drink our own death ahead of time, in loving union with his death, instead of always demanding that others die. We preemptively walk right into the mystery of death, and like him, trust its other side, which is resurrection. "Whenever you do this, you are proclaiming his death" (1 Corinthians 11:27)—and yours too, which you desire to do in the same way!

Remember, homeopathic cures always include a slight touch of the disease. Each time we eat and drink, we agree to die with him, in him, for him and because of him. The eating says to our very body that henceforth our lives are not our own, and "my life is not about me"! If we did not have such an incarnational mystery as Eucharist, we would have to create something similar.

The tradition always insisted that the meal was also a sacrifice (a letting go) and a "memorial" or act of solidarity with Jesus' letting go— so that we could ride on his coattails, as it were (see 1 Corinthians 11:23–27). Thus we could trust the outcome together with him, because we are incapable of such trust and rest alone. Unfortunately, we made it into Jesus' heroic sacrifice that we could thank him for, instead of an invitation to the same—"through him, with him and in him" as the Eucharistic Prayer rightly ends (taste those three prepositions!).

Every denomination and century has embroidered Jesus' home-spun ritual (remember, he was breaking with his Passover tradition, partially changing its meaning and creating his own ritual) for its own purposes. We have surrounded it with candles, vestments, polyphonic music, incense and elaborate words; we've built huge cathedrals in which to celebrate this mystery. But we still have people who don't get the basic mime of what we have to do. Ours became a Platonic world of heavenly ideas instead of the simple embodiment, and ongoing proclamation of Incarnation and transformation *now.*

It was always easier to "convince" bread and wine of its true identity, than it was to convince humans! We spent much of our history arguing about the "how" and the "if," and who could do it ("transubstantiation" of the bread), instead of simply learning how to *be present* ourselves ("contemplation"). We made it into magic to be believed instead of transformation of ourselves.

In contemplation there is no argument about Real Presence. People who can simply be present will know about presence, union and even ecstasy, and they would not think of denying God's availability in the material world. They know that Eucharist is a distilled and focused statement about the objective Incarnation. It is the ongoing Incarnation continued in space and time to tell creation what it is afraid to believe: "My dear people, we are already the children of God, but what we are to be in the future has not yet been revealed, all we know is that when it is revealed, we shall be like him"! (1 John 3:2).

It seems obvious to me that God is calling everyone and everything home, not just picking and choosing a few. In fact, the few are only for the sake of the many, or as Paul put it "the dough is for the whole batch" (Romans 11:16 ff.).

We all are saved in spite of ourselves—and for one another. It never was a worthiness contest. If God is love and if grace is true, then what exactly is the cutoff point? "When is God's arm too short to save?" (Isaiah 50:2). Are there any who have achieved worthiness and do not need saving? Name them, please.

You can see this promise and cosmic hope growing through plenty of bookmark places throughout the Bible: the all-embracing covenant with Noah (Genesis 8:16, 17), the shocking globalism of Jewish prophets (Isaiah 2:1–4; 56:2–8), the confident universalism of early Christian hymns (Ephesians 1:9–10; Colossians 1:15–20), the "universal restoration" *(apokatastasis)* promised in Peter's first sermon (Acts 3:21), or just in the clear will and desire of God (1 Timothy 2:4; John 3:17).

Can God not achieve God's purposes? Are we in control? Does our sin have the last word? Or is God in control and victorious? If God is all powerful, it is no accident that we often began prayers with the appellation, "All powerful and merciful God," because God's power is precisely used for mercy throughout the evolving Bible.

What could possibly be allowed to frustrate this divine desire or God's capacity for true victory? Paul says, "Nothing!" (Romans 8:38–39). He says that after listing all of the usual supposed obstacles to God's victory, and asserting that "When God acquits, no one can condemn" (8:32). Why do we not use Peter's power of the keys to *unbind* the world in this way, and to offer it the full victory of God's love? Why do we prefer binding to unbinding; when Jesus clearly gave us *both* (Matthew 16:19)?

In human history it seems to me so very little is really resolved or solved, settled or answered. We live in the in-between, holding the tensions, discovering and even loving the paradoxes, realizing we ourselves *are* the contradictions visualized by the geometric image of the cross.

That living space, the ultimate liminal space, is called faith, and Jesus praises it even more than love. For inside that force field, inside the economy of grace, is where everything new, including love, can always happen.

Symeon the New Theologian (949–1022), a saint and mystic, revered to this day by Eastern Christians, wrote some words that point beautifully to this new force field, that we call the Body of Christ.

Symeon describes this cosmic embodiment created by God's grace and our response. Hymn 15 in his *Hymns of Divine Love* beautifully names the divine union that all the Bible is forever inviting and edging us toward. It is probably my favorite piece of religious verse, and so I wanted to sum up all of the prose of this book with twenty-seven mystical lines that honestly say it all.

This is the final thin slice, because it moves all we have said to the now, to present experience, to the living force field wherein we will know all this to be true for ourselves; we will no longer rely upon belief systems or even Scripture quotes. Here, in Symeon's hymn, Scripture has become spirituality:

> We awaken in Christ's body,
> As Christ awakens our bodies
> There I look down and my poor hand is Christ,
> He enters my foot and is infinitely me.
> I move my hand and wonderfully
> My hand becomes Christ,
> Becomes all of Him.
> I move my foot and at once
> He appears in a flash of lightning.
> Do my words seem blasphemous to you?

—Then open your heart to him.
And let yourself receive the one
Who is opening to you so deeply.
For if we genuinely love Him,
We wake up inside Christ's body
Where all our body all over,
Every most hidden part of it,
Is realized in joy as Him,
And He makes us utterly real.
And everything that is hurt, everything
That seemed to us dark, harsh, shameful,
maimed, ugly, irreparably damaged
Is in Him transformed.
And in Him, recognized as whole, as lovely,
And radiant in His light,
We awaken as the beloved
In every last part of our body.[2]

"Test yourselves: Do you acknowledge that Jesus, the Christ, is really in you? If not, you have failed the test."

—2 Corinthians 13:6

notes

frontispiece

1. Saint Symeon, "What Is This Awesome Mystery," from *Hymns of Divine Love*, Stephen Mitchell, trans. (New York: Harper and Row, 1989).

introduction

1. Malcolm Gladwell, *Blink* (New York: Little Brown & Co., 2005), pp. 33 ff.

chapter one

1. D.H. Lawrence, *Studies in Classic American Literature* (New York: Seltzer, 1923).
2. Rosemary Haughton, *The Knife Edge of Experience* (London: Darton, Longman and Todd, 1972).
3. Walter Brueggemann, *Theology of the Old Testament: Testimony, Dispute, Advocacy* (Minneapolis: Fortress, 2005), pp. 215 ff.
4. Gerald May, *The Dark Night of the Soul: A Psychiatrist Explores the Connection Between Darkness and Spiritual Growth* (New York: HarperOne, 2004).
5. Walter Brueggemann, *The Message of the Psalms* (Minneapolis: Augsburg, 1984).

chapter two

1. Thomas Merton, *The Inner Experience: Notes on Contemplation* (New York: Harper Collins, 2003), p. 35.
2. Julian of Norwich, *Showings,* Edmund Colledge and James Walsh, eds. (New York: Paulist, 1978), pp. 148 ff.

chapter four

1. Karl Rahner, *The Shape of the Church to Come* (New York: Seabury, 1972).

chapter five

1. John of the Cross, *The Living Flame of Love,* second redaction, 3:59.

chapter six

1. This idea comes from Heinrich Zimmer.
2. With thanks to William Johnston, S.J.

chapter seven

1. James Alison, *The Joy of Being Wrong* (New York: Crossroad, 1998).

chapter eight

1. The New Baltimore Catechism, question 101.
2. Walter Brueggemann, *Theology of the Old Testament.*
3. Isak Dinesen, "Babette's Feast," *Anecdotes of Destiny* (New York: Vintage, 1993), p. 45.
4. Dinesen, p. 52.

chapter ten

1. William Wordsworth, from "Intimations of Immortality from Recollections of Early Childhood."
2. Saint Symeon the New Theologian, from *Hymns of Divine Love.*

annotated bibliography

Abrams, David, *The Spell of the Sensuous* (New York: Random House, 1996).

Alison, James. *The Joy of Being Wrong* (New York: Crossroad, 1998). I would recommend any of the brilliant theological writings of James Alison to help you unpack the implications of Rene Girard's scapegoat mechanism.

————. *On Being Liked* (London: Darton, Longman and Todd, 2003). All of James Alison's books are highly recommended in this regard, but they do demand a bit of theological background to stay with his tight (but very clear) gospel logic.

Borg, Marcus. *Meeting Jesus Again for the First Time* (San Francisco: HarperSanFrancisco, 1994). Borg is a major force in bringing us back to an honest reading of Jesus, and a very clear writer to boot!

Bourgeault, Cynthia. *The Wisdom Way of Knowing* (Hoboken, N.J.: Jossey-Bass, 2003).

Brueggemann, Walter. *The Message of the Psalms* (Minneapolis: Augsburg, 1984).

————. *Theology of the Old Testament* (Minneapolis: Fortress, 1997).

Delio, Ilia. *The Humility of God* (Cincinnati: St. Anthony Messenger Press, 2005). In reading this treasure of a book, I realized how much my Franciscan view of God had uncovered for me what I believe is the actual biblical revelation.

Documents of Vatican II. All documents of the Second Vatican Council are available online at www.vatican.va.

Girard, Rene. *Violence and the Sacred* (Baltimore: Johns Hopkins University Press, 1977). You might also want to review good (and more reasonably priced) summaries in *The Girard Reader* (New York: Crossroad, 1996). See also his *Things Hidden Since the Foundation of the World, The Scapegoat* and *Sacred Violence.*

Hart, Tobin. *From Information to Transformation* (New York: Peter Lang, 2001). This is a brilliant analysis of much of our confusion with stage of consciousness, as are many of Ken Wilber's books.

Ingham, Mary Beth, "Holding the Tension: The Power of Paradox" A recorded conference that we did together in 2006, or "Jesus and Paul as Non-Dual Teachers," Center for Action and Contemplation, Albuquerque, N.M., www.cacradicalgrace.org.

Jaynes, Julian. *The Origin of Consciousness in the Breakdown of the Bicameral Mind* (New York: Houghton Mifflin, 1976).

Lane, Belden. *The Solace of Fierce Landscapes* (New York: Oxford University Press, 1998). I find Belden's presentation of the two streams especially readable and convincing, as are all his writings.

May, Gerald. *The Dark Night of the Soul* (San Francisco: HarperSanFrancisco, 2004). This excellent presentation of the actual psychological and spiritual meaning of Teresa of Avila and John of the Cross is highly recommended.

Peterson, Eugene H. *The Message* (Colorado Springs, Colo.: NavPress, 1993). This is one of the most brilliant scholarly paraphrasing of the Scriptures I have ever read.

Robinson, J.A.T. *In the End God* (New York: Harper & Row, 1968).

Rohr, Richard. *Adam's Return* (New York: Crossroad, 2005).

———. *Everything Belongs* (New York: Crossroad, 1999).

———. "The Divine Dance" and "The Shape of God," recorded conferences available at the Center for Action and Contemplation, Albuquerque, N.M., www.cacradicalgrace.org.

———. *The Great Themes of Paul* (Cincinnati: St. Anthony Messenger Press, 2004).

———. *Job and the Mystery of Suffering* (New York: Crossroad, 1995).

———. *Soul Brothers* (Maryknoll, N.Y.: Orbis, 2004).

———. "The Spirituality of the Two Halves of Life" (Albuquerque, N.M.: Center for Action and Contemplation, 2003). These are recorded conferences with Ron Rolheiser and with Paula D'Arcy. We are all three convinced that the clarification of these major two stages offers much pastoral help and theological insight into the spiritual journey.

————. "The True Self and the False Self." Recorded conference available at Center for Action and Contemplation, Albuquerque, N.M., www.cacradicalgrace.org.

————. *From Wild Man to Wise Man* (Cincinnati: St. Anthony Messenger Press, 2005).

Schumacher, E.F. *A Guide for the Perplexed* (New York: Harper & Row, 1977).

Schwartzentruber, Michael, ed. *The Emerging Christian Way* (Incline, Nev.: Copperhouse, 2006). Although I would not necessarily agree with everything in this fine book, it is naming the growing consensus very well. The future of the church is clearly ecumenical, it seems to me, because each denomination has to pretend to be certain about things that can only be "known" by faith, yet each preserves a part of the mystery.

Tolle, Eckhart. *The Power of Now* (Novato, Calif.: New World, 1997). This brilliant book takes centuries of mystical teaching, on what we called "the sacrament of the present moment" and made it accessible to our time. If you want to learn more, Thomas Keating and I did a conference called "The Eternal Now: And How to Be There," recorded and available from the Center for Action and Contemplation, Albuquerque, N.M., www.cacradicalgrace.org.

Townsend, Mark. *The Gospel of Falling Down* (Winchester, U.K.: O Books, 2007). A very creative and experiential based book realigns "the beauty of failure in an age of success."

Watts, Alan. *Behold the Spirit* (New York: Random House, 1947). I think this book is an undiscovered gem, and validated for me much of my own experience. The Bible's primary concern is mystical, not moral.

Weaver, J. Denny. *The Nonviolent Atonement* (Grand Rapids, Mich.: Eerdmans, 2001).

Wilber, Ken. *One Taste* (Boston: Shambhala, 2000).

————. *Sex, Ecology, Spirituality* (Boston: Shambhala, 1995).

Young, Jeremy. *The Cost of Certainty: How Religious Conviction Betrays the Human Psyche*, (Lanham, Md.: Cowley, 2005).

See Web sites and resources at www.cacradicalgrace.org and at www.SAMPBooks.org

appendix a

Two apparent subtexts in the history of Western biblical spirituality emerge as the main text. They unfold below and lead toward some examples for North American readers.

subtext I. the way of the wound

We open to God by doing it wrong more than by doing it right. The call is to divine union more than private perfection.

MOSES
>   (the chosen stutterer and murderer who leads the enslaved to freedom)

JEREMIAH
>   (the reluctant, rejected, seduced prophet)

SUFFERING SERVANT OF ISAIAH
>   (a mystical foretelling of the pattern)

JOB
>   (wounded and restored by God)

JESUS
>   (crucified humanity personified, and the pattern presented as redemption)

PAUL
>   ("when I am weak, I am strong")

DESERT FATHERS *&* MOTHERS
>   (detachment over achievement)

ISAAC OF NINEVEH
>   ("the way of tears")

EPHREM THE SYRIAN
("the way of tears")

CELTIC SPIRITUALITY
(compassion and healing for the broken)

SYMEON THE NEW THEOLOGIAN
("experience teaches you, not moralism")

FRANCIS & CLARE OF ASSISI
(poverty as the way)

JULIAN OF NORWICH
("your wounds will be your honors")

JOHN OF THE CROSS
(darkness preferred to light, suffering to consolation)

Almost a four-century hiatus, as Catholics and Protestants battle for worthiness systems, and in fighting the Enlightenment and modern secularism, becoming rationalistic and perfectionist themselves. The Catholic mystics still continue to value suffering and descent, however.

THÉRÈSE OF LISIEUX
("The Little Way")

SIMONE WEIL
(dramatic solidarity with the pain of humanity and the outsider)

TWELVE-STEP SPIRITUALITY
(the American contribution to the history of spirituality)

HENRI NOUWEN
(spirituality of the wounded healer)

Recovery of the HOSPICE, BEREAVEMENT & HEALING ministries as central to the gospel

subtext II. the way of mystery/paradox/non-duality (apophatic tradition)

MOSES

>   (who knows God, but through the cloud)

JOB

>   (none of whose questions are ever answered)

JESUS

>   (the first non-dual teacher of the West)

PAUL

>   (a dialectical mystic, who was interpreted by a dualistic tradition)

DESERT FATHERS *&* MOTHERS

>   (no need for systematic theology but only inner experience)

EVAGRIUS PONTICUS

>   (introduces the way of "unknowing," grandfather of the Enneagram)

CAPPADOCIAN FATHERS

>   (Trinity as the way into mystery)

AUGUSTINE

>   ("If you understand it, it is not God")

PSEUDO DIONYSIUS

>   (the classic teacher of the apophatic way)

CELTIC CHRISTIANITY

>   (nature based and healing based, not in the head)

JOHN DUNS SCOTUS

>   ("intuitive cognition" as the balance to "rational cognition")

BONAVENTURE

>   (the Godself is itself a coincidence of opposites)

MEISTER ECKHART

>   (classic non-dual mystic and teacher)

THOMAS AQUINAS

(if his statement "All my writings are straw" is true)

AUTHOR OF THE "CLOUD OF UNKNOWING"

(the classic text)

NICHOLAS OF CUSA

(formal teacher of the coincidence of opposites)

JOHN OF THE CROSS

("luminous darkness" and inner experience)

JACOB BOEHME

(coincidence of opposites, Protestant mystic)

GEORGE FOX

(Quaker appreciation for silence, inner light, nonviolence)

Another long hiatus as contemplation largely becomes identified with "saying" prayers, separation from the world, and introverted personalities.

THOMAS MERTON

(almost single-handedly retrieves the tradition for the West)

BEDE GRIFFITHS, JOHN MAIN, CYNTHIA BOURGEAULT, THOMAS KEATING, LAURENCE FREEMAN, RUTH BARROWS

(each, in his or her own way, making use of the language of modern psychology, Eastern wisdom on the process of transformation, and the postmodern critique of knowledge, Centering Prayer/Meditation Movement)

KEN WILBER

("Everyone is right!" Tries to hear the level of truth in every opinion)

COSMOLOGISTS

(who are making use of science, quantum physics, and our knowledge of the universe to lead us back into a reappreciation for "non-knowledge" and mystery)

appendix b

unresolved issues of dualistic thinking

Below is a listing of issues that have played out strongly in our tradition, where Christianity has been forced into an arbitrary and often artificial choice:

- Creationism versus evolution

- Justification by faith versus justification by good works

- Eucharist as meal versus Eucharist as sacrifice

- Sacredness of life in the unborn versus sacredness of life of someone on death row

- Iconoclasm toward the past of most reformations and revolutions versus true enlightenment which includes all the previous stages

- Myth of private perfection versus call to divine union

- Christianity as power versus a gospel of powerlessness

- Dominative power versus nonviolence

- Body versus spirit

- Leadership versus community

- Homosexual dilemma

- Maintaining the container versus experiencing the contents

- Group identity versus inclusivity

- Cross as necessity versus cross as gift

index

Abel, 42

Abrams, David *(The Spell of the Sensuous)*, 129

Adam, 31, 34, 39, 139

Adam's Return: The Five Promises of Male Initiation (Rohr), 46

Albertz, Rainer, 128

alienation, 40–41

Alighieri, Dante *(Divine Comedy)*, 112

Alison, James *(On Being Liked; The Joy of Being Wrong)*, 102, 151

Ananias, 50

Andrew, 66

Anne, Saint, 92

Anselm, Saint *(Cur Deus Homo?)*, 196

apocalyptic language, 117

apophatic tradition, 20

Apostles' Creed, 100

Aquinas, Thomas, 196

atonement, 195–200

Augustine, 100, 187

authoritarianism, 87

authority, inner vs. outer, 5

"Babette's Feast," 180–183

basilica, 99

Beatitudes, 15, 117

Benjamin, 91

Bible. *See* Scripture

birth control, 125

Blixen, Karen. *See* Dinesen, Isak

Body of Christ, 24, 212

Bonaparte, Napoleon, 88, 194

Bonaventure, Saint, 33, 63

Borg, Marcus *(The Emerging Christian Way; Meeting Jesus Again for the First Time)*, 114, 159

Bourgeault, Cynthia, 94, 122

Brueggemann, Walter *(Theology of the Old Testament)*, 10, 17, 128, 164–165, 169

Buber, Martin, 60, 179

Buddhism, 123–124

Burrow, Ruth, 122

Cain, 42

Christ. *See* Jesus

Christianity, ecumenical character of, 4

church, defined, 56

circumcision, 46

Clare, 102

Cloud of Unknowing, 119

Confucianism, 189

Constantine, 99, 161

Copernicus, 30

"cosmic egg," 14–15, 20–26

criticism, 137–138

Cupid, 54

Cyrus, 187

D'Arcy, Paula, 17

Dalai Lama, 73

David, 17, 42, 48, 93, 134, 164–165, 166–167

Dead Man Walking, 134

Delio, Ilia *(The Humility of God)*, 93

De Lubac, Henri, 13

Deborah, 17

demonic possession, 60

Desert Fathers and Mothers, 119

dignity, 56

Dinesen, Isak ("Babette's Feast"), 180

Dionysius the Areopagite, 119

dualism, 17, 32, 42

Duns Scotus, John, 127, 196–198

Eckhart, Meister, 65, 165–166
Edict of Milan, 161
ego, 30, 68, 75
Einstein, Albert, 14, 57, 161
election, 44
Elijah, 17
Eliot, T.S., 211
Elizabeth, 91
encyclicals, papal, 116
Enlightenment, 115
Ephraim, 91
Esau, 93
Esther, 17
Eucharist, 49, 62, 157, 188, 215–218
Eve, 34, 39, 139
Ezekiel, 17, 97, 169

false self, 12–13
fertility rites, 46
Flags of Our Fathers, 134
forgiveness
    healing of, 23
    graces in, 37
    in letters of Paul, 37
    See also under Jesus
Francis, Saint, 33, 83, 93, 102, 103, 104,
    168
Freeman, Lawrence, 122
From Wild Man to Wise Man (Rohr), 166
Fry, Christopher *(Thor, With Angels),* 158
fundamentalism, 3, 120

Gandhi, Mohandas, 152
Garden of Eden, 210–211. *See also* Adam;
    Eve; Genesis, book of
Genesis, book of
    as spiritual account, 32
    Cain and Abel in, 42

creation story in, 27–28, 32
    Fall in, 37, 39–40
    Noah's ark, 36–37
    Trinity in, 35
Gerasene demoniac, 150
Ghost Ranch, New Mexico, 123
Gideon, 42, 94, 145
Girard, Rene, 11, 47, 139
Gladwell, Malcolm *(Blink),* 2
God
    as Absolute, 72
    as community, 35
    "control" of, 9, 10
    desires of, 35–36
    experience of, 129–131
    fear of, 9
    feminine images of, 42
    generosity of, 155
    images of, 43
    masculine images of, 41–42
    names for, 69, 110
    nonviolence of, 140, 147
    as Pantocrator, 93, 100
    presence in ordinary, 16, 17, 18
    relationship with, 53–54
    revelation of, 15, 53
    soul's union with, 28
    surrender to, 19
Good Samaritan, 150
gospel, defined, 8
group identity, 23

Hannah, 91, 92
Hart, Tobin, 125–126
Haughton, Rosemary, 7, 10–11
heaven, 112–113
Heidegger, Martin, 61
hell, 171
Hildegard of Bingen, 45

Hinduism, 123–124

homeopathic images, 191, 216–217

Holocaust, 135, 143

Holy Spirit, 74, 97, 98, 138, 148, 213

homosexuality, 29, 125

Hopkins, Gerard Manley, 175

human sacrifice, 47

humanity
    depravity of, 28–29
    as image of God, 28

humility, 15, 38, 56

Husserl, Edmund, 61

Ignatius Loyola, Saint, 137

Incarnation, 17

Incarnational Mysticism, 131

individuality, 54

indulgences, 160

Ingham, Mary Beth *(Scotus for Dunces)*, 127

integrity, 59

Ionesco, Eugene, 7

Isaac, 91

Isaiah, 42

Isaiah, book of
    inclusivity in, 146
    Jesus on, 25, 110
    "Servant Songs" of, 25, 146, 187

Islam, 119–120

Jacob, 91, 187

Jaffa, 147

James, 100

Jaynes, Julian *(The Origin of Consciousness in the Breakdown of the Bicameral Mind)*, 74

Jeremiah, 17, 42

Jesse, 93

Jesus
    on "beginner's mind," 8
    crucifixion of, 185–193
    as fulfillment of the Scriptures, 141
    forgiveness of, 31, 149–153
    imitation of, 36
    as Jew, 4
    as Job, 25
    on judgmentalism, 37
    as living water, 45
    and metanoia, 137
    on orthodoxy, 113
    parables of, 34, 44, 117, 126
    on "poverty of spirit," 8, 15
    as prophet, 77
    Resurrection of, 191
    as scapegoat, 189, 193–195
    Sermon on the Mount, 77–78, 117, 201
    teaching style of, 126–127
    Transfiguration of, 118
    on violence, 125
    vulnerability of, 9–10
    on wealth, 125

John (disciple), 100, 177

John of the Cross, 39, 68, 110

John Paul II, Pope, 172, 173

John the Baptist, 45, 65, 91, 144

Johnston, William, S.J., 120

Jonah, 42, 43, 146, 187

Jordan River, 45

Joseph, 93, 187

Judaism
    as archetypal religion, 105
    covenant love in, 10
    purity codes in, 105–107, 159
    scapegoat ritual in, 142. *See also* scapegoating
    self-criticism in, 19

Judas, 177

Julian of Norwich, 39, 45

Jung, Carl, 14, 163, 193

kataphatic tradition, 115, 122
Keating, Thomas, 122
King, Martin Luther, 152

Labre, Benedict Joseph, 102
Lane, Belden, 114–115
Last Supper, 121, 176, 177
Lawrence, D.H., 7
Left Behind series, 117
Levinas, Emmanuel, 61, 179
Lewis, C.S. *(Till We Have Faces: A Myth Retold),* 54
Lucifer, 116

Mary Magdalene, 55
Mary
    Annunciation to, 31–32
    chosenness of, 43
    egolessness, 32
    Magnificat, 92
    sinlessness, 63
    virginity of, 91
Mass, 81, 161–162
May, Gerald *(Dark Night of the Soul),* 55
McBrien, Richard, 80
McLuhan, Marshall, 4
Mechtild of Magdeburg, 45
Merton, Thomas, 28, 122
The Message (Peterson), 170–171
midrashim, 61
minyan, 84
monotheism, 57–58
Moore, Sebastian *(The Crucified Jesus Is No Stranger),* 186
moral theology, 37
Moses, 17, 19, 42, 44, 55, 90, 118, 172
Mother Teresa, 66
Mount Sinai, 55, 117
mysterion, 62

Nathan, 93, 134
Nathanael, 66
New Age, 23, 115
The New Baltimore Catechism, 156
New Jerusalem Community, 164
Noah, 139, 170. *See also* under Genesis
Nostra Aetate, 23

Obadiah, 17
orthodoxy, 110

parousia, 16
paschal mystery, 62–63
Paul, Saint, 8, 17
    on Adam vs. Christ, 34
    chosenness of, 43, 177–178
    conversion of, 49–50
    on election, 44
    as first Catholic, 147–149
    on freedom, 31
    on forgiveness, 37
    on hope, 36
    on initiation, 103
    on "inner spirit," 12
    on Jewish people, 43
    on law, 78–79, 81–82
    letters of, 11, 33, 67, 72, 149
    on pride, 43
    on prophecy, 138
    on spiritual teaching, 125
Pentecost, 97
person, defined, 54
Peter, Saint, 43, 66, 147, 177
Philip, 66
Platonism, 17, 207
poverty of spirit
    in reading Scripture, 30
    See also under Jesus
prayer

centering, 122
defined, 5
God's gaze and, 50
Jesus on, 5
necessity of, 124
Prejean, Sister Helen, 134
"prosperity gospel," 160
Protestant Reformation, 115, 158
Psalms, 19, 95–97, 201

Qoheleth, 116

Rahner, Karl *(The Shape of the Church to Come)*, 80
Real Presence, 64. *See also* Eucharist
Rebecca, 91
Red Sea, 45, 90
relativism, 71
Revelation, book of, 145
Robinson, J.A.T., 173

Sampson, 91
Samuel, 42, 91, 93
Sarah, 91
satan, defined, 136
scapegoating, 135–136, 139, 142, 153
Schumacher, E.F. *(A Guide for the Perplexed)*, 14
scholasticism, 126
Scripture
banquet, as symbol in, 155–162, 174–177
blood sacrifice in, 46
central ideas in, 3
character development, 3
context of, 14
Hebrew Scriptures, 3, 10, 18

interaction with, 13
interpretation of, 124
Law, 72–73, 95
nature as, 32
patterns in, 188
on power, 85–86
Prophets, 72, 95
revelation in, 4, 11, 15, 17
second–person language in, 68–69
theme development, 3, 12
translations of, 5
tribal thinking in, 54, 141
violence in, 133
Wisdom, 72, 75, 95
See also specific books of the Bible
Second Vatican Council. *See* Vatican II
shadow self, 75–77
sin
culpability in, 33–34
defined, 29, 137
original, 33–34, 37
Sistine Chapel, 100
Socrates, 2, 163
Sombrero Galaxy, 176
Song of Songs, 42
Stephen, 144
"subject–object split," 40, 210
suffering
God in, 25
meaning in, 25
symbiosis, 2
Symeon the New Theologian *(Hymns of Divine Love)*, 219–220
Syro-Phoenician woman, 150

temple, architecture of, 105–108
Teresa of Avila, 20, 45, 57, 163
Tetragrammaton, 129
theophany, 9
theosis, 7

Thérèse of Lisieux, 41, 102

"thin slicing," 2

Thompson, Francis ("Hound of Heaven"), 156

Tolle, Eckhart *(The Power of Now)*, 16

Topeka, Kansas, 12

Townsend, Mark *(The Gospel of Falling Down)*, 89

Tradition, 19–20

transformation

  blood as symbol of, 46

  leading others to, 44

  moral moments vs., 49

  prayer and, 124

  suffering and, 124

Trinity

  in Genesis, 35

  Holy Spirit in, 98. *See also* Holy Spirit

  humility of, 93

  power of, 87

  relationship in, 56

  in Scripture, 57

Twelve–Step Programs, 90

union, divine

  Eucharist as, 49

  invitation to, 45

universalism, 146

Vatican II, 13, 23

Vincent de Paul, 102

Violence and the Sacred (Girard), 47

water, symbol of, 49

Weaver, J. Denny *(The Nonviolent Atonement)*, 199

Weil, Simone, 102

Wilber, Ken *(Sex, Ecology, Spirituality)*, 86, 207

Williams, Charles, 57, 212

women

  barren, 91

  spiritual advantage of, 103

wounding, sacred, 24–26, 42

Young, Jeremy *(The Cost of Certainty)*, 38

Zacchaeus, 150

Zechariah, book of, 192

Zimmer, Heinrich, 111